MULTINATIONAL CORPORATIONS AND THE THIRD WORLD

Multinational Corporations and the Third World

EDITED BY C.J.DIXON, D.DRAKAKIS-SMITH, AND H.D.WATTS

CROOM HELM
London & Sydney

© 1986 C.J. Dixon, D. Drakakis-Smith and H.D. Watts
Croom Helm Ltd, Provident House, Burrell Row,
Beckenham, Kent BR3 1AT

Croom Helm Australia Pty Ltd, Suite 4, 6th Floor,
64-76 Kippax Street, Surry Hills, NSW 2010, Australia

British Library Cataloguing in Publication Data

Multinational corporations and the Third World.
   1. International business enterprises —
   Developing countries
   I. Dixon, C.J.   II. Watts, H.D.   III. Drakakis-
   Smith, D.W.
   338.8'91724   HD2932

ISBN 0-7099-0876-8

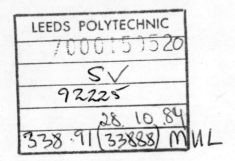
Printed and bound in Great Britain
by Billing & Sons Limited, Worcester.

Contents

List of Tables and Figures

Tables

Preface

The purpose of this volume is to examine the varied roles played by multinational corporations in the economies of the Third World countries. Since the early 1960s there has been an explosion of publications on multinational corporations, however comparatively few have focused directly on multinational activities in the Third World.

The present volume has its origins in the papers presented at a conference held in November 1983 at the University of Birmingham under the auspices of the Developing Areas Research Group and the Industrial Activity and Area Development Study Group of the Institute of British Geographers.

Abbreviations

BIAC	Business and Industry Advisory Committee of the OECD
c.i.f.	Cost, Insurance and Freight
CMEA	Council for Mutual Economic Aid
DC	Developed Country
DoD	Department of Defense (USA)
FDI	Foreign Direct Investment
FMS	Foreign Military Sales
GATT	General Agreement on Tariffs and Trade
GDP	Gross Domestic Product
ILO	International Labour Office
IRM	Institute for Research and Information on Multinationals
ISI	Import Substitution Industrialization
ISIC	International Standard Industrial Classification
LDC	Less Developed Country
LSI	Large Scale Integrated-circuitry
MNC	Multinational Corporation
MNRC	Multinational Resource Corporation
NIC	Newly Industrializing Country
NIDL	New International Division of Labour
NIEO	New International Economic Order
OECD	Organization for Economic Cooperation and Development
OPEC	Organization of Petroleum Exporting Countries
R & D	Research and Development
SIPRI	Stockholm International Peace Research Institute
UNCTNC	United Nations Centre for the Study of Transnational Corporations
UNELA	United Nations Economic Organization for Latin America
UNIDO	United Nations Industrial Development Organization
VLSI	Very Large Scale Integrated-circuitry.

INTRODUCTION

C.J. Dixon, D. Drakakis-Smith
and H.D. Watts

The International Context

Multinational corporations have been of significance in the
world economy since the colonial era. Lenin (1916), for example,
analysed the increasing flow of capital to the 'colonial and
semi-colonial territories' as well as the emergence of multinational production and finance corporations.   These developments were explained at the time largely as responses to higher
potential rates of return on capital (Lenin, 1916; Bukharin,
1917).
     Steady acceleration of this process occurred through the
late colonial and early independence periods, although fluc-
tuating world commodity markets acted as a moderating influence.
It is really since the 1960s that MNCs (Multinational Corporations)
have emerged as a dominant force.   During the last twenty-five
years the world economy has been characterized by a growing
internationalization of production and finance, together with
increased concentration of ownership.
     Such processes have been closely linked to fundamental
changes in production, distribution and communications which
have enabled spatial separation of, for example, manufacturing,
research, marketing and management across a global scale.   A
driving force behind these developments was the falling level of
profit in many industries, but particularly the labour intensive
ones, in most advanced economies.   The emergence of the multinational corporations to their present dominant position in the
world economy was both an integral part of this process as well
as a consequence.
     Since the 1960s, therefore, the structure of international
finance and production has undergone a qualitative transformation.   Analysis of this new structure has given rise to a
series of new terms, most notably the New International Division
of Labour (NIDL), Newly Industrializing Countries (NICs) and deindustrialization.   These terms did not represent a marked departure in the form of analysis of the world economy, rather
they were responses to the challenge of understanding a quali-
tatively different situation.   In this analysis multinational

corporations were found to be playing an increasingly dominant role and to have formed the focus of an increasing volume of literature.

From the late 1970s the extent of the deceleration in the world economy, which had begun a decade earlier, was exposing basic structural weaknesses. The long post-1945 boom and its financial and production underpinnings were showing signs of collapse. In 1971 President Nixon ended the parity of the US dollar with gold, heralding the breakdown of the Bretton Woods based structure of international finance. This and subsequent events, such as the oil price rises of 1974 and 1979, the collapse of commodity prices between 1979 and 1981, and the drying up of recycled petro-dollars as a major source of international finance, were all symptoms of the changes in the world economy rather than causal factors.

During these events the multinational corporations continued to expand their activities not only in terms of manufacturing or resource exploitation, but also as major sources of finance. The multinationa's provided a steadily increasing proportion of the foreign direct investment flowing into the Third World. These expanding financial activities of the multinational corporations, together with those of the multinational banks, have become decisive factors in Third World economic activity.

As a consequence, despite the deepening recession, those Third World countries with extensive and largely multinational controlled and financed manufacturing sectors continued to exhibit rapid rates of growth for both GDP and exports. For example, between 1970 and 1980 the South Korean economy maintained an average annual growth rate of 10.1 per cent for GDP and 37.2 per cent for exports. Even economies with comparatively small manufacturing sectors participated in this growth with Thailand, for example, maintaining an average annual GDP growth rate of 6.9 per cent for the same period.

From 1981, however, the deepening recession affecting the developed economies and the associated growth of protectionism resulted in a collapse of many of the major markets for third world manufactured goods. In consequence, some of the NICs have been affected by major crises of debt, balance of payments and near zero growth; although other NICs, such as Hong Kong and Singapore, have attempted to avoid the worst effects by shifting into the promotion of high-value, high-technology industries.

It is against this background of rapid structural change in the world economy that this present volume of essays examines the activities of multinational corporations in the Third World. But not all influencing factors are global, there are also regional, national and even corporate contexts to take into account.

Introduction

The Regional and National Context

It is tempting, particularly within broad global analyses based on models of the NIDL or comparative advantage, to see a straight-forward dichotomy between the labour intensive production of the Third World and the capital intensive, technologically sophis-ticated manufacturing of the developed nations. However, the reality of the situation is far more complex, with several of the major production centres in the NICs having developed con-siderable pools of skilled labour and high technology, albeit through the medium of foreign investment.

At the regional level within the Third World, therefore, marked divisions of labour are now emerging. These are based on differential levels of skill, labour cost and 'risk' assess-ment by the multinationals. But although the location of industrial investment is primarily determined by MNCs, at the national level state governments can and do exert some influence over those macro-level decisions. From the early 1960s onwards a variety of incentives have thus been offered to MNCs to entice them to certain national or urban locations. The incentives, such as tax holidays, remission of tariffs, or full repatriation of profits, are frequently reinforced by policies aimed at keep-ing labour costs low, particularly by control of labour organ-izations, and giving a general impression of political and financial stability. Often such incentive packages are spa-tially wrapped up into special production zones, known by a varied nomenclature, into which indigenous labour is allowed to move on a daily basis to work and to withdraw to localized areas of labour reproduction when the shift is over, a pattern not dissimilar to the spatial organization of labour in South Africa.

During the 1980s many Third World nations that had pursued policies intended to attract MNC investment have been faced not only with economic but also with political dependence, confusion and chaos. The Philippines, in particular, bears strong wit-ness to such problems. There the growing international disen-chantment with the economic and political foibles of the Marcos regime has posed a far more significant threat to its survival than domestic disillusion.

The Corporate Context

The international economy and its regional variations provide the backdrop to the material in this volume, but the internal policy decisions of the multinational firms themselves, as with those of state governments, cannot be neglected. As the par-ticular economic forces that affect multinational companies have changed over the years, so have their individual responses. Indeed, with the deepening of the world economic recession such responses have become more volatile and less predictable. This is particularly related to the fact that the process of global industrialization has not only been spatially uneven but has also been very erratic within the various sectors of economic activity.

Thus in recent years it has become increasingly difficult to generalize about corporate activity either in developed or developing countries and as with so many research analyses, it has been found to be more intellectually and practically re-warding to narrow the focus to geographically and/or productively specific areas. This is, consequently, the approach chosen by several of the individual chapters in this volume.

An Overview of the Contributions

A common and important theme that runs through all of the essays in this book is the realization that a full appreciation of multinational activities in the Third World must incorporate all levels of economic change outlined above, irrespective of the particular focus of the individual investigation. As might be expected this focus changes throughout the volume, with the first three essays, in particular, adopting a more pronounced global perspective. Subsequent contributions concentrate more closely on regional, national, sectoral or corporate levels.

It must also be pointed out that the contributors vary considerably in the nature of their approach towards the acti-vities of multinational firms. Some are essentially specialists in Third World development and tend to have formulated their interest in MNCs because of the impact such firms are having within the development process of individual countries of re-gions. Other contributors have been more concerned with economic development in a broader context and their interest in the impact of MNCs is directed more towards the rewards they bring to the developed nations in which they are theoretically based. This dual interpretation of the operations of MNCs should not be considered as depriving the volume of a cohesive focus; on the contrary, it offers a balance of views that is too often missing.

In Chapter One Ian Hamilton provides an overview of multi-national corporations. This chapter underpins the subsequent ones by providing an introduction to the main trends in multi-national development, the emergence of a body of literature on multinational activities and the main areas of debate. The elements of a theory of multinational development and operation are outlined and the inevitability of the development of multi-national activity under capitalism is stressed.

Gerald Manners in Chapter Two continues with the broad inter-national perspective but narrows the focus to consider those MNCs that are concerned with the exploitation of non-renewable re-sources. These corporations, which may be termed MNRCs are a distinctive if varied group. In general they are involved in large-scale long-term investments which makes them much more sensitive to uncertain economic and political conditions than those corporations concerned, for example, with labour inten-sive manufacturing processes. Over the last fifteen years the MNRCs have become increasingly risk averse; as a result they have reduced their role in the production and trade in non-renewable resources in general and in the Third World in particular. For many corporations higher cost production in more 'secure' developed countries has become a more attractive option than Third World activities.

In Chapter Three Sue Cunningham follows up and elaborates a number of the issues raised by Ian Hamilton in Chapter One. The role of MNCs in the financial and industrial restructuring of Latin America which since the early 1970s has taken place as both a response to, and an integral part of, the changing world economy, is examined. In this discussion particular emphasis is laid on the role of FDI (Foreign Direct Investment) in underpinning the activities of MNCs. Additionally the increasing role of the multinational banks both as lenders and orchestrators of MNC activity is examined. Overall since the early 1970s the industrial sectors of most Latin American states have been orientated increasingly away from 'traditional' or 'basic' consumer good production and towards higher technology sectors in which MNCs are coming to control an increased share.

Since the early 1970s the restructuring of the Latin American economies has resulted in them being much more firmly integrated into the world economy and under increasing control by a small group of OECD states.

Steve Williams in Chapter Four focuses on an area of multinational enterprise that is extremely powerful in its impact and yet little investigated, so well are the activities of the arms trade underplayed and concealed. The chapter documents the dimensions of its production and distribution and indicates clearly the way in which arms manufacture in the Third World is subject to the same constraints and controls as any other MNC activity, condoned only too eagerly by governments anxious to spend their limited revenues on military rather than more basic needs.

In Chapter Five Jeff Henderson employs the theory of the new international division of labour to examine the nature of the American semiconductor industry as it is structured in Southeast Asia. He illustrates that, in contrast to conventional wisdom on this matter, a distinct subregional division of labour has emerged in which cities such as Singapore and Hong Kong play a crucial role. The social, economic and spatial consequences of these new developments are immense but as yet imperfectly understood and Henderson finishes his narrative with some timely pointers for future research directions.

Bob Gwynne in Chapter Six provides an analysis of MNC activity at state level in Latin America which complements the more internationalist perspective provided by Sue Cunningham in Chapter Three. The main focus of the chapter is on the varied and changing roles of MNCs in the association of state, private and multinational activity, frequently termed the 'triple alliance' which typifies much of the recent industrial development in the region. Particular attention is given to the differential reaction of MNCs to the progressive 'opening up' of

Latin American economies to the influences of the world economy.

In Chapter Seven Chris Rogerson and Barbara Tucker bring together two under-researched areas: the emergence of Third World regional based MNCs and the role of MNCs in the commercialization of traditional rural production. The chapter focuses on a longitudinal study of the development of MNC control over the indigenous sorghum brewing activities of Central Africa. This study demonstrates the value of longitudinal research in revealing the activities of MNCs in the Third World. Of specific interest is the documenting of the existence of a small group of Third World based MNCs whose activities are limited to a particular region because of their concentration on the production of commodities that are tied to localized cultural tastes.

Rick Auty in Chapter Eight examines the problems posed in small, relatively resource-rich countries, of trying to ensure that the benefits are distributed fairly throughout society. He makes it clear that the constraints on such actions lie not only with the companies themselves but also with the weak, often self-interested, governments of those countries. His detailed examination of resource exploitation by MNCs in Jamaica, Trinidad and Guyana reveals that it is often in situations where greatest sensitivity and cooperation are needed, that the MNC and the relevant government have the worst relations to the detriment of all.

References

Bukharin, N. (1917) *Imperialism and the World Economy*, (in Russian), 1st English edition 1929, Martin Lawrence, London.
Lenin, V.I. (1916) *Imperialism, the Highest Stage of Capitalism*, (in Russian), 13th English edition 1966, Progress Publishers, Moscow.

Chapter One

THE MULTINATIONALS: SPEARHEAD OR SPECTRE?

F.E.I. Hamilton

In the late 1950s a London theatre successfully staged a play entitled *Stop the world - I want to get off!* A 'zany comedy', it nevertheless conveyed the analogy of one of the most serious challenges to social scientists in general and to economic geographers in particular: namely, trying to catch up with, and then keep abreast of, real-world change and processes of change. Once one has 'caught up' with the world, it is then a major task to unravel the essentials of change from the ever-rising tides both of information and, to an extent, disinformation. There is a need to distance oneself from reality for a while to build up a balanced perspective. By then, though, the real world has changed yet again.

The study of the phenomenon called the MNC (Multinational Corporation) is a classic example of this type of problem. By the mid-1960s, despite Lillienthal's introduction of the term (Lillienthal, 1960:119), a great gap had opened up between the vastly increased real-world significance of MNCs and the very limited interest in, or investigation of, them. Several explanations can be suggested for this unsatisfactory situation. First, political and linguistic barriers in North America and Western Europe largely stultified the dissemination of Lenin's (1916) penetrating pre-Revolutionary analysis of mainly American and German 'monopolies', 'combines' or 'big enterprise' which formed a key part of his *Imperialism: The Highest Stage of Capitalism*. Second, in part this reflected the ascendancy in the West of neo-classical economic theory which had both diverted scientific attention away from the more classical 'real world' economics of Alfred Marshall for instance, and yet also underpinned the thinking behind anti-trust legislation in a number of countries. And third, the rise of Keynesian economics from the 1930s unleashed a growing preoccupation amongst economists, geographers and policymakers with national social and economic issues and their concomitant 'blinkering' to the operation of many international forces.

Nevertheless, about the time *Stop the world - I want to get off!* was playing to full houses in London, the foundations

1

were being laid (*e.g.* Balogh and Streeten, 1960; Chandler, 1962; Dunning, 1958; Hymer, 1960; Seers, 1963) for what became from the late 1960s an explosion of publications in economics and business studies attempting to identify, define, describe, analyse and predict the character, significance, strategies, structures, spread and behaviour of MNCs (for an extensive recent bibliography, see: Hood and Young, 1982). Much of this literature covers the same ground but incremental conceptual progress and major syntheses were made, particularly by Caves (1971); Dunning (1974); Hood and Young (1982); Kindelberger (1969); Parry (1979); Rugman (1981); Vernon (1977). Economic geographers have contributed modest quantitative yet significant qualitative additions to the debates on MNCs (see, for instance: Hamilton, 1976, 1981; Jansen and Van Weesep, 1980; Hamilton and Linge, 1981; Taylor and Thrift, 1982). Nevertheless, while the mass of publications provide in-depth examination of MNCs in general, and a few firms in particular, important gaps remain in our knowledge of past trends and experience; and yet there are signs that the character and behaviour of MNCs and national attitudes to them are again changing under the stressful politico-economic conditions of the mid-1980s.

PROBLEMS OF DEFINITION

A basic problem lies in the continuing debate concerning what is an MNC (see Linge and Hamilton, 1981:48-58). There is neither a single nor a simple definition: criteria such as size of enterprise, degree of 'transnationality', ownership, and focus of control all have pitfalls. There is also confusion over terminology. Before 1974 the term 'transnational' was being applied to a specific sub-set of multinationals, namely to firms whose owners were located in two countries (*e.g.* Unilever which is an Anglo-Dutch firm). The establishment by the United Nations in the mid-1970s of both a Centre and a Commission on Transnational Corporations has probably stimulated the more popular (and confusing) interchangeable use of the terms 'multinational' and 'transnational'. The UN may have preferred the latter to meet objections from socialist countries to the term 'multinational', especially if the work of its bodies was to encompass the overseas activities of enterprises fully or partly owned by CMEA (Council for Mutual Economic Aid) - Bulgaria, Cuba, Czechoslovakia, the German Democratic Republic, Hungary, Mongolia, North Korea, Poland, Romania, the Soviet Union and Vietnam.

Although size is an important criterion for distinguishing multinationals from other enterprises, one should differentiate between absolute and relative size. Certainly the largest firms account for a very significant proportion of the world's stock of foreign investment and they wield substantial economic and political power, with the total sales of many corporations singly exceeding the Gross National Products of many nation

states (see Linge and Hamilton, 1981:50). Yet a far wider range
of enterprises have become significant as MNCs because of their
relative size, *i.e.* their dominance of particular segments of
international markets for specialized products or services:
many MNCs are quite small in terms of value of sales when measured against the world's top 500 corporations.

This, however, ties in with the problem of the degree of
'transnationality' for a firm to be an MNC.   Most authorities
would accept production in one foreign country (*i.e.* two countries in all) as a minimum requirement for such a description.
Barnet and Müller (1975) argue, however, that 'transnationality'
should not be measured only by where firms operate but also by
the degree of internationalization of the management, stock
ownership and control of foreign affiliates.   Ownership chains
have become so complex in many corporations that major research
must be undertaken to unravel 'who owns whom'.   The source of
control may be equally elusive not only because majority ownership of an affiliate abroad is not needed to achieve control
(which may be possible with as little as 3-10 per cent shareholding) but also because of the increased use by MNCs of non-
equity arrangements such as licensing, franchising and co-production in foreign countries without the need for the MNCs to
establish a physical presence inside their borders.

There is in reality, therefore, a complex 'hierarchy' of
MNCs in size, structure and spatial spread. Yet as Parry (1980:
1) states:

> the stereotype multinational enterprise [demonstrates]
> (1) a structural involvement in more than one nation mar-
> ket, with a 'significant' proportion of enterprise op-
> erations based in more than one nation; and (2) an
> organizational commitment to decision-making on the
> basis of global resources available to and global op-
> portunities facing the enterprise.

The MNC thus ties together (and makes interdependent) the fortunes of the areas of the home and host countries where it is
located: this is its key geographic significance.

TOWARDS A THEORY OF MULTINATIONAL CORPORATIONS

Classical international capital flow theory explained reasonably
well the pattern of predominantly portfolio investments overseas
before the Second World War.   With the rise of FDI (Foreign
Direct Investment) from the 1930s involving international transfers of technology and skills, however, only theories which
embraced a range of decision parameters and also took account
of the important distinctions between *initial* and *on-going* FDI
have sustained much credibility.   Thus theoretical support for
the international spatial structures of MNC activities must be

sought in combinations of:
1.   The supply-orientated theory of location allocating
production to least-cost centres, a theory which is further
underpinned by the basis of comparative costs and advantages in
international trade theory.
2.   The market-orientated theory of location allocating
FDI to profit-maximizing centres and incorporating both the interdependent behaviour of oligopolistic competitors in search of
spatial monopoly positions in national markets and the risks of
follow-the-leader entry by rivals.   This approach is further
supported by real-world international trade distortions introduced in host country markets by national tariff and other
barriers or by distance and transport time/cost imperfections
which may induce MNCs to make either defensive FDI to maintain
their share of global sales or aggressive FDI to exploit profit
opportunities.
3.   Restrictions on factor mobility imposed by national
ownership of resources or by labour immobilities gave birth to
the product life cycle theory of international trade, innovations
and production which attempts to explain the dynamics of MNC
activity from exports to FDI and subsequent changes in the
character and location of FDI.   (For a discussion see: Linge
and Hamilton, 1981:21-3.)
4.   Industrial organization theories which stress the significance of firm-specific advantages associated with oligopoly
in FDI in general (and when combined with product differentiation,
associated with horizontal FDI in particular);   economies of
scale; and economies of internalization of various transactional costs through the firm's exploitation of its organizational,
accounting, marketing or other skills.
5.   Marxist analysis which emphasizes the capital deepening
process with capital/labour substitution and restructuring in
places of rising wages (or real labour costs) and the displacement of more labour-intensive functions to lower labour-cost
areas.
6.   Finally, market imperfections in host countries introduced by artificial tariffs and other measures may simultaneously
offer MNCs second-best profit opportunities and yield a loss of
real income to the host country itself (Parry, 1980).
However, as mentioned above, Lenin (1916), following Marx
(1848) had already elaborated basic elements of some of these
theoretical points in his analysis of the emerging new technology based on monopolistic firms of the early twentieth
century.

THE WORLD IMPORTANCE OF MNCs

The Apparent Stability of the Role of Multinationals
Recent research by Dunning (1982) has suggested that FDI
was as important in the world economy before 1914 as it became

in the 1960s and 1970s;   the signs are, however, that as a
proportion of total assets, FDI is now much more significant
in the mid-1980s than before 1914 or in the 1970s.   In reality
Dunning's somewhat surprising finding is explained by the very
serious 'sag' or decline which occurred in FDI (and hence MNC
activity) between 1914 and 1960.   Several factors account for
this.   They may be grouped into two sets of forces.   The
first, world economic recession in the 1920s and particularly
the depression of 1929-32 seriously restricted overseas investment opportunities in all but the newest industries as markets
contracted, sales revenue fell, over-capacity grew and sufficient profit rates disappeared.   This macro-economic constraint
on FDI operated in spatially differentiated degrees, however,
mainly because of the operation of the second set of forces,
notably state policies in selected countries.   Such policies
varied from country to country and had differential effects on
the world pattern of much reduced FDI:
    1.   Economic nationalism, expressed in government pol-
icies for greater tariff protectionism in some already industrialized countries and in the newly independent states seems
to have had complex push-pull effects.   On the one hand, particularly in Eastern Europe, it fragmented into small markets
or truncated the wider markets of former Empires (especially
the Austro-Hungarian market) that could have sustained optimum
or minimum efficient facilities;   on the other hand, protectionism is some larger developing economies (such as Argentina,
Brazil and Chile in Latin America) undoubtedly provided a sufficiently profitable basis to encourage the entry and to support
the operation locally of foreign industrial firms.
    2.   Nationalization of some or all foreign assets in
countries experiencing socialist revolutions led to the closure
to the operations of MNCs of very large regions of the world,
notably the USSR after 1917, Eastern Europe and the Chinese
People's Republic in the late 1940s, and some other Third World
countries after 1950.   State-initiated and managed industrialization in such countries often precluded MNC involvement until
recently.
    Such policies effectively reduced the attraction of host-
country environments for FDI.   Yet other policies - in addition
to the effects of the 1930's depression - constrained the abil-
ities of the source countries of FDI to invest abroad:
    3.   Anti-trust policies especially in the USA in the
inter-war years broke up cartels which had formed nationally
and internationally in some of the newer and profitable electrical and chemical industries and may have reduced the capabilities of individual firms to find the resources to establish
production facilities abroad.
    4.   Restrictions imposed by the US government on the
outflow of American capital had similar effects into the 1950s.
    5.   International political and institutional controls
placed on the re-formation and operations of large West

5

German and Japanese enterprises after the Second World War in
the 1940s and 1950s similarly slowed the rise of MNCs based in
those two leading industrial nations.

Since 1950 three sets of factors have greatly encouraged
the expansion of existing, and proliferation of new MNCs. First,
the huge expansion of world demand for existing, improved and
new manufactures and services that has emanated from:

1.   The post-war reconstruction of Western Europe and
Japan till the early 1950s which depended largely on American
corporate supplies and was further induced by the technology
gap between the USA and these war-devastated economies.

2.   The rapidly expanding capital-goods and consumer-
goods markets in Western Europe and Japan which led, after 1950,
either to entry of US corporations (especially in the former
region) or to US technology transfer through licensing
(especially in Japan).

3.   The entry of NICs (Newly Industrializing Countries)
and some LDCs (Less Developed Countries) into various branches
of mining and manufacturing on the basis of imported know-how,
technology and, partly, capital.

4.   The colossal expansion and global diffusion of the
production and purchase of weapons, armaments and sophisticated
'hearing', 'seeing' and 'sensing' information-gathering equipment as a result of the Cold War between East and West, the
spread of their ideological conflicts into newly independent
states, and the rise of political and military friction between
the developing countries themselves. Although this may not have
led directly to so much foreign output of military or militar-
ily-usable products by MNCs, indirectly it generated sufficient
sales revenues and technological advances for their home production base to facilitate their expansion overseas of *non-
military* production (see chapter 4).

A second major factor encouraging the rise of MNC activity
has been the liberalization of trade in goods and services until
the late 1970s, and latterly money, mostly between the industrialized nations and, to a much lesser extent, between them
and the Third World. Yet residual (or new) barriers erected in
the larger LDCs and NICs which have achieved some measure of
political independence have also operated as important stimuli
to the selective international spread of functions by MNCs.

Third, technological innovations, often made (or quickly
and effectively adopted) by large corporations, have greatly
reinforced their own internationalization capabilities. Prop-
rietary or firm-specific advantages in product and process
technology endow some MNCs with global monopoly advantages in
certain sectors. More generally, innovations have rapidly reduced the costs and the time spent on:

1.   the transport of raw materials, energy, semi-manufac-
tured and manufactured inputs and outputs;

2.   the travel of personnel on decision-making and executive tasks; and

6

3.   the collection, processing and transmission of information. These various kinds of savings have enabled corporations to reduce greatly internal transactional costs while also centralizing their control over operations in widely separated locations.

The Global Dynamics of MNCs

Even if one concedes, therefore, that the proportion of world economic activity controlled by MNCs in the mid-1970s was not significantly different from that in 1914, FDI has fluctuated greatly through time and is now confined spatially to barely 75 per cent of the world's land area c. 1914.   Yet this must not mask the even more fundamental changes that have occurred in patterns of FDI.

The first since then is the growth in the scale of MNC activity. According to Dunning (1982) the estimated stock of accumulated FDI rose from US$14.3 billion in 1914 to US$386.2 billion in 1978, although the most rapid growth - a six-fold increase from US$63 billion - took place between 1960 and 1978.   A related change is that the largest MNCs today concentrate relatively more MNC business (in US$ sales revenue terms) than they did in 1914.

The second is the shift in the character and qualitative structure of MNC investment.   As the world economy has progressed from a dominantly extractive through an increasingly industrialized to an 'information-orientated' (rather than a 'post-industrial') one, MNCs have:

generally entered and come to dominate more sectors (both manufacturing and non-manufacturing), most especially being the main catalysts of expansion of activities where technology is advanced and capital requirements high or rapidly rising in relation to labour; and

often diversified their activities individually from their initial or 'traditional' sector into other industrial or non-industrial sectors.

Before 1914 the majority of MNCs engaged in portfolio investments or were trading companies handling the movement and processing of materials and agricultural produce.   Yet by then a new generation of mainly UK, USA, French and German based MNCs had begun to emerge to dominate the then newest, capital-and-technology intensive chemicals, electrical, engineering and mass-produced consumer-goods industries. Thus the period 1875-1914 saw the infancy and adolescence of the type of activity which has become most common since 1960, $i.e.$ the location of branch production facilities in foreign countries.   Although MNCs continue to invest in oil-drilling and metals, FDI in the extractive sectors has greatly declined as a proportion of MNC activity in general.   One reason lies in the impact of state policies in many Third World and OPEC countries where attempts

7

have been made, with greater or lesser success, to indigenize ownership of plantation agriculture and mineral extraction. Far more important, however, has been the growth in the importance of manufacturing abroad by MNCs especially since 1955.   Still more recently, MNCs have emerged in selected and apparently more profitable sectors concerned with either servicing indus- trial MNCs (*e.g.* with capital, other banking and accountancy services, insurance, transport and communications) or marketing their products (*e.g.* advertising, media, wholesaling, retailing and catering).   The 1980s appear to be witnessing the emergence of new MNCs and the link-ups of existing MNCs to penetrate and to internationalize research and development in a number of high technology fields.

One of the most significant aspects of this process is the interlocking spread of MNC business, a factor underestimated in past industrial studies.   Research in the 1970s certainly rev- ealed the clustered entry of American MNCs in linked and oligo- polistic sectors into the West European market in the inter-war and post-war periods.   The classic example was the vehicle as- sembly industry dominated by the 'big three' US manufacturers (General Motors, Ford and Chrysler) which brought in a wide range of US vehicle components producers (*e.g.* Goodyear: tyres; Borg-Warner: gearboxes; Lockheed or Eaton: brake systems, etc.). In retrospect this work served only to highlight the narrow industrial bias of researchers who overlooked that such entry was also accompanied by a wider cluster of linked non-manufac- turing sectors to finance the manufacturers (*e.g.* US banks and insurers) or to sell their products (US advertisers; or US car-rental firms such as Avis, Budget and Hertz).   Thus the 'progression' of MNC activity through various economic sectors should be seen as an interdependent process.

Third, the geographic patterns of home and host countries of MNCs have undergone major changes during the past seventy years.   Against the background of the enormous rise in FDI, the main trends regarding the countries of origin of MNC invest- ment have been:

1.   A big relative decline in the importance of the for- mer Western European colonial states (notably the UK, France, Belgium, Italy and the Netherlands) from *c.* 70 per cent of FDI in 1914 to *c.* 25 per cent in 1978.

2.   The rise of US multinational FDI from *c.* 18 per cent in 1914 to a peak of around 55 per cent in the mid-1960s, de- clining to *c.* 43 per cent in 1978.

3.   The recent expansion of West German and Japanese firms into MNCs accounting for 8-9 per cent each in 1978 as against about 1 per cent each in 1960.

4.   The slow emergence of developing countries as very modest centres of MNCs, the entire Third World registering a rise from *c.* 1 per cent in 1960 to 3 per cent in 1978.

The most striking features of the pattern of location of FDI since 1914 have been the increasing localization of MNC

activity in the developed countries and a concomitant sharp relative decline in the importance of FDI in the developing countries.   These broad trends, however, hide several other significant geographical shifts through time:
1.   The relatively 'cyclical' pattern of flows of FDI into the USA, with 'peaks' in 1914, 1960 and 1978 and 'troughs' in 1938 and 1971.   In aggregate, the most marked growth has resulted from the inflow of West European and Japanese investments in the 1970s, mainly into manufacturing and services; but the USA had never hosted more than 14 per cent of world FDI before 1978, although that level may be exceeded by the mid-1980s.
2.   The greater prominence of FDI in Canada than in the USA, an especially large rise being apparent during and after the Second World War so that by 1960 Canada localized 23.7 per cent of world FDI, much of it in the form of US-owned branch plants.
3.   The spectacular and sustained rise of MNC activity in Western Europe from c. 7-8 per cent before 1939 to 38 per cent in 1978, mostly as a result of post-war US and UK FDI in the EEC 'Six', although the UK still retained its position in 1978 in the region as the leading host country (recording a fairly consistent 8 or 9 per cent of world FDI between 1960 and 1978).
4.   A 'cyclical' pattern of investment in Australasia and South Africa, peaking at 10 per cent of world FDI in 1971, partly as MNCs responded to changing world market conditions for minerals and local market opportunities.
5.   Extremely limited FDI in Japan, despite a rise from 0.2 per cent in 1960 to 2 per cent in 1978.
6.   All regions of the Third World have declined in relative importance as host countries for FDI since the 1930s, yet it is notable that since 1960 the rise of the NICs in Latin America (Brazil, Mexico) and in Southeast and East Asia (Hong Kong, Korea, Malaysia, Singapore, Taiwan) has ensured that these two world regions have maintained a fairly stable share of total FDI respectively of 15 per cent and 7 per cent.
Interestingly enough, fourthly, the spatial distribution of numbers of manufacturing subsidiaries between 1914 and 1960 shows a broadly contrary trend to that of aggregate FDI: the proportion located in the industrialized countries declined from just under 80 per cent to just below 66 per cent.   There are several possible explanations for this phenomenon:
1.   The greater capitalization, larger size and vertical integration of manufacturing plants established in the developed countries than of those set up in the LDCs.   Related to this factor is
2.   The different sectoral composition of manufacturing activities located by MNCs in the 'North' as opposed to the 'South', with an emphasis on more advanced technology sectors in the former and their comparative or complete absence from the latter.

9

3.   The increasing importance of the diffusion of non-manufacturing MNCs into developed host-country markets relative to manufacturing in contrast to their limited location in developing countries where industrial subsidiaries remain more significant.   Thus the structure of the spread of MNC activity globally is somewhat analogous to the displacement in developed countries manufacturing from highly urbanized regions into more peripheral and rural areas.

4.   The increased importance of the Third World for manufacturing subsidiaries is linked in part to the proliferation of new sovereign states and the initiation in them of so-called import substitution policies by the new governments.   Such an environment encouraged MNCs to establish small, often non-integrated, plants behind tariff walls to serve national markets of restricted size.   The only exception to the general trend in subsidiaries in the 1946-61 period were the UK multinationals which located 80 per cent of their subsidiaries in developed countries, especially Europe, not only because of the market growth potentials of this region but also because of perceived political uncertainty in the longer term in newly independent or remaining British colonies in Africa or Asia.

Data on subsidiaries for the 1961 to 1978 period are as yet unavailable; but it is necessary to refer here briefly to some components of change which have occurred during the past twenty-five years.   First, 'recommended', 'fashionable' or apparently 'successful' government policies for industrialization in Third World countries have altered markedly from an almost total dominance of so-called 'import substitution' measures to the greater prominence of 'export orientation'. This has had very significant consequences for the international pattern and type of MNC activity in the Third World:

1.   A relative shift from resource-based FDI, this being one reason for the relative decline of MNC involvement in the LDCs.

2.   A slowdown has occurred in the construction of partially-integrated or non-integrated and sub-optimal plants assembling imported materials and components into finished goods to serve small national markets protected by tariff walls.

3.   A rapid growth in the development of 'export platforms' in locations overseas of more optimal larger-scale and specialized manufacturing or other facilities designed to serve global or international markets at highly competitive prices.   Within this category it may be important to distinguish between those facilities which are:

(a) exporting to broad consumer-goods markets through retailing and wholesaling outlets, although some of these may be large national or MNC monopolistic retailing firms (such as C & A, Spar or Habitat) subcontracting production from NICs and LDCs, and

(b) those 'exporting' to other capital-goods markets often as 'cogs in the chain' or production of individual

MNCs and so, in effect, becoming internalized in their 'intra-firm' trade.

A second set of forces which, as yet, has unclear implications for developing countries concerns the interactions between capitalist MNCs and state-managed or worker-managed enterprises in the socialist countries. Although begun by Yugoslavia as early as 1953 (for the licensed production of Fiat cars), it will be the 1970s that will probably be remembered as the decade of East-West detente which spawned the rapid rise of joint ventures, licensing and non-equity resource flows between (mainly European) MNCs or European subsidiaries of US-owned MNCs and enterprises in CMEA countries. A complex tripartite East-West-South system of cooperation began to develop which helped to reduce capital construction costs in the recession of the late 1970s and stimulated more industrialization in selected Third World countries (see: Gutman and Arkwright, 1981). Increased international tension since 1979 has seriously weakened this interaction and, from the MNC's viewpoint, has sometimes been exacerbated by Western governments' restrictions on the export of 'high technology' to the CMEA countries. Only time will tell whether the current interest of the Chinese People's Republic in Western technology transfer for both its onshore and offshore development will create a sufficient geographic shift in East-West trade to compensate for shrunken CMEA markets.

The other side of this set of interdependencies relates to the growth of the so-called 'red multinationals'. Evidence is fragmentary, but McMillan (1979) identified a majority of the 544 CMEA enterprises operating in OECD and Third World countries as marketing CMEA products in European OECD countries (307), while 185 located in developing countries engaged in marketing (78), mining and raw-material processing (51) and services (56). Manufacturing seems to be completely localized within the CMEA itself.

Although by no means a new phenomenon amongst MNCs, the 1970s and 1980s have witnessed a third trend: an accelerated rate of liquidations of, and divestments in, some (occasionally all) overseas affiliates.   The following aspects of this should be noted here:

1.   Most liquidations have been carried out by MNCs operating in low or mature technology sectors in which entry barriers are falling (or have been made to fall by state or cartel policies, as in petroleum) and especially by firms which are competitively weaker on costs, design, product reliability, marketing and delivery dates.   In many instances this is an integral part of the 'cross-investment' pattern under conditions of recession (*e.g.* the cutbacks in overseas operations, almost in a clustered fashion, by US and UK motor vehicle and components manufacturers in the face of continental European and Japanese competition and FDI).   Some experts see this as the 'zero-sum game' in which MNC competition results solely in

11

displacement in mature markets.

2.   Voluntary divestment in the interests of global or
regional rationalization of corporate activities may also involve liquidations.   Recent examples here are the sales by
large petroleum-refining MNCs of their chemicals or refining
plants to OPEC-based organizations as the MNCs diversify or
shift into more profitable lines of production (*e.g.* Exxon into
business machinery and office automation).

3.   Forced divestment as a result of nationalization.

A fourth trend involves the recent changes in the locational
pattern of MNC activities.   The recessionary conditions of the
past eight years in particular, exacerbated by the demise of
detente and by military conflicts around the globe, have led to
a very substantial shift of standardized or routine functions
by MNCs of all 'national' origins into places which offer cost-
cutting advantages.   Relocation has been a necessity for many
manufacturing MNCs to maintain their market share and to minimize the fall in their rates of profit.   'Push' factors in
this situation have been inflation in wages in the MNCs' home
countries (in the case of Japan also land-price inflation and
pollution costs) and in currency exchange rates (especially in
the UK, Netherlands, Switzerland, West Germany and, most recently, the USA).   'Pull' factors have been the low - often many
times lower - labour costs per unit output mainly in Third World
(and especially population-rich Asian) countries.   Two points
must be added.   It is not only Third World countries which
have been (albeit selectively) recipients of relocated and relatively labour-intensive functions: the Mediterranean periphery of Europe from Portugal to Turkey also 'gained' FDI for this
reason.   And, in addition to low labour costs, a major factor
attracting industrial development or relocation by MNCs in the
short term has been the proliferation of capital and operational
cost-cutting facilities offered by government subsidies, infrastructure or tax holidays in selected regions, export-processing
or free trade or enterprise zones located in developed, newly
industrializing and developing countries. In the long term such
policies may be self-defeating and also result in a 'zero-sum
game' of spatial displacement: in the present world conditions
of simultaneously shrinking manufacturing and industry-related
job opportunities and escalating inter-governmental competition
for those opportunities, it is a leading question as to how
'generous' can governments afford to make the subsidies or how
'low' can the human living and working conditions be 'maintained' (in the LDCs) or be 'reduced' and 'worsened' (in the developed countries).   *Ceteris paribus* this should enhance the
attractiveness of LDCs for the location of manufacturing.

A fifth trend, which has recently become more pronounced,
overtly warns us however, that the shift to LDC is unlikely to
continue for very long: the apparent coincidence or partial
interdependence - authorities argue over this - between the
economic depression since 1979 and the trough between Kondratiev

long waves that implies a major shift between technologies and
hence in economic structures. Rapid innovation of new technologies threatens to eliminate the labour-cost advantages of LDCs
and to recentralize MNC activities in developed countries where
capital and know-how are sufficient to support sophisticated
automation, robotization, and hence R & D (research and development) activities (Hamilton, 1984).
       Reinforcing these new constraints on Third World indus-
trialization are the outcomes of: the OPEC-led oil price inflation which has increased capital investment costs per unit
capacity; the recycling of petrodollars which encouraged banks
in developed countries to extend large loans to many developing
countries; the monetarist and protectionist responses of some
Western governments to their national economic crises (espec-
ically the USA and UK) which have greatly inflated interest
rates on loans to developing countries while simultaneously
restricting the export markets for goods from those countries.
At the end of 1983 the twenty-five largest Third World debtor
nations owed an estimated US$530 billion to banks in advanced
industrial nations: one could speculate on the basis of
Dunning's estimates for 1978 (see p. 7 above) that total Third
World debt currently equals, if not exceeds, the stock of all
accumulated FDI. Moreover, as interest rates have risen, the
debt-servicing ratios have increased from averages for 1977 of
13, 11 and 28 per cent per annum to averages for 1983, of 21,
24 and 42 per cent per annum respectively for the Middle East,
Africa and Latin America (including the Caribbean). Whereas
these countries have sustained average debt payments of c.
US$50-60 million annually from 1979 to 1984, interest payments
have risen in the same period from c. US$35 million to c. US$75
million annually. Under these conditions fewer MNCs have the
incentive or the capability to establish subsidiaries in either
LDCs generally or in the Latin American NICs: and the longer-
term political and economic uncertainties associated with rising
social unrest (itself related to the debt problem) act as
further deterrents to FDI in these countries.

MULTINATIONALS: SPEARHEAD OR SPECTRE?

MNCs as a species are an inevitable product of the capitalist
process. It could be argued that their phenomenal growth in
recent years has made them the major determinants of the course
of that process. MNCs are thus the spearhead of the capitalist
system and become identified equally in the eyes of critics and
adversaries with the very spectre of capitalism itself.   In
reality the pertinent questions that must be raised are not
whether MNCs are either a spearhead or a spectre; but rather
to what extent, in which ways, for what purposes, why and where
are they spearheads or spectres.   Undoubtedly some MNCs are
predominantly spectres, others mainly spearheads; most may be

one or the other at certain times, in certain ways and certain
places.   In any situation, however, the issues are complex and
the outcomes may only be judged from a variety of viewpoints as
well as from the perspective of what would be were there no MNCs
in any given situation.

Perceptions of MNCs

Value judgements abound in the evaluation of MNC activities:
and they would almost inevitably continue to be in evidence
even if MNCs were forced to reveal all their secrets and accounts publicly.   As is outlined elsewhere (Linge and Hamilton,
1981:78-81) there are broadly three viewpoints supporting FDI
in principle and practice ((a) the business school, (b) norm-
ative economic, and (c) neo-traditionalist economic approaches)
and three opposing it ((d) nationalists, (e) dependency
theorists, and (f) Marxists).   While these may appear to be
somewhat 'armchair' or 'lectern' categories, yet even allowing
for significant nuances between them some are very clearly
identifiable with various real-world actors.   MNC managements
and shareholders undoubtedly subscribe to (a), economic advisers
to governments and corporations may support (a), (b) or (c)
while government officials and politicians may identify themselves more with (d) and, in some countries and parties, with
(e) or (f).   Recent political shifts to the 'right' in developed countries and the persistence or ascendancy of similar
political or military factions in many LDCs and NICs mean,
however, that in very large areas of the world governments and
bureaucrats may be sympathetic to, or believe in (a), (b) or
(c) and hence seek to court MNCs. By contrast, it is not at all
certain that workers, households and the public at large very
clearly support any one of these viewpoints: their interests
are primarily 'bread and butter' and thus they may favour (or
not oppose) MNCs when these provide jobs, security of employment, career prospects and good wages or salaries, but they
will resent them when they do not (or cease to) do so.
     One of the major conflicts of our time is that between (a)
corporations which become ever more international and global,
organized and integrated across national frontiers, continents
and oceans, and (b) the sovereignty of nation states and of life
in their constituent regions (see Hamilton and Linge, 1981).
Politicians, the vast majority of the people they represent (or
say they represent), and government advisers are all 'prisoners
of their territorial bailiwick' which for the capitalist corporation 'the world is an oyster' (Barnet and Müller, 1975).
     Given that MNCs often successfully remain secretive about
their intentions, operations and performance, perception is a
major ingredient in any assessment of them.   A recent report
by the Corporate Responsibility Centre (1983) suggests that
there is an 'opinion abyss' regarding MNC activities between MNC

decision-makers and diplomats (of many national backgrounds)
working in LDCs.   While 85 per cent of MNC managements surveyed
thought that MNCs 'behaved well', 75 per cent of the diplomats
interviewed believed that MNCs were involved in, among other
things, corrupt practices or policies detrimental to the societies, economies and environments of LDCs. Building bridges of
confidence over this abyss for the mutual benefit of the future
cooperation and interaction between the Third World and the MNCs
may prove to be as difficult as re-establishing East-West
detente or reversing the arms race.   Yet it may have more chance
of success, at least selectively between countries and MNCs,
given the pressing needs in most countries to create jobs and
to generate higher-value manufactured exports.

Centralization and Concentration:
Keys to MNC Global Dominance
It is perhaps symptomatic of the MNC's 'great crusade for
understanding' to bridge this gap that the dominant vision
amongst executives of US corporations interviewed by Barnet and
Muller (1975) sought a 'genuine government-business-labour
partnership' in which government's real job was to foster the
best possible environment for business:

> stabilize the economy ... with wage and price controls
> ... pump-prime [it] with capital investment in military,
> social and infrastructure programmes ... to smooth ...
> changes in the location and function of MNC activity by
> training and moving workers ... not to protect old
> industries ... and to educate the population to be ef-
> ficient and respectful corporate workers
> (Barnet and Müller, 1975: 111-113)

Statements made by managing directors of major European MNCs at
The *Financial Times*/IRM Conference on 'Multinationals and the
EEC' in London in June 1984 broadly concurred with this stance.
Executives frequently argue that their firms create wealth for
society, that society should thus be grateful and leave the
MNCs unfettered.   Of course, they fail to add that this is
tantamount to shirking social responsibility, that in reality
the wealth created is very unevenly distributed, and that apart
from satisfying the monetary appetites of the shareholders the
company accountants do everything possible to launder money out
of society's sights.
     Such then, is the power of the MNCs that they have been
able individually or collectively to bargain to obtain many
concessions from governments in a large number of developed
OECD countries and in almost all bigger or smaller NICs and
LDCs.   Collectively, they have steered the course of capitalism
in such a way as to convince governments that their 'supportive'

policies are necessary if they are to attract FDI. In attempts
to grapple with world recession, and its more localized sub-
national impacts, governments have become ever more intensely
locked directly and indirectly into cut-throat inter-governmental competition for MNC 'favours' through tax concessions,
regional aid and free-trade zone policies and, more recently,
through their sectoral aid, infrastructure-improvement policies
or innovations-orientated incentives.   While some, like Franko
(1982), may argue that proliferation of MNCs and especially of
MNC source economies 'has vastly reduced the bargaining power
either of individual MNCs or of MNCs from any particular
country', few would disagree with the observation that MNCs
individually have succeeded in 'dividing and ruling' with regard
to state intervention in First and Third World countries; their
'success' has been enhanced in recession as competition between
more nations for fewer jobs or less new capacity has enabled
any single MNC to threaten more countries that it will 'locate
elsewhere' unless they meet its terms.
     Apart from recession which may be a relatively shorter-
term phenomenon (albeit already a decade long), the key long-
term factors underpinning the increased bargaining power of MNCs
are two.   First, growth rates in MNC overseas investment have
consistently, and often substantially, exceeded national economic growth rates in OECD countries, including even those of
the NICs.   Thus collectively MNCs progressively concentrate
more on the assets, jobs and value-added tax of the capitalist
world.   And concentration increases towards the top of the
MNC 'pyramid'.   This natural capitalist process has not just
led to the creation of a dual or segmented economy in advanced
as well as developing countries but as MNC activity has spread
in interlocking fashion into extractive, manufacturing and non-
manufacturing functions it is fashioning an MNC economy and a
residual economy.   (And financial practices are increasingly
supporting the former and marginalizing the latter.)
     Second, MNCs have become far more highly centralized
'supra-national' powers, even though the degree of centralization of decision-making, control and finance varies between
industries, activities and MNCs within the same broad industry
group.   Centralization is a science refined and sophisticated
by modern communications technologies.   Although these technologies permit spatial separation and decentralization of more
routine tasks, it has removed much decision-making and control
from former decision centres to a smaller number of headquarters places.   Centralization thus lies at the roots both of the
'North-South' problem and of the increasing differentiation of
national or international space between 'core' global-city
regions (and there is also a hierarchy of these) and specialized
industrial-distributive hinterlands/peripheries.   MNCs have
undermined local and regional economic and social autonomy.

It is now widely recognized that geographers have neglected for far too long the importance of finance.   The major constraint on corporate growth is a sufficient supply of capital. The rate of profit is thus fundamental to the 'success' of the MNC. Evidence suggests that firms are induced to become MNCs when their economic strength and efficiency is such that they can generate surplus capital for investment which cannot - for reasons of scarcities in factor supply, rising costs, or stag-nating sales at home - realize a sufficient rate of profit in the home country, but which can do so abroad.   Multinational-ization is thus encouraged by the ability to earn higher rates of profit abroad than at home.   The exact combination of stimuli to the firm for realizing those higher profits is related to resource extraction, tariffs, protected markets, comparative costs and superior corporate attributes in management, marketing or technology as outlined by the theories of MNC. According to US Department of Commerce surveys in the 1970s the dependence of US-based MNCs on foreign profits has grown at an accelerating rate since the mid-1960s and there is every reason to believe that a similar trend since the early 1970s holds true for West European and Japanese firms.

The reasons why profit rates tend to be higher - sometimes many times higher - abroad are numerous.   The leading factors are: lower production costs, especially resulting from lower labour costs; ability to transfer outdated technology abroad and charge high rates for its use; managerial ability of the corporation to indulge in transfer pricing so that weaker econ-omies (or states with weaker governments) subsidize the corpor-ation's home country activities, especially long-term and expensive R & D or advertising; the ability of MNCs to derive a double comparative advantage so reducing costs and raising profits by trading internationally with itself (the internal-ization theory); ability to bargain 'good deals' with governments and to minimize or effectively eliminate taxation or other controls; and the capability to attract local capital at fav-ourable interest rates. Normally in the long run, there is thus a net outflow - sometimes a very large net outflow - of finance from host countries.

Since 1970 a combination of factors has led to a rapid concentration and centralization in the banking sector. Inter-nationalization of finance capital has become inextricably in-terwoven with the internationalization of production and all other services.   Economic geographers considered it essential for growth in production to have access to cheap capital.   The past decade in particular has seen a rapid rise in the cost of capital borrowing with two important effects: first, it is far harder for small firms to borrow: MNCs are in a relatively stronger position to borrow, restructure and expand to cope with changing economic conditions; and second, profit rates to banks

have risen; their growth and multinationalization has perhaps
been the most spectacular change in the global economic scene
in the 1970s and 1980s, aided by major changes in the organization of money markets, currency exchange and laws. There is
now, in effect therefore, a large group of MNCs in banking which
form the top of the pyramid *above* and amongst the very largest
industrial corporations (including the petroleum companies).
Because of their high profitability the MNC banks have drawn in
large sums of money from the OPEC and LDC countries, often pre-
empting scarce local funds which might have been used to finance
locally-controlled projects. While, therefore, banks have
innovated many changes in the liberalization of capital and
currency flows, their large resources and power can be regarded
as a 'spectre'. Whether the individual or collective indebtedness of Third World countries as a threat to the stability of
the very banking system itself is either a sufficient condition
or a desirable one to encourage banks to aid Third World development more generously is a moot point: pressure from US
interest rates seems to be operating in the opposite direction.
     What is worrying is that contemporary needs in capital in-
vestment, especially in R & D for new industries such as space
communications, robotics, and biotechnology and the ability of
large MNCs to accumulate capital, are leading to the creation
of yet a 'higher' order of MNCs. That echelon currently comprises
consortia of banks or, in the case of robotics for instance,
oligopolistic link-ups between US, European and Japanese for R
& D, design and ultimately co-production. Moreover, firms which
started in the newest and most profitable activities - information processing and media - have rapidly diversified into
finance, technology and trade and become leading MNCs (*e.g.* RCA).
And centralized information control may be economically more
potent and politically and socially less desirable than financial
centralization.

Labour Market Impacts

Barnet and Müller (1975) argue that workers and their dependants
are probably the biggest losers from MNC activities. True, MNC
superior technology, marketing and profit rates often enable
them to pay higher salaries (for equal? work) than other firms
and *as a whole* (though only in selected locations) they may
employ a higher white collar:blue collar ratio of workers than
national or local firms. In LDCs they may pay higher wages,
too. Working conditions and workers' facilities may also be
better but there is usually a trade-off between these and higher
labour productivities.
     The spectre of MNCs for labour derives from four major
sources:
     1.   The ability of MNCs to escape from national government
regulations, welfare policies, or union pressures regarding the

quality of working conditions and hence ultimately from rising
real labour costs in their home countries.

2. Thus the consequential overseas movement of MNCs in
the long-term leads to significant job losses in the developed
countries, and to the weakening of workers' bargaining power,
partly through 'thinning' labour union membership and inter-
union conflicts in trades threatened with significant job losses.
As a result, of course, opportunities for workers in NICs and
LDCs to gain better wages and working conditions are likely
also to be fewer, although their ability to obtain jobs *per se*
may be greater.

3. The creation of global labour markets in effect by MNC
activity *ceteris paribus* works ultimately towards depressing
labour compensation rates especially, but not only, in semi-
skilled and unskilled categories towards the lowest wage rates
and poorest working and living conditions per unit output or
service for employees engaged in various stages of MNC operation.
Here the feedback loop effects of MNCs relocating production to
locations first in, and then sequentially amongst, lesser developed countries could be (or even already is) devastating on
workers in NICs and advanced countries.

4. Despite apparent movement of MNCs through time up the
scale from lesser to greater skill functions, at least in manufacturing, from capital-and-raw material intensive, the effects
are unevenly distributed globally. MNCs have simultaneously
redistributed their functions with the traditional core-region
of the MNC in its home (developed) country experiencing some
replacement of lost skilled, semi-skilled and unskilled jobs
especially by capital deepening, although more usually new types
of semi-skilled jobs have been created in existing and in new
locations in the periphery. The de-skilling debate implied in
this, however, is a very complex and controversial one particularly with respect to the jobs created by MNCs in NICs and LDCs.
It is linked with the issue of technology transfer.

Technology Transfer

The transfer of technology is usually seen as a major factor in
development. Yet it is generally accepted that, first and
foremost, MNCs (at least in manufacturing) transfer older technologies to host countries. Not only does this maximize their
profits from R & D but it also ensures greater 'in-house' control of the process of technology diffusion. Too much competition might result and too quickly (limiting profits to
sustain R & D) if up-to-date technology were transferred and
copied. (Many US corporations now regret having sold technology licences to Japanese firms in the 1950s and 1960s.)
Second, frequently MNCs prohibit exports by NICs or LDCs (and
even some advanced countries) using the technology transferred:
there is much UN documentation on such 'restrictive practices'.

While third, a large proportion of equipment transferred to NICs
and LDCs is often considered to be 'inappropriate' on grounds
that it is capital-intensive (and hence is insufficiently job-
creating in countries mostly with a labour surplus) and usually
produces goods suitable for (or capable of) consumption only by
the elite classes.

By contrast, Emmanuel (1982) argues that while lower technologies (than those introduced by MNCs) may create more jobs
they also generate little value-added and hence little capital
or wealth creation.   And if LDCs are to become NICs they need
up-to-date technologies in order to export and to compete in
world markets on price, quality, design and delivery dates. A
related issue here, however, is that MNCs' activities are also
'inappropriate' in LDCs because they create 'enclave' production
systems with few direct or indirect linkages with, and hence
multiplier effects on, the local economy. And by absorbing local
capital, MNCs using capital-intensive technologies may raise
the opportunity costs of LDC development since a proportion of
the capital invested in the MNCs from local sources is denied
to potential or existing indigenous entrepreneurs.   However,
Parry (1980:155) argues that the critical issue is that

> Absorptive capacity really determines the extent to which
> *potential leakages* take the form of *actual linkages* be-
> tween the MNC and the host economy.   Very often ... min-
> imal impacts [result from] the lack of absorptive capacity
> in the host economy rather than the unwillingness or
> inability of the MNC to link up with [it].

One interesting point here is that the foregoing debate
relates to the major MNCs from developed countries.   Research
recently (*e.g.* Linge and Hamilton, 1981; Lall, 1983; Linge,
1984) has turned attention to the embryonic emergence of Third-
World headquartered MNCs.   Insofar as these are engaged in
manufacturing, one might expect from the theory of MNC that
these firms would have a competitive advantage in small-scale,
labour-intensive technologies for producing undifferentiated
price-competitive goods and in LDC markets.   Lall (1982) has
demonstrated that, while India is certainly not a very important
Third-World source country for FDI (*cf.* Hong Kong or Korea), it
is Indian-based MNCs which transfer most technology amongst
LDCs.   Despite their small scale, inefficiency, and lack of
very significant innovation, however, Indian firms seem able to
lead in technology transfer on account of a combination of environmental conditions at home and in other LDCs. In particular
the Indian environment contains strong 'push' factors for overseas technology sales.   Poor domestic profit and plant expansion
prospects are related to tight and slow Indian bureaucratic
procedures.   Import substitution policies of the Indian government have combined with a relatively large-scale national and
regionally fragmented market to stimulate growth of a diversity

of capital goods industries within India, many or some of which
do not exist in other LDCs. And, in addition, severe Indian
state restriction on MNC entry has forced local firms to inno-
vate at least to an extent which might not be true in other LDCs.
Thus, in the context of Third World export markets, Indian
manufacturers suffer no competitive disadvantages and, significantly, are often favoured by governments and entrepreneurs in
other LDCs who prefer to opt for technologies not controlled by
capitalist MNCs or stage-managed (CMEA) socialist enterprises.
Research is yet to show how important Indian traders living outside India might be as intermediaries in this technology transfer process; judging from evidence on Chinese communities in
South and East Asia as media for Hong Kong or Taiwanese MNC
expansion (Linge, 1984), ethnic networks could offer major explanations. And yet, finally, Indian technologies are often
well tested in physical, social and economic environments
similar to those in other LDC countries purchasing equipment
and hence may be viewed in host countries as the most
appropriate.

SOME FURTHER CONTROVERSIES

This chapter has stressed the dynamism of MNCs in the global
economy of the twentieth century and some of their relationships
with concentration processes, finance, labour and technology
transfer in the capitalist world. A broad canvas has been
painted to which ensuing chapters specifically concerned with
Third World experience can be related. Any assessment of the
impacts of MNC activity, however, must attempt to forecast or
predict the achievements and effects of alternative development
paths in host countries had MNCs not entered their national and
regional economies. The situation prior to MNC entry would
provide indications, but subsequent development trajectories or
non-development would have to be predicted on the basis of local
entrepreneurial activity or government initiatives or both.
Obviously the impacts with or without MNCs vary greatly from one
host country to another, from one social formation to another.
In the broadest terms, though, the trade-offs that a potential host country could expect are quite clear. Development
by indigenous entrepreneurs frequently involves low productivity
and low capital accumulation but also more jobs; yet while
probably slow adaptation to external and internal changes might
raise the risks of import penetration and job loss (unless
protected), it might also smooth social adjustments. By contrast, the entry of MNCs from developed countries usually means
implantation of new activities and (for the host country) new
production organization and technologies. These tend to yield
high productivity and relatively higher wages but, if the MNCs
introduce manufacturing of consumer goods or agricultural tools
traditionally handcrafted in the country, then, the ensuing job

losses and social upheavals can be substantial. And while the presence of MNCs may stimulate or contribute to the upgrading of local infrastructure and skills, it also means the locking of the local economy into the international economy with risks of significant net financial loss.

Potential host countries, however, also have the option of adopting state enterprise as a development medium. The socialist countries, and to an extent India, demonstrate the capabilities of very substantial state-managed industrialization based on substitution of imports mainly of intermediate and capital goods and strict trade controls. In that way, between 1950 and the 1970s these countries were able to develop strong backward and forward linkages within their frontiers in contrast to the majority of Third World countries whose policies led to import substitution mainly in finished and consumer goods with long backward linkages *overseas* often as part of MNC intra-firm trade. Since 1970, however, state-managed economies have shown far less capability of shifting to export-orientation which requires innovation and innovativeness: the NICs, sometimes using MNC know-how (see Hamilton and Linge, 1981), have been able to displace many CMEA products from world markets. As earning foreign exchange through exports of higher value-added goods may be the main (or only) path that LDCs can follow to narrow the gap with the 'North', their governments will have to make it attractive and worthwhile for MNCs to locate manufacturing there. One may then witness the actions of MNCs operating as the most potent force in convincing the governments of the advanced nations that they must lower or remove their tariff and non-tariff barriers to imports from NICs and LDCs. The MNC would become in some sense a spearhead for the Third World; till now it has been so only or mainly for the developed world.

REFERENCES

Balogh, T. and Streeten, P.P. (1960) 'Domestic versus foreign investment', *Bulletin of the Oxford University Institute of Statistics*. 22: 213-224.

Barnet, R.J. and Müller, R.E. (1975) *Global Reach: The Power of the Multinational Corporations*, Jonathan Cape, London.

Brooke, M.Z. and Remmers, H. (1970) *The Strategy of Multinational Enterprise*, Longman, London.

Caves, R.E. (1971) 'International corporations: the international economics of foreign investment', *Economica*, 38 (149): 1-27.

Chandler, A.D. Jr (1962) *Strategy and Structure: Chapters in the History of the American Industrial Enterprise*, MIT Press, Cambridge (Mass.).

Dunning, J.H. (1958) *American Investment in British Manufacturing Industry*, Allen & Unwin, London.
Dunning, J.H. (1971) *The Multinational Enterprise*, Allen & Unwin, London.
Dunning, J.H. (1982) 'The history of multinationals during the course of a century', unpublished paper, Multinationals in Transition, Institute for Research and Information on Multinationals Conference, Paris, November 1982.
Emmanuel, A. (1982) *Appropriate or Undeveloped Technology*, Wiley, London.
Franko, L. (1982) 'Relative decline of American multinationals or decline of multinationals in general?' unpublished paper, Multinationals in Transition, Institute for Research and Information on Multinationals Conference, Paris, November, 1982.
Gutman, P. and Arkwright, F. (1981) 'Tripartite industrial co-operation between East, West, and South' in Hamilton, F.E. Ian and Linge, G.J.R. (eds.), *Spatial Analysis, Industry and the Industrial Environment* Vol.2: *International Industrial Systems*, Wiley, London/New York: 185-214.
Hamilton, F.E. Ian (1976) 'Multinational enterprise and the European Economic Community', *Tijdschrift voor Economische en Sociale Geografie*, 67(5): 258-278.
Hamilton, F.E. Ian (1981) 'Industrial Systems: a dynamic force behind international trade', *Professional Geographer*, 33 (1): 26-35.
Hamilton, F.E. Ian (1984) 'Industrial restructuring: an international problem', *Geoforum*, 15(3): 349-364.
Hamilton, F.E. Ian and Linge, G.J.R., (eds.) (1981) *Spatial Analysis, Industry and the Industrial Environment*, Vol.2, *International Industrial Systems*, Wiley, London/New York.
Hood, N. and Young, S. (1982) *The Economics of Multinational Enterprise*, Longman, London.
Hymer, S. (1960), 'The international operations of national firms: a study of direct investment', PhD thesis, MIT, Cambridge (Mass.).
Jansen, A.C.M. and Van Weesep, J. (eds.) 'Foreign investment in industrialized countries', *Tijdschrift voor Economische en Sociale Geografie* (Special Issue), LXXI(1): 1-68.
Kindelberger, C.P. (1969) *American Business Abroad*, Yale University Press, New Haven.
Lall, S. (1982) 'Third World multinationals', unpublished paper, *Multinationals in Transition* (Institute for Research and Information on Multinationals Conference, Paris, Nov.1982).
Lall, S. (1983) *The New Multinationals: The Spread of Third World Enterprises*, Wiley, Geneva and Chichester.
Lenin, V.I. (1916) *Imperialism – The Highest Stage of Capitalism*,(in Russian), 13th English edn 1966, Progress Publishers, Moscow.
Lillienthal, D. (1960) 'The multinational corporation' in Anshen M. and Bach G.L. (eds.) *Management and Corporations*

1985, McGraw-Hill, New York: 119-158.
Linge, G.J.R. (1984) 'Developing-country multinationals: a
    review of the literature', *Pacific Viewpoint*, 25(2): 173-
    195.
Linge, G.J.R. and Hamilton, F.E. Ian (1981) 'International
    industrial systems' in Hamilton, F.E. Ian and Linge G.J.R.
    (eds.) *op. cit:* 1-117.
Marx, K. (1848) 'The Communist manifesto' reprinted in Mendel
    A.P. (ed.) (1961) *The Essential Works of Marxism*, Bantam
    Books, London.
McMillan, Carl H. (1979) *A New Dimension in International
    Enterprise. Direct Foreign Investment by the Comecon
    Countries*, Carleton University Working Paper No.8, Ottawa.
Parry, T.G. (1980) *The Multinational Enterprise*, Jai Press Inc.
    Greenwich (Conn.).
Rugman, A.M. (1981) *Inside the Multinationals*, Croom Helm,
    London.
Seers, D. (1963) 'Big companies and little countries', *Kyklos*,
    26(4): 599-607.
Taylor, M.J. and Thrift, N. (eds.) (1982) *The Geography of
    Multinationals*, Croom Helm, London.
Vernon, R. (1977) *Storm over the Multinationals*, Harvard
    University Press, Cambridge (Mass.).

Chapter Two

MULTINATIONALS AND THE EXPLOITATION
OF NON-RENEWABLE RESOURCES

G. Manners

Convincing generalizations about the nature and the behaviour of
undifferentiated MNCs (Multinational Corporations) are extremely
elusive.   The number and the diversity of MNCs increases re-
lentlessly.   By any objective definition, Arthur Anderson,
Atlas Copco, British Leyland, Cambridge University Press, the
Kuwait Petroleum Company, Laura Ashley, Marks & Spencer, the
Moscow-Narodny Bank, the National Coal Board, Reuters, and Trust
House-Forte are all 'multinational'.   Yet huge contrasts exist
in the many goods and services that they produce, in the size
of their annual turnover, in the countries from which they originated, in the geography of their activities, and in the
international transfers of capital, personnel, expertise and
technology that they generate.   For reasons related to this
diversity alone, the present chapter seeks to narrow the focus
of discussion and to consider a limited but strategically important group of MNCs that clearly have a broad affinity.   These
are companies that are primarily concerned with the production,
processing and transport of non-renewable resources, both energy
raw materials and minerals.   They can be termed the MNRCs
(Multinational Resource Corporations).

THE DISTINCTIVENESS OF NON-RENEWABLE RESOURCE EXPLOITATION

The business of finding, extracting, processing and transporting
energy and mineral raw materials is exceptionally capital intensive.   From this viewpoint alone, the distinctiveness of the
MNRCs is clear.   Large sums of capital have to be invested with
unusually long lead times - and sometimes, in periods of market
weakness, the capital yields a relatively low rate of return.
In consequence, the MNRCs are aware of, and are highly sensitive
to, their exceptionally high exposure to political as well as
economic uncertainties.   Their notions about acceptable target
rates of return, in different markets and in different political
environments, is inevitably influenced by these circumstances.
An appreciation of their reality is essential if the process and

problems of Third World development are to be fully understood.
Amongst the many products won by these corporations, by
far the most valuable is oil.   Its exceptional importance to
the world's economy is well known.   In 1983 it still satisfied
over 40 per cent of the world's energy demands (compared with
46 per cent a decade earlier).   Complex political sensitivities
surround its ownership and exploitation;   there can be very few
other industries that in recent years have been more affected
by changed and still changing market and political circumstances
and that play such a central role in the development and management of national economies both in the developed and developing
worlds alike.   These facts alone bestow upon the MNRCs a unique
role.

Of the other key minerals that are exploited, transformed
and traded by the MNRCs, the most important in terms of both
volume and value is iron ore.   However, the growing economic
importance of bauxite and aluminium, the renaissance of the international coal trade, and the expanding international trade in
natural gas collectively give both a rich variety and a complexity to the MNRCs and their operations.   As a result, the
search for valid generalizations about even their collective
behaviour - in both the Third and the First Worlds, since the
two are closely related - requires more than a degree of caution.

THE CHANGING ECONOMIC AND POLITICAL ENVIRONMENT

The oil shocks of the 1970s, and the related global recession,
formed an important watershed in the evolution of the MNRCs.   The
previous decade, and indeed much of the post-war period, had
been characterized by sustained economic growth, buoyant demand
for resources and, despite the decline in real energy prices,
relatively high levels of profitability.   It was also a time
when, in the wake of post-colonial political nationalism, the
more assertive governments in the Third World first modified
and then radically revised the legal conventions surrounding
the activities of MNRCs.   Increasingly, they insisted upon new
concession agreements, demanded a substantial share of the equity
ownership of oil and mineral company operations in their countries, and sought to acquire the greater part of the economic
rent from any natural resource development (Manners, 1977, 1978;
Mikesell, 1979; see also Chapter 8).

The events of 1973, however, reinforced by those of 1979,
ushered in a quite different period in which the generality of
energy and mineral industries throughout the world were faced
with a persistent surplus of production capacity. The expression
of this surplus varied considerably between resources.   In the
case of the oil industry, for example, excess capacity was substantially hidden by the production quotas imposed by OPEC. The
relatively high price of the cartel's oil triggered new demands
for natural gas, coal and uranium.   In time, however, overcapacity

began to affect these industries also and by 1984 all three were suffering from the excessive demand expectations which had guided private and public investment decisions in the 1970s. In the minerals sector producers were faced with mounting surplus capacity as a result of the persistently depressed level of demand after 1974 and the steady commissioning of new mines, and their associated transport and processing facilities, most of which had been planned and started during the preceding years of rapid economic expansion. In some instances, and particularly in many countries in the Third World, the motive behind the development of new capacity was either a desire for national self-sufficiency in particular minerals, or an urgent need for greater foreign exchange earnings. In other cases, it followed from a desire to create and diversify employment, or from a growing market for a co-product or a by-product. Incorrect price and market expectations, on the part of the MNRCs and governments alike, also lay behind this growth of surplus capacity. The result, of course, was a decade or more of low mineral prices and relatively low profitability for many, if not all, of the mineral activities of the MNRCs.

Amongst others, the Business and Industry Advisory Committee of the OECD (BIAC, 1982:6) called for the early correction of the market. *Inter alia*, it pleaded for the withdrawal of the highest cost producers from the market, ensuring that 'efficient producers, regardless of their ownership, have an opportunity to compete in the marketplace'. Indeed, the Committee considered this adjustment process to be a 'far more important problem today than [that of] encouraging investment in new mines and primary processing plants' (BIAC, 1982:6). However, high cost production facilities are often no simpler to close in developing countries than they are in the developed world; the market prospects and the political difficulties facing British coal and Swedish iron ore mines, for example, have their parallels in Africa and Latin America. The Bolivian tin industry is a classic case in point.

In such circumstances, the MNRCs naturally came to be increasingly risk-averse. Heightened uncertainties about future rates of economic growth in different parts of the world, the difficulty of disentangling the structural and the cyclical components in the changing patterns of resource needs, and the widely accepted necessity to revise downwards most energy and mineral demand forecasts, resulted in an increasingly cautious approach towards new investment decisions. It was not surprising, therefore, that the evaluation of the political risks surrounding investment security came to rank substantially higher in the deliberations of MNRCs than previously, and that the tendency to shift resource investment away from the Third World became more pronounced. Inevitably, perceptions of the nature and the scale of political risks surrounding resource investments in the Third World varied between corporations, countries and resources, as well as over time. The risks were always measured against the potential rewards. Despite Namibia's tortured political circumstances, the exploration and development of its uranium reserves was judged to be an acceptable risk in the middle and late 1970s, in the context of the existing plans for nuclear power station construction and the presumed future worth of the processed ore. The overall effect, however, was a distinct geographical shift in the pattern of international capital flows for resource development in favour of such developed and politically stable countries as Australia, Canada and the United States, and away from the Third World in general and the countries of Africa north of the Zambesi in particular (British North-American Committee, 1976; European Group of Mining Companies, 1976; Radetzki and Zorn, 1979) noted that

> The decline in the efforts which transnational corporations are devoting to the exploration and development of petroleum and gas resources in developing countries is a matter of serious concern not only to these countries but to the international community as a whole. The leading transnational corporations have redirected their investments towards locations that they consider to be least exposed to risk. As a result seismic prospecting in developing countries fell during the 1970s while corresponding activity in the developed countries increased considerably.

In time predictably, this tendency began to generate a new set of political attitudes. By the early 1980s the governments of the Third World were becoming increasingly concerned about their growing failure to attract development capital and began to understand much more clearly the potentially beneficial role that MNRC capital - plus the associated flow of energy and mineral exploitation technology and management expertise - can play in the development of their natural resources. They also came to recognize more clearly the nature of the restraints upon capital and other factor mobility. Their policies in consequence began to change. Increasingly, the MNRCs came to be offered by governments an increasing variety of inducements in order to encourage their involvement in Third World energy and mineral developments once again. Simultaneously, in a number of countries, experience gained with state-owned resource corporations subsequent to their nationalization was being realistically evaluated for the first time, and new policies were emerging towards them as a result. In a report to the Committee on Natural Resources of the Economic and Social Council, the Secretary-General of the United Nations (1983a:3) observed that

> In the early 1970s, investment legislation was predominantly directed towards screening, monitoring and imitating foreign investment; more recently the emphasis has shifted from restriction to selective and

> controlled promotion and encouragement ... while up-
> holding the principle of permanent sovereignty over
> natural resources, financial incentives ... can be
> used to promote and guide investment activities. ...
> Few countries not employing investment incentives
> seem to have achieved a rate of mineral industry
> growth equal to that in countries employing incentive
> schemes.

A year later, the Secretary-General of the United Nations (1984:19), following a survey of the energy investment require-ments of developing countries, concluded that

> the capacity of domestic energy enterprises ... to
> generate sufficient cash from their own operations
> to finance their own investment programs appears very
> limited. At the same time, given the enormous overhang
> of foreign debt already burdening some developing
> countries, increments to that debt, even for fully
> economic energy projects, will be difficult to acquire,
> at least for several years.

The conclusion led inevitably to the consideration of possible new vehicles for the international transfer of capital for the development of energy resources in the Third World - vehicles such as an energy affiliate of the World Bank, an Exploration Insurance Fund, and an Energy Development Fund - and the personal stumbling block to their creation, the lack of a political con-sensus and will. Even if that consensus were to be forged, however, the resource corporations would still have an important role to play in assisting with the exploitation of energy resources in the developing world, a role that is more likely to be more fully realised under 'new concepts in exploration and development agreements which would facilitate cooperation between trans-national corporations and host governments' (Secretary-General of the United Nations, 1983a:65).

The growing involvement of the centrally planned economies in the exploitation of, and international trade in, resources has added a further element to the changing economic and political environment facing, especially, those MNRCs operating in the Third World. As Soviet resource exploitation has moved pro-gressively further eastwards, to exploit the previously untapped resources of Siberia, as well as to satisfy the rapidly growing demands of the Pacific Basin, so has the scale of the USSR's international trade in resources increased substantially. The persistent and increasing Soviet need for hard currency is per-haps the principal motor of this development. The result, however, is often a powerful influence upon the prices at which energy and minerals are sold in Western and Third World markets. Soviet gas exports are the most recent case in point. The rest of the CMEA (Council for Mutual Aid) countries - where they are endowed with marketable natural resources - have followed suit.

Polish exports of coal and copper are but two examples. In addition, Eastern Europe has increasingly looked 'South' to participate in equity joint ventures and to negotiate barter deals with countries in the Third World. In this way the CMEA has secured access to new resources and also found new outlets for its manufactured goods. More recently, there are increasing signs that China is not only anxious to quicken the pace of its resource exploration and development, but that it could well become a major net exporter of energy and minerals towards the end of this century. Such developments have a considerable impact upon the MNRCs; at times they afford opportunities to sell their technological skills - exploration for Chinese offshore oil is a case in point. More generally they affect the size and the geography of the markets that the MNRCs might prospectively serve.

THE CHANGING ROLE OF MNRC CORPORATIONS

Simultaneous with the changing economic and political environment of the MNRC corporations over the last ten to fifteen years, a fundamental restructuring of the world's energy and mineral industries has been taking place. A growing share of global energy and mineral production is no longer in the hands of the MNRCs. Since 1973, for example, not only have those multinationals with oil interests had to accept a price regime which has been powerfully influenced, and at times determined, by the OPEC cartel, but the ownership of the world's oil production facilities has substantially passed out of their hands. Increasingly, host governments and/or national oil companies have come to own and control the production of oil. In 1970, for example some 61 per cent of the world's crude oil output was in the hands of the seven largest oil multinationals, known as the 'Seven Sisters' (Exxon, Royal Dutch/Shell, British Petroleum, Gulf Oil, Texaco, Standard Oil of California and Mobil); only 6 per cent was produced by state production companies and the remaining 33 per cent was won by smaller MNRCs. By the end of that decade, however, the share of the 'Seven Sisters' had been reduced to 25 per cent, and the smaller resource companies to 20 per cent. The state production companies, on the other hand, of which there were by now more than 100, had increased their share to 55 per cent of the total (UN Centre on Transnational Corporations, 1983:197). Over the same period, rather less change occurred in the structure of the international oil trade. Nevertheless, in 1970 the seven largest oil companies handled 50 per cent of product trade, and smaller MNRCs 41 per cent; state enterprises in that year handled a mere 9 per cent. By 1979, in contrast, the 'Seven Sisters' had lost about 10 per cent of their share of the trade; the smaller corporations had increased theirs by 1 per cent; and the state enterprises had doubled their share to some 18 per cent.

In the case of minerals, there has been a similar progressive reduction in the control of production by the MNRCs.   In 1976 companies based in the developing world already controlled 66 per cent of tin production; that share had increased to 83 per cent by 1981.   By then, the role of MNRCs had been reduced to a minority ownership of an equity interest in tin mining enterprises, or to agreements with state-owned companies under which they provided assistance with or the full management of the production process.   In the case of copper, the same tendency can be traced over a somewhat longer period.   In 1948, seven large MNRCs produced some 70 per cent of the world's copper; by 1960 their share had fallen to 60 per cent; by 1970 it was just over one third; and by 1981 it had fallen to 23 per cent of the world output (UN Centre on Transnational Corporations, 1983:207-8).

Criticism of the 'traditional' relationships between MNRCs and host governments over the years has encouraged the development of new types of contractual relationship between them.   In the case of oil for example, the legal framework surrounding the MNRCs' relations with host governments was at one time almost invariably the concession agreement; virtually no management or control functions were retained by the host governments and national resource companies simply did not exist.   By 1980, however, not only was the greater part of crude oil production in the hands of state companies, but a substantial part of the rest was won under production-sharing arrangements or service contracts between the MNRCs and national governments.   In consequence, in the case of crude oil production, governments can now generally capture between 80 and 98 per cent of the rents or profits derived from the exploitation of their country's resources.   Similarly, host governments and national companies have increasingly come to own the greater part, and sometimes all, of the equity in many mining ventures in their own countries - and in the process have had to take a commensurate part of the commercial risks of mining enterprise.   In addition, they have taken advantage of management contract agreements with MNRCs, to overcome the scarcity of domestic management resources, and where necessary, have forged commercial arrangements for the transfer of mining technology. The traditional form of mining concession held by an MNRC as a consequence, has become increasingly rare.

Following various resolutions of the General Assembly, the Economic and Social Council and the Committee on Natural Resources invested much time and money during the 1960s and more especially, the 1970s, encouraging the adoption of new legal and contractual frameworks for resource exploitation in the Third World.   Their success, in the sense of encouraging change, cannot be denied. By the 1980s, however, the declining volume and the falling share of resource investment in the Third World had become a matter for growing concern.   Experience with the new legal and contractual relations had begun to accumulate, and by 1983 the United Nations Committee on Natural Resources noted that

> A comparative financial analysis of various types of [resource development] agreement shows that the form is of little importance; indeed, States have often lost revenue through some of the 'innovative' arrangements advocated in the 1970s. In many instances the problem seems to be how to uphold the principle of permanent sovereignty over natural resources and to secure adequate state control without having to pay the price of full ownership. In some cases, majority representation in the main decision-making organs of the operating company without commensurate equity perticipation achieves this.

To some degree, therefore, attitudes towards, and perceptions of, the role of MNRCs is in the process of being re-evaluated once again (Walde, 1984:52). It is noteworthy that in Chile, for example, the legal status of the mining concession has been strengthened against nationalization; as in the 1982 Mining Law of the Federal Republic of Germany, the mining concession is now a real property right and can be used as collateral for raising finance. Throughout the Third World in general, many of the new mining and investment laws of the 1980s for the first time place some emphasis upon incentives and guarantees, propositions that would have been unthinkable a decade ago.

Meanwhile, of course, MNRCs have become much more varied in structure, origin and size. Some state oil companies in the Third World - such as those of Venezuela and Mexico - have become involved in overseas ventures and so have become MNRCs themselves. Kuwait financial interests have bought the Santa Fe Corporation, with its considerable oil and mineral resource activities and the Gulf Oil Company's downstream interests in Western Europe. The Hyundai Corporation of South Korea, which is already larger than, for example, Britain's RTZ Corporation, is heavily involved in various international resource developments. The late 1970s saw a growing number of oil corporations taking over mining companies as part of their diversification ambitions; BP, for example, took over Selection Trust, whilst Sohio (its US-based subsidiary) acquired Kennecott, America's biggest miner of copper. This was a trend however which, in response to the depressed market conditions of the early 1980s, was reversed a few years later; more recently, several of the major oil companies have begun to sell off their mineral interests as a result of their sustained losses. Thus, large, medium and small companies, from different countries of origin, with varied patterns of ownership, with a range of management characteristics and objectives, and with contrasting attitudes towards commercial and political risks, today comprise the complex and changing corporate component of energy and minerals exploitation, in both the developing and the developed world. It is a very different set of actors to those who held the stage twenty years earlier.

SOME ISSUES SURROUNDING THE RESOURCE CORPORATIONS

The 1960s and much of the 1970s witnessed a surge of interest in, and widespread criticism of, resource corporations and spawned a number of debates in political, corporate and academic circles. These debates included: the definition and the most appropriate ways in which to assert permanent sovereignty over a country's natural resources; the most appropriate contractual bases for natural resource development; pleas for an international investment agreement, that would provide an investment counterpart to the GATT; and the search for a definitive code of business practice for MNRCs. In the very different economic circumstances of the 1980s, all these issues have either been overtaken by events or have come to be regarded as relatively unimportant.

The principle of permanent sovereignty over natural resources - implying the freedom of each country to dispose of its natural resources in accordance with its own priorities, policies and objectives - is now beyond substantial dispute. Its relative importance in the changed market context of the 1980s has, however, been substantially reduced (Secretary-General of the United Nations, 1983b). The variety of forms that the contractual bases for resource development might take has been fully explored, and advice is now widely available to all host governments, ensuring a much greater equality of knowledge between the contracting parties. For example, the Natural Resources and Energy Division of the United Nations' Department of Technical Cooperation for Development advises governments and state enterprises on such matters as the identification of investment policies, the formulation of exploration and development agreements, the drafting of resource legislation, and advice on tax regimes. The multiplication in recent years of a variety of bilateral agreements on investment protection is, in the judgement of many, rapidly overtaking the need for a more comprehensive convention concerning international capital flows. The publication of the OECD guidelines on the business behaviour and ethics of MNCs, plus once again the transformed world market circumstances, have prompted a less urgent search for a United Nations code.

As one set of problems has been resolved or defused, however, another group has become more important. Four, in particular, deserve attention. The first is the reduced stability of the world's materials supply system, in terms of both prices and investment flows. In the past, the large North American and Western European MNRCs provided a valuable element of stability in the world's resource supply system. Their size and their substantial degree of vertical integration may have posed problems and invoked criticism, but these corporations did take a long-term view of resource needs, were of a size to be able to withstand short-term setbacks, and generally organized an efficient flow of materials from source to market. As a consequence of their reduced importance, the associated stability of the supply system that they engendered has been eroded. An extreme example is provided by the international oil industry. A considerable degree of vertical integration between upstream (crude production) activities and downstream (transport, refining and marketing) functions within single corporate structures has in the last decade been replaced: first, in the 1970s, by long-term contracts between the producer interests on the one hand, and the refining and marketing interests on the other; and then in the 1980s by the growth of shorter-term trading. The long-term crude oil contracts of the 1970s for perhaps 250,000 barrels per day supplied over several years have not only been substantially replaced by smaller contracts of the order of 20,000 barrels per day delivered over several months, but also by an increasingly important 'Rotterdam' spot market with its highly volatile prices. That market was once in essence a 'balancing market', handling a mere 2-3 per cent of internationally traded oil; by 1985, however, it had become a major link in the oil supply chain, and at times a significant factor in the determination of oil prices. It has been estimated that spot market contracts now comprise between 20 and 30 per cent of internationally traded oil (Shell Briefing Service, 1984). Moreover, some of the longer-term contracts that remain are agreed bilaterally between governments, who might or might not be permanent participants in the oil market. Whilst it can be argued that these developments beneficially allow a fuller expression of market forces in the determination of oil prices, they also impose penalties on the resource supply system. Market uncertainties for the resource industries are heightened, with detrimental effects upon investment for the medium and longer term. Third World oil producers are faced with major questions about the scale of the rents they are likely to obtain for national development purposes; Third World energy users generally must plan their development programmes in the context of additional foreign exchange risks. The dimensions of these uncertainties undoubtedly deserve fuller investigation.

A second set of problems centres more directly upon the process of resource investment and disinvestment. Given the extended world recession, and the increasingly diverse nature of the resource industries, the traditional questions of when and where to invest in an uncertain market are now paralleled by the equally important issue of when and where to abandon marginal capacity. Many production facilities have become permanently obsolete, but the most appropriate timing of closures often requires judgements about whether recent changes in demand are simply cyclical or more permanently structural. The Business and Industry Advisory Committee of the OECD in 1982 concluded that

> securing a broad balance between supply and demand, and ensuring that all efficient producers, regardless of

their ownership, have the opportunity to compete in
the marketplace is a far more important problem today
than encouraging investment in new mines and primary
processing plants ... Today's need is to assist the
market to remove capacity that is permanently obsolete
because it is in the wrong place or because its cost
structures have been outmoded by technical and economic change.

There is too little research into how, and the efficiency with
which, this might be achieved - both in the world's energy and
mineral markets in general, and in the Third World in particular.
    The question is particularly acute in the case of tin, for
example. By 1985, after two and a half years of stringent export controls by the six largest producing members of the International Tin Agreement, countries such as Malaysia and Bolivia
faced buffer stock holdings equal to about four months' supply
and likely to have a major depressing influence upon the market
for many years to come. This issue also faces the MNRCs themselves. British Petroleum finally came to insist in 1985 upon
the voluntary liquidation of Seltrust - its Australian mining
finance subsidiary - and an increasing number of major American
oil companies such as Standard Oil of Indiana and Atlantic
Richfield have decided to reverse their earlier policies of
diversification into mineral production. Difficult investment
and disinvestment decisions also surround the downstream processing activities of the MNRCs. Thus, the retreat of the
aluminium smelting industry from such high energy cost locations
as Japan, and the need to adjust the scale on the geography of
oil refining both to lower levels of world product demand (at
the same time as some producing countries in the Middle East
have decided to increase the scale of their refining activities),
together illustrate the increasingly complex environment of
resource investment in the 1980s. Sometimes the changing market and institutional forces serve the interests of the Third
World well. The expansion of Brazilian iron ore output and
Colombian coal mining, whilst older iron ore production facilities
in Eastern Canada and Scandinavia and relatively expensive coal
mines in Britain and France are forced to contract, are cases
in point.
    A third set of problems particularly concerns the smaller
MNRCs to the extent that they appear to be more risk-averse
than the larger corporations. Large MNRCs understandably
approach many investment uncertainties with rather greater confidence than do their smaller counterparts. Indeed, the
financial and other resources of the large corporations allow
them to take rather greater economic, technical and political
risks. With the relative importance of the large MNRCs having
been significantly reduced in recent years, the non-renewable
resource supply situation of the late 1980s and 1990s is much
more likely to swing from 'feast to famine'. The price of energy

and minerals could as a result become increasingly volatile, to the particular disadvantage of those Third World host countries that are heavily dependent upon the production and export of non-renewable resources for their economic wellbeing.

A final set of problems for the 1980s and 1990s centres upon the difficulties faced by host countries in their desire, not only to stabilize the worth of their energy and mineral output (and hence their national income and export earnings from these activities) but also to add value to their resource production. The likelihood of producer associations and of the various compensatory finance schemes making a significant impact upon price stability is severely constrained by market realities. Aspirations to become further involved in the 'downstream' marketing of resources and resource products, and more directly involved in the processing of resources when substantial value is added to their worth, have too frequently been frustrated in the past. Sometimes the causes stem from the economics of location; at other times the explanation lies in the industrial structures that have been handed down from an earlier phase of world economic development. A case in point is the relatively small international market in pig iron which, in considerable measure, is a function of the long-established integrated mode of iron and steel production developed in the industrially advanced countries, and which has limited the ability of iron ore producers to add value to their resource beyond beneficiation and palletization. The task now is to monitor and understand more fully than hitherto the economics of existing downstream investments in resource-rich Third World (and, indeed, First World) countries, to learn the lessons of success and failure, and to gain new insights on the extent to which their extension and replication has merit.

Each of these four issues - the reduced stability of the world's materials supply system, the questions surrounding the process of resource disinvestment, the growing role but the risk-averse behaviour of the smaller MNRCs, and the variable but uncertain returns to investments in resource processing in the Third World - is important in its own right. An improvement in our understanding of them, however, additionally has the potential of not only enhancing the prospects of sound economic development in the Third World, but also throwing much needed light on the distinctive and changing role that the MNRCs are playing (and can prospectively play) in furthering that growth. There is no reason why it should not be assumed that a fair balance of interest cannot be struck between those Third World countries with energy and mineral endowments and multinational corporations. As in the past, however, that balance will tend to change not only with time, but also with place and resource.

REFERENCES

Auty, R.M. (1983) 'Multinational Corporations and Regional Revenue Retention in a Vertically Integrated Industry: Bauxite/Aluminium in the Caribbean', *Regional Studies*, 17(3): 3-17.

Bosson, R. and Varon, B. (1977) *The Mining Industry and the Developing Countries*, Oxford University Press, Oxford.

British North-American Committee (1976) *Mineral; Development in the Eighties: Prospects and Problems*, BNAC, Washington DC.

BIAC (Business and Industry Advisory Committee of the OECD) (1982) *The Role of the Private Sector in the Development of Non-Fuel Minerals, Report of the Working Group on Raw Materials Investment*, OECD, Paris.

The Economist (1983) 'Here Come the Multinationals in the Third World', 23 July: 61-62.

European Group of Mining Companies (1976) Raw Materials and Political Risk, a paper submitted to the President of the Commission of the EEC, Brussels.

Guinet, J. (1983) Aluminium: Restructuring an Energy-Intensive Industry, *OECD Observer*, 124(3): 3-8.

Lall, S. (1984) 'Transnationals and the Third World: Changing Perceptions', *National Westminster Quarterly Review*, May: 2-16.

Makdeshi, Z. (1976) *The International Politics of Natural Resources*, Cornell University Press, Ithaca, New York.

Manners, G. (1977) 'Three Issues of Minerals Policy', *Journal of The Royal Society of Arts*, 125: 386-401.

Manners, G. (1978) 'The Future Markets for Minerals: Some Causes of Uncertainty', *Resources Policy*, 4: 100-105.

Mikesell, R.F. (1979) *New Patterns of World Mineral Development*, BNAC, Washington DC.

Radetzki, M. and Zorn, S. (1979) *Financing Mining Projects in Developing Countries*, Mining Journal Books, London.

Secretary-General of the United Nations (1983a) *Development of the Energy Resources of the Developing Countries, A Report to the Economic and Social Council*, E/1983/91, United Nations, New York.

Secretary-General of the United Nations (1983b) *Permanent Sovereignty over Natural Resources, A Report to the Economic and Social Council*, E/C.7/1983/5, United Nations, New York.

Secretary-General of the United Nations (1984) *Development and International Economic Cooperation: Development of the Energy Resources of Developing Countries, A Report to the General Assembly*, A/39/420, United Nations, New York.

Shell Briefing Service (1984), *Trading Oil*, SIPC, London.

United Nations Centre on Transnational Corporations (1983) *Transnational Corporations in World Development, Third Survey*, United Nations, New York.

United Nations Centre on Transnational Corporations (1984) *Main Features and Trends in Petroleum and Mining Agreements*, United Nations, New York.

Walde, T. (1984) 'Third World Mineral Development: Recent Literature', *The Centre on Transnational Corporations Reporter*, 17: 52-57.

Chapter Three

MULTINATIONALS AND RESTRUCTURING IN LATIN AMERICA

S.M. Cunningham

This chapter considers the role of MNCs (multinational corporations) - including multinational banks - in the industrial and financial restructuring of Latin America. Detailed evidence is also presented for Brazil. A central theme of the chapter, applicable beyond the Latin American region, is that MNCs' involvement in LDCs (Less Developed Countries) is one of the principal factors in the increasing internationalization of the means of production and related consumption patterns. As such, multinationals channel the spread of a mass-consumer ethos (which arose essentially in western industrialized countries with high income profiles) among what are predominantly low to middle income populations. This is perhaps most readily appreciated in relation to the now well researched activities (and internationally renowned products) of the manufacturing and mining companies whose FDI (Foreign Direct Investment) in the post-1945 period underpins the spread of multinational subsidiaries worldwide. Yet, much more recently - roughly since the early 1970s - a further but less well documented aspect of MNCs' involvement has been evident: *viz.* the profound deepening of their financial penetration through the mechanism of foreign commercial bank lending. This development harnesses the societies concerned even more firmly into the structures controlled by a select group of OECD countries.

Accordingly, there are two main strands to be explored here: the expansion, and in many cases reorientation, of industrial production towards the output of consumer durables and even capital goods; and the restructuring of the financial base. Both aspects emphasize increasing links to the international system and the central role of MNCs is brought into the forefront of the analysis. However, this does not presuppose that the LDCs involved, notably those in Latin America, are simply passive recipients of MNC production facilities (including technology) or finance. Moreover, while there are clear reasons why changes at the core of the international economy help to explain some of the restructuring process on the periphery, in fact by far the greater part of the explanation resides in the particular stance

adopted by the individual Latin American state.   Indeed, from
the outset it is recognized that MNCs are enmeshed in highly
interdependent, but not necessarily equal, relationships with
other interests, be they from the public or private sectors, and
wherever in the world they operate (Chapter 6 presents further
discussion and empirical material built around the so-called
'triple-alliance' between these different interests).

RESTRUCTURING OF THE INTERNATIONAL ECONOMY

Chapter 1 contained an overview of the changes in multinational
organization and related developments of the international
economy; this section elaborates some points which have particular relevance to Latin American economies in particular and
LDCs in general.

The Broad Setting for Industrial Change Since 1945

The greater part of the period between 1945 and the early 1970s
was characterized in the DCs (Developed Countries) by increasing
prosperity, tariff liberalization, trade growth, decolonization
and a tendency to implement full employment policies.   Simultaneously, developments in the fields of international finance,
technology and business organization, combined with further innovations in communications and transport, paved the way for
increased internationalization of production and the division of
labour associated with it (Wallerstein 1979; Fröbel *et al*, 1980).
     New flows of capital and technology were central to the
changing structure of the world economy. Between approximately
1945 and 1960 these flows were dominated by the United States of
America.   In that period, the activities of the rapidly expanding USA-based corporations were important in channelling FDI
into new manufacturing subsidiaries in Canada, Western Europe
and Latin America (Dunning, 1977).   From the mid-1950s the
dominant position of the United States was eroded by changing
forms of industrial organization elsewhere, and by the economic
recovery of the two nations most devastated by the Second World
War, West Germany and Japan.
     In the developed countries, the expansion of industry was
underpinned by major technical innovations which gave rise both
to new products and production processes, especially in the
electrical, electronic, petrochemical and motor vehicle fields.
These developments hastened the decline of most DC traditional
industries, especially textiles, steel and shipbuilding, a trend
to which Japan, with its post-war industrial reconstruction,
remained an exception.
     With respect to labour, the nature of technical changes in
DCs involved decreased labour requirements and also allowed
further specialization and disaggregation of the production
process.   Meanwhile, organized labour in DCs often demanded
higher wage levels and improved job security.

The above factors, in conjunction with the lower labour costs, market potential and other advantages of LDCs, suggest a variety of corporate motives for the spread of the subsidiaries of MNCs to the Third World as well as setting in context the broad conditions for industrialization of the 'periphery', especially during the 1960s and 1970s.   This in fact is only one side of the equation since governments and other local interests in particular LDCs intensified their drive for industrial expansion throughout this period.   In doing so they also devised new measures to capture investment to attract foreign enterprises and to set in motion technology transfer.   (See: Fitzgerald, Floto and Lehmann 1977 for a discussion of Latin America; Fransman 1982 for a discussion of Africa; Sen 1982 for India; and Balassa 1981 and Kemp 1983 for a variety of examples.)

Rapid Changes During the 1970s into the 1980s

Events during the 1970s altered the bases of the post-1945 international economy, and ended the period of sustained prosperity hitherto enjoyed by the developed economies.   Among the principal events of the early years of the decade was the breakdown in 1971 of the fixed exchange rate system set up at Bretton Woods in 1944-5 and its replacement by floating exchange rates.   This change contributed to the climate of growing financial uncertainty which was compounded during 1973.   In quick succession the end of the Arab-Israeli war, the oil embargo by Arab states and the action taken by the OPEC cartel resulted in a four-fold increase in world oil prices.   New inflationary and recessionary pressures were thus added to an international economy which, according to some observers, was already suffering from a crisis of overproduction (Mandel, 1978).

Since 1974 the advanced western industrial economies have been forced to adapt to higher energy costs, while at the same time, the capital surplus of OPEC countries and other oil exporters has provided a massive influx of funds. Major modifications to the existing world financial superstructure were rapidly introduced.   The most important was the recycling of the OPEC capital surplus, through on-lending by multinational banks. This meant that foreign direct investment took second place as unregulated sources of finance (notably through a much expanded Eurodollar market) acquired a new significance for both private enterprises and governments in DCs and LDCs (governments in particular needed large inputs of these funds to finance balance of payments deficits incurred as a result of the oil price rises).   To a certain extent, the new dimensions of international finance overshadowed other developments, such as the quickening pace of industrial reorganization engendered partly by the wider diffusion of microelectronic-related innovations in manufacturing production and industrial design, as well as by new waves of corporate mergers and takeovers (especially in the USA and UK).

While developed industrial countries experienced some economic recovery during the period 1975 to 1979, growth rates did not return to previous levels. Further oil price increases in 1979, and tighter monetary policies in the USA and UK particularly (which spawned a marked upward rise in international interest rates) spelt the return of world recession. An upturn among leading OECD economies (led by the USA) was evident by 1983 and was continuing less strongly during 1985. Central obstacles to sustained recovery include the combination of an overvalued US dollar and high real interest rates, which in turn are related to the escalating defence expenditure and a mounting budget deficit in the USA. It remains to be said, of course, that despite some erosion of US economic hegemony within the west in recent decades by the strengthened positions of the EEC and Japan, the enhanced role of the dollar as the world currency, and hence the demand for dollars worldwide, have tied more countries into the dollar orbit.

Financial Restructuring Trends During the 1970s.

From 1974 the international recycling of petrodollars and other adjustments in the wake of the OPEC price rises (including the easing by the US government of restrictions on overseas lending by American banks) gave impetus to further financial restructuring which affected some LDCs as well as DCs. Two main elements can be singled out. The first relates to the changing pattern of FDI, a process in which MNCs are heavily involved. As can be seen from Table 3.1 the interpenetration of FDI inflows continued to be well below the level of outflows (on average, 40 to 50 per cent below). For the LDCs as a whole, the reverse was true. Despite some increase in inflows after 1974, outflows continued to be at least double the level of annual inflows. This suggests that a large share of profits generated in LDCs were being used to shore up ailing DC economies. However it can be seen that the Latin American region is exceptional in the Third World, in that during 1976 to 1980 inflows began to exceed outflows. So not only was this region the major LDC recipient of new investment, mostly originating from multinationals in DCs, but by implication, a higher proportion of funds generated by MNC subsidiaries were reinvested there.

The second element in the post-1974 financial restructuring is of crucial significance to this chapter. This is the growth of unregulated sources of finance, in particular through the Eurocurrency markets, which reflects the escalating operations of multinational banks. As can be seen from Table 3.2, these funds were far more substantial (for both DCs and LDCs) than the amounts involved in FDI during the 1970s. Also in the second half of the 1970s more than half the annual total of Eurocurrency credits worldwide went to LDCs. This represented a marked shift in practice by multinational banks. Previously LDCs did not enjoy easy access to sources of private funds on international markets. In fact, after 1974 although the *majority*

TABLE 3.1 FDI Inflows and Outflows[1] by Region, 1970-1980   (US$ mn)

		1970	1972	1974	1976	1978	1980
DCs	Inflows	7,906	10,314	14,930	11,238	22,423	27,494
	Outflows	3,462	4,467	7,212	8,122	10,904	15,963
LDCs	Inflows	1,834	2,585	508	2,830	7,447	7,654
	Outflows	5,693	5,510	10,856	8,700	11,979	15,833
Latin America	Inflows	815	1,019	1,894	1,174	4,059	5,249
	Outflows	1,696	1,489	2,190	1,594	2,239	2,717
South and East Asia	Inflows	486	,780	1,445	1,690	1,888	3,230
	Outflows	1,206	1,733	1,900	1,808	2,904	5,624
Africa[2]	Inflows	369	570	689	432	566	2 188
	Outflows	1 316	1 065	1 640	1 841	2 241	2 016

Source: UN (1983) *III Report on Transnational Corporations*, New York, (compiled from
Appendix data, Annex Tables II 13, II 2 and II 4).

1 Outflows relate to payments on FDI
2 Africa totals exclude S. Africa which is included with DCs

Table 3.2   Eurocurrency Credits: selected data, 1976-82
            (US $ bn)

	1976	1977	1978	1979	1980	1981	1982
TOTAL	28.8	41.7	70.2	82.8	77.4	113.3	85.0
DCs	11.2	17.2	28.9	27.2	39.1	86.0	42.7
LDCs	15.0	20.9	37.3	47.9	35.0	45.2	41.4
Of which:							
Brazil	3.2	2.8	5.6	6.2	4.1	5.7	5.7
Mexico	1.9	2.7	7.2	8.2	5.9	7.5	7.9

Source: Morgan Guaranty, *World Financial Markets*, various
          issues

of LDCs were still in this position, for a select group credit
worthiness improved dramatically.   Particularly favoured were
those countries in the NIC (Newly Industrializing Country)
category whose development strategies during the 1960s and 1970s
were heavily geared to rapid economic growth based on industrialization.   Also favoured were the oil surplus-producing
countries as well as countries where changes in both government
and the developmental model attracted foreign investment.   A
relatively large number of Latin American countries fitted one
or more of these criteria including Brazil, Mexico, as NICs;
Venezuela, Ecuador, Peru and later Mexico as oil producers; and
Chile and Argentina with major changes of regime.   Between 1976
and 1982 Latin America accounted for about half the Eurocredits
received by all LDCs, with Brazil, Mexico, Argentina and Chile
together receiving annually between 33 and 44 per cent of the
LDC total.
     These restructuring trends in finance are fundamental to
the thrust of recent change and adaptation in the (western) world
economy.   They emphasize above all the increasing articulation
between parts of the LDC 'periphery' and developed 'core' countries.   This process involved not only the attractiveness of
LDCs to MNC investment but also the development of multinational
banks as a major new source of finance.   The latter locked
peripheral economies even more firmly into the international
system.

MULTINATIONALS AND THE LATIN AMERICAN REGION

MNCs and Industrial Restructuring
Foreign enterprises, including the forerunners of many leading
present-day MNCs, were established in Latin America at an early
date, especially in the more populous countries.   Indeed, even

in the 1920s and 1930s, the region could boast a variety of assembly industries largely run by foreign concerns, especially in the production of motor vehicles, electrical goods and chemicals, industries which at that time were relatively new and expanding in the developed countries. However, in the early twentieth century investment in primary production, particularly mining and plantation agriculture, was the central focus for foreign firms.

It was only after 1945 that foreign investment in manufacturing industry brought the modern multinational corporations into prominence in the region. Chapter 1 emphasized the particular developments among MNCs which contributed to this, and other writers have drawn attention to the role of growing inter-corporate competition (see, for example Jenkins, 1984; Franko, 1976). These aspects are certainly important, yet it is also the case that in large measure the Latin American states represented a (if not the) leading edge of efforts to replace the assembly operations of foreign firms, largely based on imported raw materials and components, with the fuller complement of industrial processes. In the different countries a variety of government policies served to encourage further import substitution. These included the erection of tariff barriers for imported components and subsidies to firms establishing or extending full production operations, as well as the setting up of state enterprises in such basic industries as steel, chemicals and energy production. In certain respects Latin American governments were able to take advantage of inter-corporate rivalry as MNCs from different parts of the world sought to hold on to and expand their markets for what had become from the 1950s a rapidly diversifying range of consumer durable products and capital goods.

By the early 1970s, after virtually two decades of expansion by manufacturing multinationals in most major and some minor countries in Latin America, a substantial share of the newly-diversified industrial base was controlled by MNCs. However, it remains a difficult task to detail the penetration of MNCs into the industrial ownership, production, sales and employment structures of individual countries. Even in 1983, a study made by the United Nations Centre on Transnational Corporations (UN 1983) produced only partial evidence covering the period up until 1978 for: Brazil, Chile, Colombia and Peru. An extensive review of available data from a variety of published and unpublished sources made by Jenkins (1984) yielded information only up to 1975 at best, with results for most countries sampled *circa* 1970. Some of his findings which utilized value of production data for all manufacturing and selected industrial sectors are presented in Table 3.3. This shows the sectoral concentration of MNCs in the dynamic industries whose expansion was crucial, not simply to the industrialization of LDCs, but also to the cycle of post-1945 prosperity within the multiple cores of the international economy.

TABLE 3.3 Foreign Shares in the Value of Production of Selected Manufacturing Sectors Among Seven Latin American Countries

	Argentina (1963)	Brazil (1970)	Chile (1968)	Colombia (1974)	Mexico (1970)	Peru (1969)	Venezuela (1971)
				Percentage Share of Total:			
All manufacturing	23.8	50.1	29.9	43.4	34.9	44.0	13.8
Dynamic sectors							
Basic metals	21.1	(12.0)[1]	16.9	54.7	46.6	82.7	7.2
Chemicals	34.9	49.0	61.9	66.9	50.7	66.7	16.5
Electrical equipment	27.6	83.7	48.6	67.2	50.1	60.7	23.2
Transport equipment	44.4	88.2	64.5	79.7	64.0	72.9	31.1
Other machinery	35.6	70.0	6.7	29.6	52.1	24.8	12.8
Additional sectors							
Food	15.3	42.1	23.2	22.0	21.5	33.1	10.0
Drink	24.1	30.9	20.3	3.1	20.0	18.0	5.5
Textiles	14.2	34.2	22.9	61.9	15.3	39.7	12.9
Clothing/shoes	10.4	29.5	24.2	11.4	6.2	21.5	2.1
Furniture	1.2	16.0	6.4	6.0	3.8	19.0	11.5

Source: Jenkins, (1984) *Transnational Corporations and Industrial Transformation in Latin America* (Macmillan, London), Table 2.4: 34.

1. Estimate – no figure in original source table.

46

Table 3.4 shows the extent to which the overall industrial structure of most of the main Latin American countries had become orientated away from the traditional or basic consumer industries, and towards the dynamic or higher technology sectors, represented mainly by ISIC (International Standard Industrial Classification) categories 35, 37 and 38 (chemicals, metallurgical, machinery, electrical-electronic and transport). From this it is apparent that the full thrust of dynamic industry expansion (where MNCs are dominant) was especially strong in the three major markets: Argentina, Brazil and Mexico. In Colombia, Peru, Ecuador, Venezuela and Chile the impact is rather less marked although even relative newcomers in the industrial field such as Ecuador and Venezuela do display a substantial increase in this sector's share during the 1970s. World Bank (1983) data for 1980 reinforce the view that Argentina, Brazil and Mexico had developed manufacturing profiles which were much closer to those of the advanced industrial countries, than those considered typical in the Third World. While it should be emphasized that the output from dynamic industries controlled by MNCs has been predominantly directed to national and regional markets in Latin America, it is also the case that from the mid-1960s the three major industrial producers (Argentina, Brazil and Mexico) began to export increasing amounts of capital goods and consumer durables (see: Nayyar, 1978; Baumann Neves, 1982).

The restructuring (as well as growth) of the Latin American industrial base is also set in context by the observation that despite relatively rapid industrial growth rates for most of the 1960s and 1970s (averaging annually 6.5 - 7.5 per cent between 1960 and 1975, and only 3 - 5 per cent between 1976 and 1980) the share of manufacturing in GDP failed to grow substantially. Moreover, industrial employment continued to occupy only about a fifth of the labour force in most countries since gains made through the addition of jobs in the newer sectors of manufacturing were often offset by job loss in more traditional sectors which had been forced to modernize their production. Suffice it to say that MNCs were a major force creating the pressure to modernize production in traditional industries as well as being the principal carriers of the 'dynamic industries'.

A detailed account of multinational penetration of Latin America at national and industrial levels is beyond the scope of the present chapter. The next section therefore concentrates on a case study of Brazil. A valuable review for the Latin American region as a whole is to be found in Jenkins (1984). However, it is important to stress the importance during the 1970s of industrial restructuring, and the overall expansion of the manufacturing base, in relation to the role of Latin America as a focus for unregulated flows of finance through the commercial banking system. In essence, the increased openings for MNCs' production during the previous decades (and the channelling of output and consumption patterns along the lines of developed industrial countries) served to open up vast new markets

TABLE 3.4   Share of Dynamic Industries (ISIC 35, 37 and 38) in Industrial Structure

Country	1950	1960	1965	1970	1974	1977	1980
(a) % Share of Industrial Employment							
Argentina	28.6	38.8		36.5		53.0	(a)
Brazil	17.5	27.6		33.9			39.9
Mexico			32.5		39.2	(b)	
Colombia			22.6	28.8	31.6	32.7	
Chile				31.7	31.5	(c)29.6	
Ecuador				16.2	(d)21.7	(e)	
Peru		20.2	27.2	27.1	28.8	(f)	
Paraguay		23.3	23.6	21.6			
Guatemala				19.6	20.1	21.2	(g)
Venezuela		20.0	(h)	25.5	28.0	36.5	
Bolivia		7.9	(h)		9.7	(i)	
(b) Share of Gross Value of Industrial Production							
Argentina	35.9	47.0		55.5		67.9	
Brazil	21.5	37.1		47.2			57.5
Mexico			41.5	45.4	48.3		
Colombia	10.7 (j)	25.3		28.9	(k)		
Ecuador				19.5	27.0		
Peru				34.2			
Venezuela		19.9	29.6	29.5		41.5	(l)
Bolivia			7.3	(m)	7.5	(n)	

Source: Compiled by the author from a variety of statistical sources for individual countries (usually industrial census data if available); ILO data (ILO Yearbook 1980) were useful in calculating employment shares for some countries.   While every effort was made to ensure comparability, differences in classification by some countries means that some qualification is necessary in inter-country comparisons.   Given the over-riding importance of the petroleum sector of Venezuela this sector was not included in the calculations for either employment or value of production.

Notes: Letters in brackets indicate that another year - other than the one shown at the column head - was used; this year applied to both tables unless otherwise stated:

(a) 1978; (b) 1975; (c) 1973; (d) 1968; (e) 1975;
(f) 1973; (g) 1978; (h) 1961; (i) 1972; (j) 1952,
(k) 1967; (1) 1976; (m) 1967   (n) 1972

for capital. This involved not only financing production itself, but also a whole range of infrastructural and servicing
activities.

Increasing Links to International Capital in the 1970s

During the 1970s, even though FDI decreased in its relative importance, the Latin American region received the largest share
of FDI inflows to LDCs (Table 3.1). More importantly, Latin
American countries absorbed over half the augmented Eurodollar
funds lent to LDCs by multinational banks in the wake of the
OPEC price rises. By the end of 1984, the region accounted for
56 per cent of outstanding bank claims on LDCs; US$243 billion
out of $435 billion). The unevenness of the patterns of both
types of external financing amongst the main Latin American
countries is shown in Tables 3.5 and 3.6 From these, the importance within the region, of Brazil, Mexico and Argentina as the
preferred locations for international capital and the resulting
debt burdens is clear. However the degree to which foreign
finance - and to a lesser extent, direct investment - increased
in the other countries shown is also remarkable. Within a
period of about eight years from 1975, Venezuela, Chile, Peru,
Colombia and Ecuador were extended substantial loans or credits
by (private) multinational banks. With interest, the total
owed by these countries to banks in mid-1982 was over US$50
billion, over 40 per cent of which was due to US banks. This
compares with US$145 billion owed to banks by Argentina, Brazil
and Mexico, over a third of which was due to US banks. Overall,
between *circa* 1974 and 1982, the economies of the major Latin
American countries became more profoundly linked into the international financial system than was the case in previous decades
during which the expansion of multinational corporations, mainly
through foreign direct investment in manufacturing industry, was
more important. Also, the external payments situation of these
countries has become more complex since large portions of debt
were contracted by sovereign borrowers *i.e.* the state or public
sector enterprises, rather than by private sector interests alone.
The degree of complexity has been thrown into sharp relief by
events since mid-1982 as countries experienced major difficulties in securing either new finance or sufficient funds to service their debts (see: Cunningham and Gwynne, 1983). With the
principal exception of Colombia and Venezuela, all these countries have been involved in debt rescheduling/restructuring
negotiations.

The escalation of lending by multinational banks to Latin
American countries during the 1970s is indicative of the heightened articulation of interests between both parties. This took
place during a period for most of which the developed country
bases of the banks involved were experiencing serious recession.
By contrast, the recipients of new bank funds in Latin America
were seeking to expand and diversify their economies against the
trend of world recession.   Implicitly, the banks involved

TABLE 3.5   External Debt Position of Major Latin American
            Countries, 1975-1982   (US$ bn)

Country	Gross External Debt End 1975	End 1982	Owed to Banks June 1982 Total	US Banks
Brazil	21.2	85.5	55.3	20.5
Mexico	14.3	80.1	64.4	25.2
Argentina	3.9	38.0	25.3	8.8
Venezuela	.2	29.5	27.2	10.7
Chile	3.6	17.2	11.8	6.1
Peru	3.1	11.5	5.2	2.3
Colombia	2.5	10.3	5.5	3.0
Ecuador	.5	6.6	4.7	2.2

Source: OECD (1977) *Development Cooperation Review* for 1975
          data;   Morgan Guaranty, *World Financial Markets*
          (various issues)

TABLE 3.6   Stock of FDI in Major Latin American Countries,
            1971-81   (Total stock, end year US% bn)

Country	1971	1972	1974	1976	1978	1980[1]	1981[1]
Brazil	5.1	6.1	9.5	9.1	13.2	15.9	17.8
Mexico	2.4	2.6	3.7	4.6	6.0	9.1	10.2
Argentina	2.2	2.3	2.7	2.2	3.3	3.5	4.1
Venezuela	3.7	3.7	3.0	2.9	3.6	3.7	3.9
Chile	.8	.7	.7	.4	1.4	1.8	2.1
Peru	.8	.9	1.3	1.8	2.1	2.4	2.6
Colombia	.9	.9	1.1	1.2	1.5	1.7	1.8
Ecuador	.3	.3	.8	.5	.7	.7	.7

Source: UN (1983) *III Report on Transnational Corporations*,
          New York.

1. Best estimates

considered that lending to the region would generate a level of profits which was unlikely to be realized domestically.

ASPECTS OF RESTRUCTURING IN BRAZIL

The State, Multinationals and Industrial Restructuring

For well over half a century the state in Brazil has had the primary role in steering the country's economy away from its agrarian base towards an urban-industrial one. This change is partly reflected in the increased share of industrial and service activities in the occupational structure that has taken place since 1940 (see Table 3.7).

From the later 1950s, the state intensified its drive to modernize existing industry and to promote the development or expansion of the dynamic industries. It did this by participating directly as a producer of intermediate goods such as steel and petro-chemicals and as a supplier of infrastructure (energy, transport and other utilities), as well as by encouraging new foreign capital and technology inputs (see Baer, Kerstenetszky and Vilella, 1973; Suzigan et al, 1976; Cunningham, 1979; Trebat,

TABLE 3.7   Brazil: Occupational Structure of the Economically Active Population, by Sex 1940-1980 (%)

	1940		1960		1980	
	Male	Female	Male	Female	Male	Female
Agriculture	70.3	46.8	58.8	30.1	35.8	14.4
Industrial	10.2	10.6	13.2	12.5	27.9	14.8
Commercial	5.8	1.8	7.2	4.3	9.2	9.7
Services	4.6	38.4	8.3	46.1	12.6	40.9
Public Administration	3.1	0.8	3.1	2.0	4.8	3.1
Transport, etc	3.8	0.5	5.6	1.1	5.2	1.2
Other	2.2	1.1	3.8	3.9	4.5	5.9
	100.0	100.0	100.0	100.0	100.0	100.0

Source: IBGE (1974) *Annuario Estatistico 1973* for 1940 and 1960; FIBEE (1981) *Tabulacoes Avancadas 1980*

Note: Total male and female economically active were as follows:

	1940	1960	1980
Male	11,958,968	18,597,763	31,757,833
Female	2,799,630	4,054,100	12,038,930

1983). In the process a fairly sophisticated institutional
structure was established to channel and control financial and
technical resources, and to further contacts at all levels with
multinational concerns. A basic framework was in place by the
early 1960s, but it expanded further after 1964 when the military took control (Daland, 1967; da Costa, 1971) and later,
after the oil price rises of 1973. Thus it was under conditions
largely orchestrated by the Brazilian state, that multinationals
came to expand their Brazilian operations (Von Doellinger, 1975;
Suzigan, *et al*, 1976).

Multinational penetration has thus affected most industrial
sectors. Indeed, by the late 1970s there were few industries
where foreign firms did not account for at least a fifth of
fixed assets, sales, equity or employment (Mooney and Newfarmer,
1981). MNCs' operations have been concentrated in the dynamic
sectors (Mooney and Newfarmer, 1981; Connor, 1977; Newfarmer
and Mueller, 1975). A study undertaken by the author using
Brazilian corporate data for the largest enterprises in 1979
revealed the extent to which MNCs controlled assets in the
metals, machinery, electrical and transport equipment sectors.
In these industries MNCs accounted for only a fifth of total
enterprises, but nearly three fifths of assets and almost half
the employment (Cunningham, 1981a). Mooney and Newfarmer (1981)
cite data for 1970 and 1977 which relate to specific industrial
products rather than whole sectors. Their findings, summarized
in Table 3.8, show foreign firms' shares are highest in the
automobile, vehicle components, chemicals, domestic appliances,
drugs, electrical products, glass, industrial machinery, office
equipment, plastics, rubber, tobacco and tractor industries. It
is also apparent that during the 1970s MNCs increased penetration
substantially in the footwear, furniture, non-metallic minerals
and vegetable oils industries.

Clearly, the pattern of industrial ownership in Brazil is
complex. Local interests, public and private, share diverse
relationships with multinational concerns. Simplifying the
position, Evans (1974, 1979; see also Chapter 6) among others,
has emphasized the 'triple-alliance' of multinational, local
private and public sector interests in this process. While it
can also be argued that, internationally, the issue of ownership
by MNCs is perhaps of less concern than it was (Ballance and
Sinclair, 1983), nevertheless the issue remains central in a
less developed country, the industrial structure of which has
shifted in recent decades so far towards the dynamic sectors
dominated by multinationals. The 'survival' of Brazilian
private enterprise in this context is thus a particular matter
for debate. It is certainly the case that local concerns had
established themselves in some branches of dynamic industries
before MNCs transferred production to Brazil, and inevitably
during the past thirty years they have been displaced and de-
nationalized. The relative strength of the domestic private
sector has come to reside principally in the traditional industries

TABLE 3.8   Foreign Firms' Percentage Share of Brazilian
             Industry in 1970 and 1977.

Industry/Products	Fixed Assets 1979	Fixed Assets 1977	Sales 1970	Sales 1977	Equity 1970	Equity 1977	Employment 1977
I Highest foreign penetration:							
Automobiles	100	100	100	100	100	100	100
Auto components	58	57	63	54	63	50	46
Chemicals	54	57	55	57	55	42	61
Domestic appliances	76	74	73	76	73	74	64
Drugs	83	82	30	84	80	74	64
Electrical products	81	86	81	79	81	84	83
Glass	53	69	49	76	73	74	79
Industrial machinery	66	51	67	59	67	47	54
Office equipment	96	91	93	73	93	76	65
Plastics	73	42	68	57	68	43	49
Rubber	67	62	71	81	71	68	70
Tobacco	91	99	95	99	95	98	96
Tractors	83	83	80	84	80	61	69
II Marked increase from low base:							
Footwear	-	26	-	32	-	28	26
Furniture	9	24	9	13	9	19	23
Non metallic materials	3	25	5	42	5	23	32
Vegetable oils	5	52	4	59	4	52	45
III Other (Trend + or - m = mixed)							
Aircraft (-)	36	7	46	20	46	13	26
Beverages (+)	16	23	13	24	13	17	17
Cement (+)	26	41	25	33	25	25	27
Metallic minerals (+)	18	36	17	21	17	21	15
Metallurgical products (-)	38	29	36	32	36	33	33
Paper (m)	33	20	23	24	23	33	33
Petroleum (m)	10	9	14	36	14	9	14
Shipbuilding (-)	45	34	30	16	30	17	30
Spinning and weaving (-)	39	37	39	34	39	29	26
All sectors	34	33	37	44	37	31	38

Source: Mooney and Newfarmer (1981)

such as food, textiles and clothing, which mainly serve basic local needs. Yet there is evidence that Brazilian private concerns have had considerable success in extending their activities into newer industries whether alone, as part of a joint venture with foreign or state enterprise, or by purchasing some form of foreign technology (Erber, 1974; Baer *et al*, 1976; Cunningham, 1982; Rattner, 1979)[1]. It is also possible to support the view that local interests have succeeded in achieving significant technological capability in a range of dynamic sector industries (Cunningham, 1983a; Dahlman, 1979; Tigre, 1983).

The Restructuring of Industrial Employment

The degree to which employment in manufacturing industry[2] has in recent decades been restructured towards the dynamic industries where MNCs are major participants, has already been noted (see Table 3.4). Here a more detailed picture is given. The basic data are summarized in Tables 3.9 to 3.12 inclusive. Attention is drawn first to the general manufacturing employment trends for Brazil as a whole during the period 1960 to 1980 shown in Tables 3.9 and 3.10. Table 3.9 reveals a pronounced shift from traditional industry measured in terms of the sector's declining share of total employment. In contrast, Table 3.10 shows the marked expansion of the machinery industry in particular as a central focus of employment growth. Similarly, the marked decline in share of the selected traditional sectors (Table 3.9) is largely related to the decline (and modernization) in the textile sector. It is also clear from Table 3.10 that despite the erosion of the employment shares in traditional - domestically owned - industry (except clothing), these sectors continued to rank as major employers, with the food industry in first place in 1980 having well over half a million employees, and textiles and clothing (ranked fifth and fourth) having over 800,000 employees between them. Overall, however, the net increase in dynamic sector employment appears to have been such (over one and a quarter million for 1960-1980, with over 450,000 in machinery alone) that it is difficult to sustain the argument that the expansion of modern, capital intensive industry - where multinationals account for a major share of assets and sales - has failed to create a substantial amount of direct employment. Indeed, it is precisely the multinational-dominated industries with their large, rapidly growing workforces, which have become the focal point of Brazil's organized labour movement, notably the metal workers' union. So, too, labour uptake in certain traditional sectors (with the main exception of textiles) appears to have increased markedly despite the pressure to modernize.

Evidence specifically related to employment in MNCs for the year 1980 is given in Table 3.11. Over a million jobs were recorded by *Quem é Quem* in these sectors (nearly 80 per cent of the total given by the Industrial Census) in that year, and multinationals accounted for some 43 per cent of the *Quem é Quem*

TABLE 3.9   Brazil: Shares of Manufacturing Employment in Dynamic and Traditional Industries, 1960-1980. (Percentage of total).

	BRAZIL			SAO PAULO (SE)			PERNAMBUCO (NE)		
	1960	1970	1980	1960	1970	1980	1960	1970	1980
DYNAMIC[1]									
Metallurgy	9.9	10.1	11.3	10.4	11.5	13.4	2.6	5.0	5.7
Machinery	3.5	6.8	11.0	5.4	8.5	14.2	.2	1.8	7.2
Electrical equipment	3.3	4.4	5.2	5.5	6.6	7.4	-	3.3	3.7
Transport equipment	4.6	6.0	5.7	7.2	9.1	7.5	.5	1.3	1.7
Chemicals	5.8	5.0	4.2	7.1	5.8	4.4	3.8	3.9	4.5
Plastics	.5	1.6	.7	.8	.7	3.3	.1	.8	2.4
Sub total	27.6	33.9	38.1	36.4	42.2	50.2	7.2	16.1	25.2
TRADITIONAL									
Wood	5.0	5.1	5.0	1.8	1.3	1.3	1.3	2.0	1.9
Furniture	3.6	3.9	3.4	3.5	3.4	2.9	2.1	2.8	2.5
Textiles	18.7	13.0	8.5	19.7	14.3	8.7	29.8	16.5	12.8
Clothing	5.6	6.2	9.2	5.3	6.1	8.3	3.8	5.6	7.6
Food	15.1	14.1	12.1	10.1	9.0	7.7	37.1	32.3	25.7
Drink	2.5	2.2	1.1	1.9	1.5	.7	3.0	5.2	2.6
Sub total	50.5	44.5	39.3	42.3	35.6	29.6	77.1	64.4	53.1
Other sectors	21.9	21.6	22.6	21.3	22.2	20.2	15.7	19.7	21.7
All sector total	100.0	100.0	100.0	100.0	100.0	100.0	100.0	100.0	100.0

Source: Calculated from Industrial Census for each year. 1. Sectors with strong multinational ownership

TABLE 3.10   Brazil: Ranking of Employment in Main Manufacturing Sectors, 1960-80

Sector	1960 Rank	1960 Employment	1970 Rank	1970 Employment	1975 Rank	1975 Employment	1980 Rank	1980 Employment
Textiles	(1)	328,297	(2)	342,839	(4)	333,776	(5)	395,792
Food	(2)	266,106	(1)	372,401	(1)	500,006	(1)	566,833
Metallurgy	(3)	174,279	(3)	266,928	(2)	442,379	(2)	526,672
Non metallic minerals	(4)	163,680	(4)	236,506	(5)	320,304	(6)	372,496
Clothing, etc	(5)	97,999	(6)	164,512	(6)	302,192	(4)	427,192
Wood products	(6)	87,822	(8)	135,979	(8)	203,856	(9)	234,124
Transport equipment[1]	(7)	81,876	(7)	158,336	(7)	221,924	(7)	264,853
Chemicals[1]	(8)	76,518	(11)	104,367	(12)	126,516	(10)	165,022
Furniture	(9)	63,471	(10)	105,322	(10)	138,544	(11)	158,454
Machinery	(10)	62,148	(5)	180,431	(3)	391,472	(3)	515,237
Manufacturing employment total (Ten sectors above plus others)		1,753,662		2,634,630		3,816,545		4,650,358

Source: Calculated from the Industrial Census for each year.

Notes: (1) The Electrical equipment sector ranked ninth in both 1970 and 1975, and eighth in 1980 (Employment total in 1980 242,017).

(2) Total manufacturing employment increased to 2.6 times the 1960 level between 1960-1980. The increases in the main dynamic sectors were above this (with the exception of Chemicals where it was 2.1) as follows: Metallurgy 3.0 times; Transport equipment 3.2 times; Machinery 8.2 times; Electrical equipment 4.1 times. With the exception of the Clothing/Shoe sector (4.3 times) in traditional sectors the employment increase was at or below the average for Brazil: Food 2.1 times; Textiles 1.2 times; Wood 2.6 times; Furniture 2.5 times.

1. Sectors with strong multinational penetration.

TABLE 3.11 Brazil: Multinationals and Employment in Dynamic Sectors of Manufacturing, 1980

| Sectors | Quem é Quem [1] 1980 | | | Industrial Census [2] 1980 |
	Employment in Multinationals	Total Employment		Total Employment
Machinery	79,558	211,520		515,237
Electrical equipment	88,997	199,542		242,017
Transport equipment	178,053	327,845		264,853
(1) Sub total	346,608	738,907		1,022,107
Chemicals, etc	94,958	262,046		222,688
Plastics	8,987	57,076		117,379
(2) Sub total	103,945	319,122		340,067
(1) and (2)	450,553	1,058,029		1,362,174

Source: Quem é Quem (Visao) 1981 and the 1982 Industrial Census.

1. Quem é Quem does not cover all establishments, but is confined to the large corporate sector enterprises.

2. The Industrial Census covers establishments of all sizes. Sectoral classification differences between the two sources and Quem é Quem's estimating procedures where necessary, also account for discrepancies in employment totals.

57

TABLE 3.12 Brazil: The Percentage Share of Labour Costs in Total Costs of Manufacturing Production, by Sector, 1960-80

Sector	1960	1970	1975	1980	1960-70	1970-80
All manufacturing	18.1	16.1	11.1	11.5	-2.0	-4.6
Non metallic minerals	36.0	30.1	21.8	20.3	-5.9	-9.8
Metallurgy	22.3	14.7	11.0	9.7	-7.6	-5.0
Machinery	31.6	30.0	24.0	28.4	-1.6	-1.6
Electrical equipment	19.7	21.9	14.0	15.1	+2.2	-6.8
Transport equipment	20.0	22.0	8.7	11.6	+2.0	-10.4
Chemicals	12.9	10.4	3.3	3.2	-2.5	-7.2
Pharmaceuticals	25.7	25.6	16.3	13.8	-0.1	-11.8
Perfumes, soaps, etc	10.8	11.3	7.8	8.0	+0.5	-3.3
Plastics	22.8	17.6	14.1	14.0	-5.2	-3.6
Wood products	26.8	21.1	18.9	20.3	-5.7	-0.8
Furniture	31.0	26.2	26.7	20.3	-4.8	-5.9
Paper and cardboard	15.8	19.1	13.7	11.2	+3.3	-7.9
Rubber	14.5	16.4	10.6	16.9	+1.9	-0.5
Leather, hides, etc	19.6	17.2	15.5	13.9	-2.4	-3.3
Textiles	21.4	18.3	10.6	11.1	-3.1	-7.2
Clothing, shoes, etc	23.1	18.7	15.6	18.6	-4.4	-0.1
Food	7.9	6.5	5.4	5.8	-1.4	-0.7
Drink	23.3	22.4	14.0	13.4	-0.9	-9.0

Source: Calculated from the Industrial Census for each year.

total and about 33 per cent of the Census total. (In certain respects, the relatively large scale of plants operated by multinationals also presents some advantages for labour organization, particularly in the vehicle industry where up to 15,000 workers may be employed in a single plant.) Women also feature significantly in the growing workforce of industries where MNCs are prominent, particularly in the electrical equipment, pharmaceuticals and plastic sectors, where they account for between 30 and 40 per cent of employment. In other dynamic sectors, women are a relatively less important but still significant component (10 to 20 per cent), while industries which have traditionally employed women, such as clothing and textiles, account for 45 to 65 per cent (see: Cunningham, 1983b; Tigre, 1983).

The Role of Labour Costs

While the lower labour costs of countries like Brazil are often assumed to be a major factor influencing MNCs to locate or expand production there, relatively little attention appears to have been given to the changing pattern of labour costs[3] in the total costs of manufacturing production during the 1960s and 1970s. Census data for the period 1960 to 1980 presented in Table 3.12 provides some evidence on this point. While caution should always be used in drawing firm conclusions from such data, taking the period as a whole, it can be observed that there was a decrease in the share of labour costs in total costs of manufacturing between 1960 and 1980. The most marked fall appears to have taken place between 1970 and 1975[4]. It is likely that this change is related to the sharp rise in the cost of energy, raw materials and capital goods after the 1973 oil price rises, whereas equivalent increases in labour costs did not take place. Particularly striking, though, is the observation that some of the largest falls in labour costs were in those main dynamic sectors which are central to the pattern of Brazil's recent industrial restructuring through greater multinational penetration (specifically transport equipment, electrical equipment, pharmaceuticals, chemicals and machinery).

The evidence considered here throws new light upon the particular role of MNCs operating in Brazilian manufacturing during the 1970s. Specifically, increased FDI and MNC operations performed a key multiplier role in the expansion of the dynamic industries which the Brazilian state was actively promoting. In the process, employment in these industries grew markedly and in 1980 MNCs accounted for between one third and one half of employment in the largest firms. At the same time, an analysis of labour cost data suggests that an important incentive for greater investment by MNCs in their Brazilian operations may have been provided through the falling short of labour costs over the 1960-80 period and more especially between 1970 and 1980. Government action to control wages in Brazil itself (Tavares and Souza, 1983) coupled with changes in relative costs

of production internationally were both important in effecting
this trend.

THE INTERNATIONALIZATION OF CAPITAL AND INDUSTRY:
BRAZIL AND THE MULTINATIONAL BANKS

Brazil's incorporation during the 1970s into the financial
structures controlled by the multinational banks is without
precedent.   Tables 3.5 and 3.6 contain some evidence of the
scale of the country's commitments to foreign banks by 1982. As
has already been stated, between 1975 and 1982 foreign banks
provided funds far in excess of other sources (including foreign
direct investment by manufacturing multinationals).   However,
it should be emphasized that a fundamental reason behind this
dramatic growth in foreign finance was the very pattern of industrial development and restructuring which the Brazilian state
was actively pursuing.
     Brazil had from 1974 sought to expand its economy against
the trend of a growing international recession, taking advantage
of the increased opportunities for foreign commercial bank borrowing which arose in connection with the recycling of petrodollars.   Such borrowing, while it was ultimately destined to
finance internal current account deficits and service balance
of payments requirements, nevertheless also allowed resources
to be channelled into major industrial and infrastructural projects.   This was especially the case in sectors where the state
itself was directly involved as a major investor and entrepreneur;
specific examples here include: the Açominas steel project,
capacity increases in virtually all existing steel and petrochemical installations, new petrochemical complexes in the
Northeast at Camaçri (near Salvador) and South at Triunfo (near
Porto Alegre), the Carajás project, the Itaipú hydroelectric
scheme, an ambitious nuclear energy programme until 1982, the
opening up of the offshore oil resources in the Campos basin,
the paving of roads and construction of rapid urban transit
systems in major cities, and further advances in telecommunications by satellite.   Yet it should also be said that private
sector manufacturers - local as well as foreign multinational
concerns - gained substantially from the public-sector led expansion of orders.   Nowhere was this more apparent than in the
capital goods field, which also received a major boost directly
through subsidies and incentives operated by the National
Development Bank (BNDE) and Industrial Development Council (CDI).
     However, the Brazilian strategy featuring economic (and
specifically, industrial) expansion underpinned by foreign
finance, encountered greater difficulty after 1979.   From that
date, the depth of international recession in the advanced industrial nations, high real rates of interest on borrowed money,
and a new round of oil price increases began to take their toll.
These changes in the international climate seriously affected

Brazil's economic performance in 1981 when the growth rate of manufacturing industry actually declined substantially for the first time in two decades. At the same time, falling oil prices (from which Brazil stood to gain as a major importer) eroded the supply of petrodollars, so increasing the competition for funds and giving further impetus to the switch, by lenders and borrowers alike, to shorter term money at floating rates of interest. The real demise of the Brazilian expansionist strategy, which had involved an effective *détente* with multinational banks for almost a decade, did not come until the second half of 1982, when, in the wake of the South Atlantic crisis between Britain and Argentina, banks (especially in the UK and USA) began to reconsider their previous lending policies toward Latin America. An immediate casualty of the multinational banks' new cautious approach to lending occurred in August 1982 when Mexico was unable to secure sufficient funds to meet its financial payments. Since then, the debt servicing problems of Brazil and other debtor nations inside and outside Latin America have been severe. Since 1983 banks have continued to lend some new money, but mainly under forced lending regimes, tied to International Monetary Fund conditionality and designed to service old debts rather than to foster economic growth.

Leaving aside a detailed discussion of the debt crisis (see: Cunningham and Gwynne, 1983; Cunningham, 1983b), an equally important point is that the new international financial regime from 1982, coupled with the further adjustments being made by business and industry worldwide, may well have thrown into sharp reverse many of the restructuring trends in both finance and production, observed in Brazil in particular and Latin American countries in general during the 1970s.

CONCLUSIONS: THE END OF AN ERA?

Given the broad concerns addressed within this chapter and the uncertainties prevailing in the international economy, it would be invidious to draw specific conclusions at this stage. Yet the evidence considered here reveals much about the uniqueness of restructuring developments during the 1970s and 1980s, especially concerning the superimposition of multinational bank finance upon an existing nexus of foreign direct investment established by other multinational corporations (especially in manufacturing). Moreover, while these changes have been strongly linked to restructuring at the international scale - in which multinationals have a dominant role to play - it is apparent that the state in Latin American countries has mediated the particular form of that restructuring in specific portions of territory. While it is recognized that not all countries in the region have the economic or political weight of Brazil, Argentina or Mexico, nevertheless the evidence reviewed suggests that the particular conditions during the 1970s allowed a wider range of

61

countries to pursue restructuring 'policies'.   In this, the
prior implantation and expansion of dynamic industries by multinationals and the state (or occasionally as in Chile from 1974
or Argentina from 1976, the onset of a new economic regime,
perhaps involving deindustrialization) opened up new markets
for finance capital which the multinational banks supplied in
increasing quantities from 1974 to 1982.   Events since the
middle of 1982 until the time of final writing (mid-1985) have
conspired to bring about a hiatus - or possibly, an end - to
this restructuring process.

Footnotes

1.   Data for the largest enterprises surveyed annually by
      Visao in *Quem è Quem* (Who's Who), show that private
      Brazilian firms control between 20 per cent and 55 per
      cent of net assets in the main dynamic sectors
      (chemicals 22 per cent, metallurgy and machinery 55 per
      cent, transport equipment 38 per cent, electrical equip-
      ment 53 per cent) and between 65 and 100 per cent in the
      main traditional sectors.

2.   Specifically, the formal sector of manufacturing, this is
      the *only* aspect of industrial employment discussed here.

3.   For a recent discussion of Brazilian industrial wage
      levels, see: Tavares and Souza (1983).

4.   The falling share of labour costs in total production
      costs in Brazil (and some other LDCs) contrasts with a
      rise in the component of costs in a number of DCs (in-
      cluding the UK) during the 1970s.

REFERENCES

Baer, W. *et al* (1976) 'On State Capitalism in Brazil   Some New Issues and Questions' *Inter-American Economic Affairs* (Winter): 69-90.

Baer, W., Kerstenetszky, I. and Vilela, A. (1973) 'The Changing Role of the State in the Brazilian Economy', *World Development*, November: 23-24.

Balassa, B. (1981)   *The Newly Industrialising Countries in the World Economy*, Pergamon Press, London.

Ballance, R. and Sinclair, S. (1983)   *Collapse and Survival: Industry Strategists in a Changing World*, World Industry Studies 1, Allen & Unwin, London.

Baumann Neves, R. (1982) 'Brazil: the expansion of manufactured exports', *Bank of London and South America Review*, 16(2): 64-76.

Connor, J. (1977)   *The Market Power of Multinationals: A Quantitative Analysis of US Corporations in Brazil and Mexico*, Praeger, New York.

Cunningham, S. (1979)   'Brazil: Recent Trends in Industrial Development', *Bank of London and South America Review*, 13 (4): 212-220.

Cunningham, S. (1981a) 'Multinational Enterprises in Brazil: Locational Patterns and Implications for Regional Development', *The Professional Geographer*, 33(1): 48-62.

Cunningham, S. (1981b)   'New Technology, Corporate Strategies and Latin American Industrialisation: The Next Twenty Years', *Journal of Area Studies*, Autumn: 29-35.

Cunningham, S. (1982)   *Brazilian Private Industrial Enterprise 1950-80*, Institute of Latin American Studies, University of London Working Papers, Series No.7.

Cunningham, S. (1983a) 'Technical Change and Newly Industrialising Countries: The Division of Labour and the Growth of Indigenous Technological Capability' (mimeo) IGU-AAG Conference, Denver, Colorado.

Cunningham, S. (1983b)   'Labour Turnover and Women's Work: Evidence from Brazil', *Bulletin of Latin American Research*, 2(2): 93-103.

Cunningham, S. and Gwynne, R. (1983)   'The Greatest Debtors in the World', *Geographical Magazine*, November: 569-572.

da Costa, J.G. (1971)   *Planejamento Governamental*, FGV, Rio de Janeiro.

Dahlman, C. (1979)   A Microeconomic Approach to Technical Change: The Evolution of the Usiminas Steel Firm in Brazil, unpublished PhD thesis, Yale University, New Haven.

Daland, R.T. (1967) *Brazilian Planning*, Chapel Hill Press, New York.

Dunning, J. (1977)   'Trade, Location of Economic Activity and the Multinational Enterprise: A Search for the Eclectic Approach' in Ohlin, B. (ed) *The International Allocation of Economic Activity*, Macmillan, London: 395-418.

Erber, F. (1974) *Absorcão e Cricão de Tecnologia na Indústria de Bens de Capital*, Finep, Serie de Pesquisas No.2, Rio de Janeiro.

Evans, P. (1974) 'The Military, the Multinationals and the "Miracle": The Political Economy of the Brazilian Model of Development', *Studies in Comparative International Development*, 9(3): 26-45.

Evans, P. (1979) *Dependent Development: The Alliance of Multinational State and Local Capital in Brazil*, Princeton, New Jersey.

FIBEE (1981) *Tabalacoes Avancadas 1980*, Vol.1, Tom 2, Rio de Janeiro.

Fitzgerald, E.V.K., Floto, E. and Lehmann, D.L. (1977) *The State and Economic Development in Latin America*, Cambridge University Press.

Franko, L.E. (1976) *The European Multinationals*, Harper and Row, London

Fransman, M. (ed) (1982) *Industry and Accumulation in Africa*, Heinemann Educational Books, London.

Fröbel, F. *et al* (1980) *The New International Division of Labour*, Cambridge University Press.

IBGE (1974) *Anuario Esatistico 1973*, Rio de Janeiro.

ILO (1980) *Yearbook of Labour Statistics*, Geneva.

Jenkins, R.O. (1984) *Transnational Corporations and Industrial Transformation in Latin America*, Macmillan.

Kemp, T. (1983) *Industrialisation in the Non-Western World*, Longman.

Mandel, E. (1978) *The second slump: a Marxist analysis of the recession in the 1970s*, New Left Books, London.

Mooney, J. and Newfarmer, R. (1981) 'State Enterprises and Private Sector Development in Brazil', United Nations Centre on Transnational Corporations (mimeo), data reproduced as Annex Table II 25 of UNCTNC *III Report on Multinationals* (1983), New York: 352.

Nayyar, D. (1978) 'Transnational Corporations and Manufactured Exports from Poor Countries', *Economic Journal*, 88: 59-84.

Newfarmer, R. and Mueller, W. (1975) *Multinational Corporations in Brazil and Mexico: Structural Sources of Economic and non-Economic Power*, US Senate, Subcommittee on Foreign Relations, GPO, Washington DC

OECD (1977) *Development Cooperation - Annual Review*, Paris.

Quem é Quem (Who's Who), annual, Visão, Sao Paulo.

Rattner, H. (1979) *Pequena e Médiqu Empresea no Brazil*, Collecão en Saio e Memoria, No.15, Sao Paulo.

Sen, A. (1982) *The State, Industrialisation and Class Formation in India*, RKP, London.

Suzigan, W. (1976) *As Empresas do Governo e o Papel do Estado na Economia Brasileiro*, Serie Monografica No.26, IPEA, Rio de Janeiro.

Tavares, M. and Souza, P.R. (1983) 'Employment and wages in industry: the case of Brazil', in Urquidi V. and Reyes S.

(eds) *Human Resources, Employment and Development*, Vol.4,
Latin America, IEA, Macmillan, London: 195-210.
Tigre, P. (1983)   *Technology and Competition in the Brazilian
Computer Industry*, Frances Pinter, London.
Trebat, T. (1983)   *Brazil's State-Owned Enterprises: A Case
Study of the State as Entrepreneur*, Cambridge UP.
UN/UNCTNC (1983)   *III Report on Multinationals*, New York.
Von Doellinger, C. (1975)   *Empresas Multinacionais na Industria
Brasileira*, IPEA/INPES Relatoria de Pesquisa No.29, Rio de
Janeiro.
Wallerstein, I. (1979)   *The World Capitalist Economy*,
Cambridge University Press.
World Bank (1983)   *World Development Report*, Washington.
World Financial Markets, various issues.   Morgan Guaranty
Trust Company, New York.

Chapter Four

ARMING THE THIRD WORLD:
THE ROLE OF THE MULTINATIONAL CORPORATION

S.W. Williams

INTRODUCTION

The growth and diversification of MNC (Multinational Corporation)
involvement in the economies of developing countries has attracted the attention of both development organizations (for
example, Brandt Commission, 1980, 1983) and academics (for example,
Hamilton and Linge, 1983).   One area, however, which has been
almost entirely neglected is the military sector.   This is all
the more surprising given the '... considerable overlap between
the arms industry and the firms which appear in the standard
listings of the major MNCs'.   Indeed, '... if one scans the
international development literature one could almost be excused
for thinking that the military sector does not exist or is of
peripheral importance' (Luckham, 1981: 1).   Clearly, there are
a number of problems associated with the delineation of a distinct subsystem of multinational arms producers.   These include
the often unclear boundary between military and non-military
production, the influence of a variety of constraints associated
with political and security considerations, and the emphasis of
non-equity arrangements as opposed to the more frequent extension of MNC influence via ownership of a foreign enterprise's
equity (Luckham, 1984; Tuomi, 1983).
    Despite these problems, which are compounded by the lack
of accurate information and analytically sound empirical studies,
the importance of large Western corporations in the armament
process in a number of developing countries cannot be denied.
Within this context the present chapter provides a preliminary
assessment of the extent to which multinational corporations
are enmeshed in the various armament strategies pursued by
developing countries.

THE CONTEXT OF THE ARMAMENT PROCESS IN DEVELOPING COUNTRIES

During the 1970s military expenditure in the Third World grew
at the rate of approximately 7-8 per cent per annum.   In

relative terms developing countries increased their share of world military expenditure from 17.5 per cent in 1972 to 26 per cent in 1981 (SIPRI, 1982; Palme, 1982; Whynes, 1979). During the same period arms imports increased even more rapidly than overall military spending, a trend which parallels the movement in developed countries towards the procurement and maintenance of armaments, and away from paying armies.   Thus, the Third World's major arms imports (aircraft, armoured vehicles, missiles and warships) were four times greater in the 1970s than the 1960s, reaching a peak of US$9567 million in 1978 (at 1975 prices). (SIPRI, 1982:191).   Indeed, during the last decade almost three-quarters of all major weapon transfers were made to Third World countries, with the USA alone accounting for 45 per cent of all transfers.

Many factors have contributed to this rapid military build-up. Perhaps the major factor in the context of Western arms transfers has been the progressive shift away from a policy of military grant aid to one of foreign military sales.   During the late 1940s and 1950s the USA provided several Third World countries, particularly those designated as 'forward defence areas' with armaments as 'gifts' under its Military Aid Program. Grants and sales were roughly equal in the 1960s, while in the 1970s grants were steadily replaced by Foreign Military Sales (FMS) and commercial export agreements (Frank, 1980; SIPRI, 1980:57-126). This latter feature is essentially the result of what was called the 'Nixon-doctrine' which urged allies of the USA to bear their own burdens of defence; implicit in this demand was the promise to supply the military hardware required (Kaldor, 1982). On the demand side a number of political and strategic factors have been influential in the growth of imports. This is particularly evident in the Middle East which accounted for 48 per cent of all Third World imports during the 1970s (SIPRI, 1980). In addition the rapid rise in crude oil prices since 1973 made it possible for many oil producing countries to make extensive purchases of armaments. Thus during the period 1975-79 OPEC countries accounted for 50 per cent of all arms imports by developing countries (Palme, 1982).

In addition, the late 1960s was a period characterized by the increased competitiveness of European armaments industries *vis-à-vis* American companies. During the 1950s, and spurred on by Cold War policies, the arms industry was dominated by the USA. Initially, many West European countries were the recipients of large American arms transfers.   However, these transfers were followed by minority participations in the industries of the allied countries and the revival of these industries with the help of American production licences. By the late 1950s, therefore, just as civilian industries became competitive, so too did the European military industries, and a major export drive took place. It was precisely during this period, however, that it became apparent that there was an over-production of weapons in the West: too many companies with too large an output and production capacity. Indeed the improved relationship between East and West simply did not justify such high levels of production. Paradoxically, the response of the armament industry to the changing environment was one of growth and expansion:

> As an hypothesis we might suggest ... that it was a fear of diminishing demand and decline of the whole military sector that pushed armaments industries into international expansion. ... As the European markets were full and production exceeded local demand the industries turned to the Third World, where the amount of weapons was still limited and expanding markets could be forecasted. The industries were not left alone in this process; on the contrary their home governments promoted new sales and arranged public funds for the purpose.
> (Tuomi and Väyrynen, 1980:5)

Nevertheless, in the 1970s many companies realized that if they wanted to secure their share of the market or occupy new ones then exports alone were not sufficient. As a result a variety of new measures were employed including offset deals, licence agreements and other forms of production cooperation contracts. On the one hand, this tendency was part of a conscious company strategy and a sign of fierce competition. On the other hand, such arrangements were increasingly demanded by the purchasers of weapons.

At the present time, therefore, Western conventional arms production and research and development capability is restricted to a relatively small number of countries (USA, UK, France, West Germany and Italy). Similarly, the actual production of the weapons is concentrated in a few large corporations many of which have become transnational as a result of large sales and technology transfers.

A final factor which accelerated the build-up of conventional weapons in many Third World countries during the 1970s was the rapid reorganization of international economic and military relationships between North and South. Although demands for NIEO (New International Economic Order) were strongly voiced by developing countries, the negotiations regarding its implementation did not make much progress in the 1970s. However, a general reorganization did take place which was dominated by the traditional power tools of the West: militarism and technology. In particular the intention was to take advantage of the differences among the developing countries and focus attention on a number of countries identified as 'regional influentials' (Tuomi and Väyrynen, 1980; Väyrynen, 1979).

In economic terms, an intensified spread of Western technology took place in regionally influential countries with the MNCs occupying a pivotal position in this process. In many cases developing countries competed in trying to attract MNCs by founding free production zones, offering cheap labour,

infrastructure and various economic incentives. The technological superiority of the West has led a number of writers to
conclude that there is a tendency in North-South relations towards what has become known as a 'new international division of
labour'(Fröbel, Heinrichs and Kreye, 1977). Specifically, this
would involve the North specializing in complex high technology
products which would be exchanged for less complex labour intensive products of the South. In many respects this new division
of labour is the MNCs' interpretation of the NIEO which would
have the dual effect of increasing MNC control over the international economy, maintaining their technological monopoly, and
also increasing the Third World's dependency on MNC and Northern
(specifically, Western) technology. This conception of the new
division of labour is evident in the armaments sector where the
West has a virtual monopoly of qualified personnel, research
and development apparatus, funding and complex production
machinery. If weapons and weapons technology are transferred
on the basis of the new division of labour, the result is the
reinforcement of the military and technological monopoly of the
West, thus furthering dependency and underdevelopment (Ayres,
1982).

STRATEGIES OF AQUISITION OF CONVENTIONAL WEAPONS
BY THE THIRD WORLD

Several strategies exist whereby a Third World country can
procure weapons and weapons technology. For the developing
countries these strategies represent a progressive integration
into the world economic and military order. From the perspective of the Western armaments industries the strategies involve
a progressive internationalization of operations (Tuomi, 1983).

The first phase consists of the import of finished weapon
systems, and for the majority of Third World countries this
represents the principal procurement strategy. From the companies' point of view intense competition has led to a buyer's
market where arms producers compete for customers - employing
both conventional and unconventional methods (Albrecht *et al.*,
1975; Lock and Wulf, 1977; Tuomi and Väyrynen, 1980; Wulf,
1979).

The second phase is characterized by developing countries
participating in the military-economic division of labour
through various licence and co-production arrangements, thus
obtaining some domestic capacity to produce weapon systems.
This would not be possible, however, without the financial contribution of MNCs and the governments of industrialized countries. Many licence agreements are concluded only for a certain
part of the weapon while the original producer reserves for itself the production of the most important and complex parts.

Licence and co-production agreements may lead to the
licensee becoming a subcontractor for the MNC supplying the

technology. The developing country thus becomes part of the vertical division of labour within the multinational armaments industry. International subcontracting is usually considered by an MNC after the benefits of subcontracting have been examined in terms of cheaper labour costs, raw material prices and other economic advantages.

Initial demands for the indigenous production of weapons in developing countries is manifested in a general increase in the local share of the value of the weapon system. However, critical dependencies remain on certain areas of foreign technology, such as engines and electronics. High production costs and large investments have resulted in many developing countries expanding their arms exports in an attempt to cover part of the costs by sharing them with potential buyers.

Argentina, Brazil, India, Israel and South Africa have all launched major investment programmes which attempt to establish an autonomous armaments industry. This strategy was expected to strengthen political independence, reduce procurement costs and save foreign exchange. Further benefits, it was argued, would be derived from the creation of new jobs, and training of local personnel and the expansion of indigenous research and development potential. In reality, dependency on industrial powers intensified in the above countries, with their productive structure being almost irreversibly dependent on foreign technology, personnel, components and patents all of which played only a minor role when military procurements were imported.

In general the ultimate aim of many developing countries to establish an indigenous armament technology independent of MNCs is, at the present time, an elusive goal. In the following sections the various strategies outlined above are considered in greater detail. It should be noted, however, that because of the military and commercial secrecy covering the operations of the military MNCs much of the available information is of a limited and incomplete nature.

ARMS IMPORTS

The import of finished weapon systems continues to be the main armaments strategy pursued by most developing countries (for general discussions see Pierre, 1982; SIPRI, 1971) (see Table 4.1). During the 1970s the Middle East (as it has been since 1945) was the largest importing region, although the positions of individual Middle Eastern importers have changed (SIPRI, 1980). During the first half of the 1970s the major importers were Egypt and Syria followed by Iran and Israel; after 1975 the participants in the Arab-Israeli confrontation gave way to the oil producers Iran and Saudi Arabia. Table 4.1 also reflects the heavy military build-up in Iraq. Recent data for 1979-81 indicate further changes, with Iran not even appearing in the

Table 4.1   Main Third World Weapons Importing Countries,
             1977-1980

Importing Country	Total Value (US$ m)	Percentage of Third World Total	Main Supply Source
Iran	3446	8.7	US
Saudi Arabia	3133	8.0	US
Jordan	2558	6.5	US
Syria	2311	5.9	USSR
Iraq	2172	5.5	USSR
Libya	2107	5.4	USSR
South Korea	1987	5.0	US
India	1931	4.9	USSR
Israel	1778	4.5	US
Vietnam	1220	3.1	USSR
Morocco	1121	2.9	France
Ethiopia	1086	2.7	USSR
Peru	995	2.5	USSR
South Yemen	964	2.4	USSR
South Africa	950	2.4	Italy
Algeria	882	2.2	USSR
Taiwan	737	1.9	US
Kuwait	664	1.7	USSR
Argentina	642	1.6	FRG
Brazil	641	1.6	UK
Egypt	594	1.5	US
Indonesia	522	1.3	US
Pakistan	512	1.3	France
Chile	482	1.2	France
Thailand	412	1.0	US
Others	5657	14.3	-
Total	39504	100.0	

Source: SIPRI (1981)

top twenty major importing countries, while Egypt has
increased its arms imports and now ranks eighth amongst Third
World importers (SIPRI, 1982).
      The second largest importing region during the 1970s was
the Far East. Imports did not decline with the ending of the
Indo-China wars in 1974-5.   Indeed, South Korea, Vietnam,
Taiwan, Thailand, Malaysia, Indonesia and Singapore have all
allocated large funds for arms imports.   Clearly the conflict
between China, Vietnam and Kampuchea in 1978-9 has been the
major factor in stimulating armament investments in the whole

region.

In the first half of the 1970s Africa became the third largest
region for arms imports. This position was further strengthened
during the period 1975-9 when Africa accounted for 21 per cent
of Third World arms imports. Some of the principal factors in
the growth of such imports to this region include the liberation wars in the former Portuguese colonies, various conflicts
in Sub-Saharan and Southern Africa, and the military build-up
of South Africa and various North African states.

Imports to South Asia have been dominated by the tensions
and consequent arms race between India and Pakistan. The largest importer in the area is India which accounted for 57 per
cent of the major arms imports in the late 1970s. In Latin
America the armament rivalry between Brazil and Argentina dominates the situation in the whole continent.

The Role of Western MNCs

Although the export justification for continued high levels of
arms transfers is usually expressed in military and foreign
policy terms, during the 1970s economic justification became
increasingly common. This type of argument suggests that arms
sales improve the balance-of-payments deficits, stimulate commercial transactions between the supplier and recipient, lower
per unit production costs, reduce unemployment and contribute
to the viability of defence industries (Hessing Cahn, 1979).
Certainly there is evidence to suggest that national per unit
production costs, particularly in high technology equipment,
are influenced by the volume of arms exports. This is clearly
seen in the case of Sweden where restricted arms exports have
resulted in raising the per unit price of its most advanced
tactical aircraft to double that of France's Mirage.

Arguments relating to the contribution of arms exports to
the entire economy, however, are somewhat less convincing. For
example, although it is frequently argued that arms sales are
particularly important to the defence production and economies
of Britain and France, the contribution of military exports to
total exports is much greater for the USA (and the USSR) than it
is for Britain and France (see Table 4.2). But in any case, as
a percentage of GNP, arms exports are relatively insignificant
in all exporting countries (Tuomi and Väyrynen 1980).

Although arms exports may not be particularly important to
national economies they are of crucial significance to individual defence sectors and particular companies. In both the United
States and Europe the aerospace industry is the most important
sector in terms of military production and exports. Thus in
the period 1968-9, for example, the production of airframes,
aero-engines and missiles accounted for 53 per cent of total
military output in Britain, 46 per cent in France and 70-80 per
cent in West Germany (European Parliament, 1978). In 1979 the
top twenty arms exporting firms in the West (see Table 4.3)
were dominated by aerospace industries (with the exception of

Table 4.2   Arms Exports, Total Exports and GNP of Selected
             Exporting Countries, 1980

	GNP (US$ m)	Arms exports	Total exports	Arms exports/ total exports %	Arms exports/ GNP %
USA	2369987	5983	200095	2.99	0.25
France	575100	2629	105182	2.50	0.46
UK	403803	1631	104385	1.56	0.40
USSR	1290841	7978	69329	11.51	0.62
China	500542	199	16106	1.24	0.04
FRG	769086	1178	174885	0.67	0.15

Source: United States Arms Control and Disarmament Agency
          (1983)

Table 4.3   Twenty Biggest Arms Exporters in the West, 1979

Top ten US exporters	FMS orders 1979 (US$ m)	Top ten non-US exporters	Sales 1979 (US$ m)
Lockheed	1400	Dassault-Breguet (France)	1170
McDonnell Douglas	638	MBB (FRG)	756
General Dynamics	518	British Aerospace (UK)	730
Northrop	456	Aerospatiale (France)	650
Sperry	249	Royal Ordnance Factories (UK)	639
Raytheon	132	Thomson-CSF (France)	625
Vinnell	110	Kraus-Maffei (FRG)	540
Textron/Bell	109	Israel Aircraft Industries	326
General Electric	101	Rolls Royce (UK)	236
Westinghouse Electric	85	MATRA (France)	210

Note Figures for US and non-US are not strictly comparable.
     United States data refers to Defense Department prelimin-
     ary estimates. Figures for non-US firms are derived from
     government and company reports.

     FMS   Foreign Military Sales

Source: *Business Week*, 24 March 1980

Vinnell Corp. and Kraus-Maffei), and aerospace products accounted for the majority of exports to Third World countries (Pierre, 1982:12).

In general the aerospace industry is dominated by American companies. These accounted for nearly two-thirds of world market sales for all aerospace business in 1975. In terms of sales the American industry was nearly three times the size of Europe in 1976 (Franko, 1979:18). Very few aerospace companies are totally dependent on military production and it is almost invariably the case that military production is carried out by the same companies who are also large civilian producers. Although beneficial from the companies' viewpoint, the coexistence of civilian and military production makes it difficult to make accurate assessments of the extent of military production and military operations. This problem is further compounded by the possibility that companies can conceal their military operations behind civilian production; this is particularly so in the case of large MNCs which can spread military technology abroad through civilian organizations. However, with regard to United States aerospace companies, a measure of the degree of militarization can be obtained by expressing DoD (Department of Defense) contracts as a percentage of sales. Table 4.4 illustrates a threefold breakdown. The first group of companies are characterized by a relatively high level of military production, and for many state funding is essential for their very existence. In the second group of companies lower levels of military production are indicative of a diversified production profile, viz. the company is in military-related production without many DoD contracts. These factors are responsible, although to a greater degree, for the lower levels of military production in the third group of companies.

Table 4.4   The Largest US Aerospace Companies and the Military Content of Production-Aircraft and Missiles, 1978

Defense Department Contracts as a Percentage of Sales

50% and over	25-50%	25% and less
McDonnell Douglas	United Technologies	Rockwell
Lockheed	Boeing	International
General Dynamics	Raytheon	Beech Aircraft
Hughes	Textron/Bell	LTV
Grumman	Northrop	Cessna
	Martin Marietta	

Source: compiled from Tuomi and Väyrynen (1980)

In assessing the importance of the aerospace industry in United States international policies, the most valuable indicator is the value of FMS (Foreign Military Sales), whereby 'the US government functions as a middleman, in effect buying military equipment from US companies and reselling it to foreign buyers' (Husbands, 1979:157; see also Reppy, 1983). Between 1974 and 1978 FMS accounted for approximately 76 per cent of all American arms transfer agreements (SIPRI, 1980:67), and in 1977, out of an FMS programme amounting to US$7.1 billion, aircraft alone accounted for one third of the total; if missiles and aviation equipment are included this figure rises to 50 per cent (Tuomi and Väyrynen, 1980:28). This is reflected in the fact that in 1978 twelve of the fourteen leading military exporting companies were aerospace producers. Whereas these companies represented 70.3 per cent of FMS in 1978 they only received 34.3 per cent of the total DoD contracts, which suggests that they are more dominant in foreign military relations than in the total defence economy (Tuomi and Väyrynen, 1980:29). A measure of the export dependency of particular companies can be obtained by expressing FMS as a percentage of DoD contracts (Table 4.5). In 1976, according to this indicator, Northrop was clearly the most export-dependent firm, followed by Grumman and Textron/Bell. By 1978 Textron/Bell had overtaken Northrop, followed by General Dynamics and Litton Industries. The importance of FMS can be best illustrated by Northrop which is developing a new FX-fighter designed specifically for sale in Third World countries.

The West European aerospace industry is dominated by France and Britain and as a whole is far more dependent on exports to the Third World than the US aerospace industry. In 1978 the total turnover of the French aerospace industry was some US$6.1 billion, 70 per cent of which was accounted for by exports. In general military sales represents 72 per cent of all French aerospace exports, compared with less than 50 per cent for the US. The export profiles of the leading aerospace companies are presented in Table 4.6. Clearly, Dassault-Bréguet occupies a predominant position and can be considered to be one of the most export-dependent military producers in the world. In 1978 the company's total sales amounted to US$1.4 billion and exports represented 75 per cent of turnover, with three-quarters of all exports being military in character.

Recent estimates suggest that in Britain approximately half the production of the British aerospace industry is devoted to military items. (*Sunday Times*, 11 September 1983; see also Pearson, 1983). Although British arms exports in general have decreased in recent years, British aerospace exports increased from just under US$400 million in 1972 to over US$900 million in 1977. In 1973 the military content of aerospace exports was estimated to be between 50 and 60 per cent, although the present ratio in unknown military exports, in particular, have undoubtedly increased (Freedman, 1978). The principal contractors

Table 4.5   Foreign Military Sales as a Percentage of Total Defense Department Contracts
in Leading American Aerospace Companies, 1976–1978

	FMS/DoD contracts 1976 %	FMS/DoD contracts 1978 %	Change 1976–78 % units	Principal items
General Dynamics	4.3	35.5	+31.2	F-16, missiles
Litton Industries	26.4	33.6	+ 7.2	aerospace and naval electronics
Textron/Bell	30.0	50.9	+20.9	helicopters
Lockheed	9.2	13.4	+ 4.2	C-130 Hercules
McDonnell Douglas	19.5	9.6	- 9.9	F-14, F-15 aircraft
Raytheon	27.9	20.7	- 7.2	missiles
Northrop	97.3	45.6	-51.7	aircraft
General Electric	18.4	9.8	- 8.6	engines
Hughes	19.1	10.5	- 8.6	missiles, helicopters
United Technologies	8.5	4.8	- 3.7	Sikorsky helicopters, Pratt & Whitney engines
Grumman	30.9	5.9	-25.0	F-14 Tomcat, early warning aircraft

Source: Tuomi and Väyrynen (1980)

TABLE 4.6   French Aerospace Exports, 1977

Company	Main business	Exports (Ffr. m)	%	% of arms production in turnover
Dassault-Bréguet	Mirage	10700	46.5	91
MATRA	Missiles	4500	19.6	49
Aerospatiale (SNIAS)	Helicopters, missiles	3000	13.0	75
SNECMA	Engines	1900	8.2	65
Thomson-CSF	Aerospace electronics	1400	6.1	33
Sum		21500	93.4	
Total aerospace exports 1977		23000	100.0	

Source: *Le Monde*, 21 January 1978; Tuomi and Väyrynen (1980), Brzoska (1983)

TABLE 4.7   British Aerospace Industries with Ministry of Defence Contracts Over £500 million in 1976-77

Company	MoD contracts	% of arms production in turnover
British Aircraft Corp.) British Hawker Siddley Group) Aerospace	Over £100 million	80
Rolls Royce	Over £100 million	70
Westland Aircraft	£50-100 million	87
Short Brothers	£20- 25 million	-

Source: Freedman (1978), Radical Statistics Nuclear Disarmament Group (1982), Brzoska (1983).

for the Ministry of Defence in 1976-77 are listed in Table 4.7. Overseas sales of military equipment from both the public and private sectors are coordinated by the Defence Sales Organization - a semi-autonomous unit within the Ministry of Defence - whose aggressive policy to make sales wherever and whenever possible has undoubtedly been an influential factor in the growth of military aerospace exports (Pearson, 1983; Pierre, 1982).

The above discussion reveals that French and British firms are far more dependent on exports than are their US counterparts.

Nevertheless, even in the US major restraints in arms exports to developing countries could result in redundancies or even a reduction of the number of firms in the defence industry (Degrasse, 1983). In Europe the situation is even more acute; major cutbacks in exports to the Third World could threaten the very existence of national design, development and production capabilities.

From the perspective of the developing countries, continued high levels of arms imports are likely to produce several adverse economic effects. These include the distortion of the trade profile; the financial burden created as a result of purchasing arms on credit; the unproductive nature of arms imports; the misdirection of the production structure of a country so as to finance arms imports; and finally, the long term effect of importing an industrial model of warfare incommensurate with a country's existing level of industrial development (Tuomi and Väyrynen, 1980; Neumann, 1979).

LICENSED PRODUCTION AND SUBCONTRACTING

Although arms imports represent the most important aspect of the armament process in developing countries, many countries are attempting to establish domestic arms production facilities with the objective of eventually becoming self-sufficient in weapons manufacture. Although a variety of industrial strategies can be employed, Lock and Wulf (1979) suggest that two basic approaches can be identified. The first, and most common, approach is part of the general 'industrialization' model whereby arms are produced through licensing, subcontracting and, less frequently, co-production agreements. The second approach involves the development of a totally independent domestic arms industry. This was the proclaimed goal of countries like Brazil, Argentina, India, Israel and South Africa - all of which have large scale investment programmes geared towards domestic arms production.

The production of weapons under licence in developing countries is in many respects a result of the highly competitive situation in the European and US arms industries. In particular, the research and development component of these industries is characterized by a

> constant innovation with a view to ... outdoing competitors in the struggle for markets. For this reason it [is] not possible to limit the technology to be transferred permanently and exclusively to the traditional finished product, nor can it consist of the transfer of the expertise that would allow competitive and technological capacity to be generated.
>
> (Varas and Bustamante, 1982:144).

Production under licence in the armaments industry follows a pattern found in many other sectors. Facilities for the maintenance and overhaul of imported equipment are followed by assembly lines producing specific components which may be re-exported back to the licensing country. In the next stage some components are ordered from local industries and the percentage of locally produced components is increased until full production under licence is possible. Licensed production is, perhaps the most important form of military technology transfer to the Third World. However, the control of the technology remains very largely outside the country, effectively retarding the growth of a local research and development capability. Many MNCs are prepared to enter into more extensive cooperative schemes and to share production with developing countries since it allows them to penetrate markets which would otherwise be inaccessible. In some cases companies may be attracted to transfer some aspects of production to developing countries with the offer of subsidies in the form of tax exemption or other low-cost production inputs. In particular instances low labour costs alone may attract a company to manufacture labour intensive components in developing countries. Such a strategy may lead to an increase in the company's total sales, insofar as re-export of locally produced components under licence may attract the local government and lead to the company being in a relatively privileged position *vis à vis* competition.

Licensed production in developing countries is also a useful mechanism whereby MNCs can make further profits from military technology and production equipment which would be considered obsolete in the supplier countries. The Northrop F-5E Tiger 2, the Dassault Mirage 5 and the Swedish Saab supporter aircraft are all outdated from the point of view of American, French and Swedish defence, but by transferring production to a developing country the item can still be profitable from the parent companies' perspective (Varas and Bustamante, 1982).

In general, however, licensed production for many developing countries amounts to no more than the assembly of components. In many instances the amount expended in foreign exchange may actually exceed the cost of importing the completed weapon. Recent estimates suggest that the cost of producing many items under licence may be 50 per cent greater than importing the finished weapon (SIPRI, 1979:250). Further costs are incurred as a result of the sale of patents, and the payment of licence fees and royalties (Väyrynen, 1978).

Table 4.8 illustrates the general pattern of licensed and indigenous production of major conventional weapons in developing countries in 1979. Clearly, production is concentrated in a relatively small number of countries, principally Argentina, Brazil, India, Egypt, and to a lesser extent, Pakistan and South Africa, although an increasing number of countries are entering into licensing arrangements. In terms of specific sectors of military production the aerospace industry is pre-

Table 4.8 Licensed and Indigenous Production of Major Conventional Weapons in Developing Countries, 1979

	Trainer	Fighter Aircraft	COIN[1]	Light Plane	Helicopter	Missiles	Destroyer/ Frigate Corvette	Submarine	Tanks/ APC[2]
Argentina	i		i	l	l i	i	l	l	l
Brazil	l		l	l	l	l i	l	l	
Egypt	l	l			l	l i			l
India	l i	l i			l	l	i		
Indonesia	i				l				
Israel		i			l	i	l		i
Korea, North		l							
Korea, South		l			l		i		
Mexico	l		l						
Nigeria					l	l			
Pakistan	l				l	l			
Peru							i		
Philippines	i		i l						
South Africa	i	l		l		l			
Taiwan	i					l	i		i
Thailand	i								

Notes: l = licensed production
      i = indigenous production

1 COIN – counterinsurgency aircraft
2 APC – armoured personnel carrier

Source: SIPRI (1980)

dominant, reflecting the intense competition between companies and the necessity for partners in other countries to guarantee the expansion of production and marketing. Licensed production also allows the firms in industrialized countries to develop a 'worldwide' production network in order to by-pass export controls and bilateral embargoes. For example, the US embargo against Turkey in 1975 did not affect the sale of Northrop spare parts produced in Taiwan. Lock and Wulf (1979:219) suggest, in fact, that 'a new pattern in the international arms transfer system is evolving, marked by an increased number of potential suppliers and by new associations of interest along North-South lines'. However, from the developing countries' point of view this incorporation into the world military network merely involves a move from one form of dependency to another; from dependence on imports to dependence on imported licences and components. It is certain that this new form of economic/military dependence will also have an impact on the political economy of many developing countries which will only serve to enforce the hegemonic position of the supplying country.

A further strategy pursued by MNCs to obtain returns on increasing investments is by subcontracting certain aspects of the production process. Two factors are responsible for this relatively recent phenomenon. First, for the military research and development industry there is an increasing necessity to identify areas of production and development which will enable it to cut costs; subcontracting in countries with relatively cheap labour is one way of achieving this goal. Second, subcontracting has become a characteristic *modus operandi* of transnational capital enabling it to distribute the different phases of its production to those areas where costs are lowest. Such subcontracting is probably most common in the electronics industry which is, in general, closely related to military markets. Thus, in 1974 approximately a quarter of all electronics products were used for military purposes in the United States and Europe; in the former the proportion was closer to 30 per cent.

An indication of the extent of subcontracting in electronics is provided in Table 4.9 which lists those electronics firms with offshore operations and who also appear in the list of the 100 leading American Defense Department contractors. According to these criteria offshore operations are concentrated in several Asian countries, in particular South Korea, Taiwan, Singapore and Hong Kong. In general the production or assembly of electronic components are located in free-production zones established to attract international business. From the developing countries' perspective, subcontracting in the electronics industry involves a transfer of highly specialized but fragmented know-how, enabling ultra-modern technology to be reproduced in part only.

Finally, it should be noted that foreign direct investment in military production plants is not a widespread phenomenon;

.9   The Extent of Offshore Operations by American
      Producers of Military Electronics, 1974

Firm and rank in DoD Contracts	Number of employees in offshore factories	Location of operations
1. General Electric	1000	Singapore
22. RCA Corporation	3000	Singapore, Taiwan, Malaysia
25. Teledyne	3300	Singapore, Hong Kong, Malaysia
36. Fairchild	13000	Hong Kong, South Korea, Singapore, Mexico, Indonesia
41. Texas Instruments	11300	Singapore, Malaysia, El Salvador, Taiwan,
63. Motorola	7800	South Korea, Mexico, Malaysia, Hong Kong
97. Hewlett Packard	2600	Singapore, Malaysia
- Eight other firms with information on offshore operations	21250	Singapore, Malaysia, Thailand, Indonesia, Hong Kong, Mauritius, South Korea, Mexico
Total	63550	

Source: Tuomi and Väyrynen (1980)

national ownership is usually preferred for security reasons.
Joint ventures and minority holdings are more common, in addition
MNCs own and operate sales offices and service plants abroad
which favour the development of an international network.   In
recent years, however, a number of MNCs have become increasingly
involved with major armament industries in developing countries.
Thus, Embraer (the Brazilian aircraft company) is 49 per cent
in private hands, the biggest shareholder being Volkswagen do
Brasil, while Aerospatiale has a stake in Helibras (the Brazilian
helicopter company).   In Argentina, Renault, Mercedes-Benz and
Fiat are all active in the arms industry. ARMSCOR, the notable
South African producer of ammunition and explosives, is jointly
controlled by ICI and the Anglo-American Corporation (Kaldor,
1982; Tuomi and Väyrynen, 1980; Wulf, 1983).   Rockwell International, a major MNC in the military sector, operates 120
subsidiaries in thirty countries including Brazil, Singapore,
Hong Kong, South Africa and Taiwan.   During the 1970s sales by

Rockwell's foreign subsidiaries increased rapidly: from 5 per cent of total sales in 1972 to 15 per cent in 1977 (Tuomi and Väyrynen, 1980:143).

INDIGENOUS DEFENCE PRODUCTION IN THE THIRD WORLD

The ultimate goal for many developing countries is the domestic production of indigenously designed weapon systems.   Most countries, however, do not produce arms for the simple reason that they lack the essential economic and technological pre-requisites (specifically, the industrial base and available skilled manpower) to launch military programmes. Even India has not approached self-sufficiency in the production of major weapon systems even though a policy of import substitution in military procurement has been pursued for the last twenty years.
The driving force behind domestic defence production in Third World countries involves a variety of factors, including security, economic and political considerations. Nevertheless, the underlying motive is the desire to eliminate or greatly re-duce dependence on industrial countries for arms deemed vital for national security (Moodie, 1979).   The prevailing attitude was well summarized by Brazil's Air Force Minister in 1977: '... the time has come to free ourselves from the United States and the countries of Europe. It is a condition of security that each nation manufacture its own arms' (quoted in Tuomi and Väyrynen, 1980:150).   Of the principal Third World major arms producers however, only Israel, India and Brazil (and to some extent South Africa, Argentina, Taiwan and South Korea) possess an indigenous base for military production.
An essential prerequisite for the indigenous production of armaments is the existence of a suitable industrial capacity. In general this capacity is indicated by a country's ability to produce capital goods.   Table 4.10 illustrates this point in-sofar as the major arms producers are also those countries which possess a relatively developed industrial base.   However, the production of capital goods in most developing countries is res-tricted to what may be termed standard-modern technology rather than highly-modern technology (Bhagavan, 1980) which is both science-related and research-intensive. While standard-modern technology tends to be diffused relatively evenly, applications of advanced-modern technology tend to be controlled and monopo-lized by the principal social carriers which almost invariably are MNCs.   In terms of the development of an autonomous military industry, therefore, even those countries with a developed in-dustrial base have been unable to attain self-sufficiency in armaments production as they are still dependent on foreign ex-pertise for highly-modern technological items.
From the MNC perspective, involvement in the development of domestic arms production industries in Third World countries has been, in terms of control and marketing, a qualified success. In

Table 4.10   Industrial Capacity of Developing Countries and
            Their Role in Arms Production

	Major arms producers[1]	No major arms producers
Countries producing their own capital goods	Argentina, Brazil, China, India, North Korea, and South Africa	Chile(p), Mexico(p)
Countries partly producing their own capital goods	Egypt, Pakistan, Philippines, Singapore, South Korea, Taiwan	Colombia(p), Cuba, Hong Kong(p), Iran(p), Malaysia, Peru and Venezuela (p)
Countries importing their capital goods	Indonesia	All other developing countries

Notes: 1 Yugoslavia, Israel and Turkey are omitted being
          relatively industrialized and predominantly
          European countries.
       (p) Potential capacity - measured by the strength of
           the manufacturing sector and the available man-
           power - to produce more advanced weapon systems.

Source: Wulf (1983); Tuomi and Väyrynen (1980)

the case of Brazil, for example, a liberal attitude towards
foreign capital has been evident in the development of the military sector.   India, on the other hand, although cooperating
with the MNCs, is determined to achieve self-reliance in military technology.   In this respect the MNCs do not have freedom
of manoeuvre and can only expect to be welcome until   India's
self-reliance in military technology is achieved.

The Case of Brazil
By the end of the 1960s Brazil had abandoned a policy of import-
substitution as the path to industrialization, and adopted instead a strategy of 'general industrialization' based on an
export-oriented industrial pattern. The Brazilian arms industry
(which has been identified, with some justification, as being
the most developed in the Third World) is closely related to
this general model of export-oriented industrialization and in
many respects is dependent on the collaboration between the
transport and machinery industries; both of which have been the
focus for major investments by MNCs (Tuomi and Väyrynen, 1980;
Wulf, 1983).

At the present time Brazil's arms industry produces a range of weapons including military aircraft, naval craft, armoured personnel carriers and small weapons. However, Brazil's military-industrial complex is basically organized around two principal companies: Embraer (Empresa Brasilieira Aeronautica) and Engesa (Engenheiros Especialisados).

Although Brazil has had experience in the production of light aircraft for twenty years, it was not until the founding of Embraer in 1969 that the country began to be noticed as a potentially important aircraft manufacturer. At the present time Embraer is the largest general aviation manufacturer outside the USA in terms of productive volume, producing eleven different types of aircraft in fifty separate models. Although many of these models are of indigenous design the avionics and engines are often imported from North America and Europe. In addition, more extensive transnational collaboration exists with the American firms of Northrop and Piper and the Italian Aeronautica Macchi (which also has a partnership with Lockheed). Embraer's most important partner is Piper; although it is principally a producer of civilian aircraft, a number of the models are suitable for military purposes. As a result of an extensive licensing agreement Piper is able (via Embraer) to enter Brazil and export to markets in third countries. In addition, Embraer subcontracts heavily for Piper; from Embraer's perspective the agreement allows for a progressive increase in the domestic content of the final product, thus leading to a greater degree of self-sufficiency.

Engesa is the major producer of combat vehicles in Brazil, and supplies both the army and the marines. Most of the carriers produced by Engesa are of indigenous design but the engines are generally produced by Mercedes Benz do Brasil. The missile industry is noticeably dependent on foreign technology, thus Commission Central de Misseis produces Cobra and Roland missiles with French (Aerospatiale) and West German (MBB) licences, while air defence systems are manufactured with the aid of the French company of Thomson-CSF.

In 1977 Brazil cancelled the twenty-five-year-old military aid agreement with the US, and in recent years European arms producers have become increasingly prominent as a source for new technology. Thus, 45 per cent of Helibras is owned by Aerospatiale. However, the overall objective has been to increase the local content of the models; in 1983 this was targeted to be 65 per cent. A major weakness in the Brazilian military-industrial complex has been the electronics industry. During the 'Brazilian miracle' a number of MNCs were active in the civilian electronics sector, and when the demand for military electronics increased many of these companies became involved in military projects (for example, AEG-Telefunken do Brasil, Philips do Brasil and Ericsson do Brasil). After 1975 the increased balance-of-payments problem resulted in a more restrictive attitude to foreign electronic companies and a reduction in the influence of MNCs. Although imports of raw materials and components were discouraged, joint ventures (such as that between Ferranti and the government-owned Digibras) is seen as one way of promoting the productivity of Brazilian military electronics.

In conclusion, therefore, Brazil has not yet become a self-sufficient producer of military technology. Nevertheless, largely dependent on MNCs for new technology, in recent years the Brazilian military industry has achieved better terms in its dealings with MNCs, increased its control of MNC activities, and enlarged the Brazilian share in armament projects.

CONCLUSION

The purpose of this chapter has been to examine the role of the military MNCs in the arms build-up in developing countries. It is evident that the MNCs play a pivotal role in the continued high level of military exports to developing countries. It is argued that the attempt by many developing countries to establish an autonomous military capability is very largely determined by the willingness of the military MNCs to transfer the requisite modern technology. From the developing countries' perspective, however, the transfer of such technology can have a profound impact on the industrialization process. The implications are well summarized by Lock and Wulf (1979:219-220)

> ... The process of industrialisation in the third world tends to be dominated by the requirements of the arms industry whenever an ambitious programme is launched. In the absence of sufficient economies of scale and lack of potential civilian applications, a highly specialised and capital-intensive suboptimal industrial agglomeration develops. Even in non-military industries, the choice of techniques is determined by the technological impera- tives of arms production. Levels of capital investment, minimum scales of productivity, and standards of quality unnecessary or too expensive for civilian production are becoming increasingly important in defining industrial goals in these countries.

It is possible to argue that the establishment of an armament industry would stimulate beneficial multiplier effects via back- ward linkages - creating a demand for local products and thus expanding economic activity. Given an appropriate geographical location, therefore, military production could contribute to the general process of regional development and industrial growth. However, such multiplier effects are likely to be limited in extent insofar as military production is generally attracted to those locations where industrial and infrastructural development is already well advanced. In consequence, military production

will tend to accentuate rather than diminish existing patterns
of geographically uneven development within a country or region.
    More specifically Wulf (1980) has noted a number of limi-
tations on the backward linkages generated by military production in developing countries.   First, military production in
general is characterized by short production runs; in developing countries this is compounded by the fact that demand for
military items is limited.   It would therefore be uneconomic
to establish factories for the production of advanced avionics
and optronics, for example, unless the host government was wil-
ling to take over the risk of investment. Second, the production
of modern weapons systems involves the incorporation of high
technology products; these products require stringent levels of
quality of precision and control not normally associated with
civilian products.   The implication is that the specifications
demanded by the armaments industry are unlikely to be utilized
economically for civilian production.   In this context the
posited backward linkages may not materialize, or if they do,
would constitute a costly and uneconomic investment. Third, in
common with industrial production in general, the production of
arms is increasingly a capital- and skill-intensive process. In
many developing countries both capital and skilled manpower are
scarce factors; in terms of the product cycle theory (Vernon,
1966) and existing factor endowments, it would make sense for
developing countries to concentrate on the production of mature
and standardized items.   However, due to technological obsoles-
cence military products rarely reach the stage of maturity,
standardization and mass production. Developing countries intent
on indigenous weapons production, therefore, have to engage in
all stages of the product-cycle, thus generating backward linkages based on previous production stages. As Wulf (1980) notes,
the adoption of this strategy may, however, have profound consequences on industrialization strategies in general insofar as
it would be determined by the technological imperatives of arms
production.
    In the context of the evolving world system, the importance
of the military MNCs may be of even greater significance.   In
recent years the rapid diffusion of MNCs in general has added a
new dimension to the classic core-periphery division of labour
(Bornschier, 1981), whereby the periphery specializes in raw
material production and the core specializes in industrial production and financial control.   The new hierarchy, which does
not replace but is superimposed on the classic core-periphery
hierarchy, involves a core-periphery division of labour within
industrial and tertiary activities.   In this context the core
specializes in control over capital, technology and innovation
processes (highly-modern technology) at the beginning of the
product cycle, whereas the periphery and semi-periphery specialize in routine production (standard-modern technology)
either for the domestic or world market.   This core-periphery
structure reflects the organization of the MNCs which link it by

their internal division of labour; as noted earlier demands
for NIEO have been superseded by the emergence of a new international division of labour, which represents the MNC conception
of the NIEO. The prominence of the military MNCs in this process is significant not only for the future internal development
of developing countries but, perhaps more importantly in the
long term, in the creation of a New International Military
Order and the militarization of the world economy. As Kaldor
(1982:142) has noted:

> ... not only armies, but also armament factories are
> reproduced abroad, so that armament culture draws both
> military and industrial organisation into a complex
> interconnected global system.

REFERENCES

Albrecht, U.,Ernst, D., Lock, P., Wulf, H. (1975)   'Militar-
    ization, arms transfers and arms production in peripheral
    countries', *Journal of Peace Research*, 12:195-212.
Ayres, R. (1982)   'Militarism in the Third World', *Marxism
    Today*, 26:32-33.
Bhagavan, M.R. (1980) *Technological Transformation of Developing
    Countries* Research Paper 6186, Economic Research Institute,
    Stockholm School of Economics, Stockholm.
Bornschier, V. (1981) 'The world economy in the world system:
    structure, dependence and change', *International Journal
    of Social Science*, 91:37-59.
Brandt Commission (1980)   *North-South: A Programme for Survival*,
    Pan, London.
Brandt Commission (1983)   *Common Crisis*, Pan, London.
Brzoska, M. (1983)   'Economic problems of arms production in
    Western Europe: diagnoses and alternatives' in Tuomi H. and
    Väyrynen R. (eds.) *Militarisation and Arms Production*, Croom
    Helm, London:59-71.
Degrasse, R.W. (1983)   'Military spending and jobs', *Challenge*,
    July/August:5-15.
European Parliament (1978)   *Report on European Armaments Proc-
    urement Cooperation*, Document 83/78, European Parliament
    Political Affairs Committee.
Frank, A.G. (1980)   'Arms economy and warfare in the Third
    World', *Third World Quarterly*, 2:228-250.
Franko, L. (1979)   'Restraining arms exports to the Third World:
    will Europe agree?', *Survival*, 21:14-25.
Freedman, L. (1978)   *Arms Production in the United Kingdom:
    Problems and Prospects*, The Royal Institute of Inter-
    national Affairs, London.

Fröbel, F., Heinrichs, J., Kreye, O. (1977)   'The tendency towards a new international division of Labour', *Review*, 1:73-88.

Hamilton, F.E.I. and Linge, G.J.R. (eds) (1983) *Spatial Analysis, Industry and Industrial Environment*, Vol.II, John Wiley, Chichester.

Hessing Cahn, A. (1979) 'The economics of arms transfers' in Neumann S. and Harkavy R. (eds) *Arms Transfers in the Modern World*, Praeger, New York:173-183.

Husbands, J. (1979) 'How the United States makes foreign military sales' in Neumann S. and Harkavy R. (eds) *Arms Transfers in the Modern World*, Praeger, New York:155-172.

Kaldor, M. (1982) *The Baroque Arsenal*, Andre Deutsch, London.

Lock, P. and Wulf, H. (1977) *Register of Arms Production in Developing Countries*, mimeograph, University of Hamburg, Hamburg.

Lock, P. and Wulf, H. (1979) 'The economic consequences of the transfer of military-oriented technology' in Kaldor M. and Eide E. (eds) *The World Military Order*, Macmillan, London: 210-231.

Luckham, R. (1981) *Transnational Corporations in the Arms Industry*, paper prepared for the United Nations Centre on Transnational Corporations, Institute of Development Studies, University of Sussex.

Moodie, M. (1979) 'Defence industries in the Third World' in Neumann S. and Harkavy R. (eds) *Arms Transfers in the Modern World*, Praeger, New York:294-312.

Neumann, S. (1979) 'Arms transfers and economic development: some research and policy issues' in Neumann S. and Harkavy R. (eds) *Arms Transfers in the Modern World*, Praeger, New York:219-245.

Palme, O. (1982) *Common Security: a Programme for Disarmament*, Report on the Independent Commission on Disarmament, Pan, London.

Pearson, F.S. (1983) 'The question of control in British defence sales policy', *International Affairs*, 59:211-238.

Pierre, A.J. (1982) *The Global Politics of Arms Transfers*, Princeton University Press, Princeton.

Radical Statistics Nuclear Disarmament Group (1982) *The Nuclear Numbers Game*, Radical Statistics, London.

Reppy, J. (1983) 'The United States' in Ball N. and Leitenberg M. (eds) *The Structure of the Defence Industry*, Croom Helm, London:21-49.

SIPRI (1971) *The Arms Trade with the Third World*, Stockholm International Peace Research Institute, Almqvist and Wicksell, Stockholm.

SIPRI (1979) *World Armaments and Disarmaments Yearbook 1979*, Stockholm International Peace Research Institute, Taylor and Francis, London.

SIPRI (1980) *World Armaments and Disarmaments Yearbook 1980*, Stockholm International Peace Research Institute, Taylor and Francis, London.

SIPRI (1981) *World Armaments and Disarmaments Yearbook 1981*, Stockholm International Peace Research Institute, Taylor and Francis, London.

SIPRI (1982) *World Armaments and Disarmaments Yearbook 1982*, Stockholm International Peace Research Institute, Taylor and Francis, London.

Tuomi, H. (1983) 'Transnational military corporations: the main problems' in Tuomi H. and Väyrynen R. (eds) *Militarisation and Arms Production*, Croom Helm, London:148-160.

Tuomi, H., Väyrynen, R. (1980) *Transnational Corporations, Armaments and Development*, Report 24, Tampere Peace Research Institute, Tampere, Finland.

United Nations Centre on Transnational Corporations (1983) *Transnational Corporations in World Development*, *Third Survey*, United Nations, New York.

United States Arms Control and Disarmament Agency (1983) *World Military Expenditure and Arms Transfers 1971-1980*, Washington DC.

Varas, A., Bustamante, F. (1982) 'The effect of R and D on the transfer of military technology to the Third World', *International Journal of Social Science*, 90:141-162.

Väyrynen, R. (1978) 'International patenting as a means of technological dominance', *International Journal of Social Science*, 30:315-337.

Väyrynen, R. (1979) 'Economic and military position of regional power centres', *Journal of Peace Research*, 16:349-69.

Vernon, R. (1966) 'International investment and international trade in the product cycle', *Quarterly Journal of Economics*, 80:190-207.

Whynes, D. (1979) *The Economics of Third World Military Expenditure*, Macmillan, London.

Wulf, H. (1979) 'Dependent militarism in the periphery and possible alternative concepts' in Neumann S. and Harkavy R. (eds) *Arms Transfers in the Modern World*, Praeger, New York: 246-263.

Wulf, H. (1980) *Transnational Transfer of Arms Production Technology*, Study Group on Armaments and Underdevelopment, University of Hamburg.

Wulf, H. (1983) 'Developing countries' in Ball N. and Leitenberg M. (eds) *The Structure of the Defence Industry*, Croom Helm, London: 310-343.

Chapter Five

THE NEW INTERNATIONAL DIVISION OF LABOUR
AND AMERICAN SEMICONDUCTOR PRODUCTION IN SOUTHEAST ASIA

J.W. Henderson

INTRODUCTION

One of the most significant features of the contemporary world-system has been the tendency towards the internationalization of capital investment. This process, which has become particularly evident in the last quarter-century, now encompasses finance and service as well as industrial capital, and has enormous implications for social and spatial development (see Hymer, 1979; Portes and Walton, 1981; Cohen, 1981; Friedman and Wolff, 1982; Castells, 1984). In this chapter I seek to examine the contours of the internationalization of one important production branch,[1] the American semiconductor industry. In particular, the chapter focusses on the development of the industry in Southeast Asia. It does so, however, in the light of one of the principal bodies of work yet to emerge to explain the origins and significance of the recent globalization of industrial production, *viz*. the theory of the NIDL (New International Division of Labour).

I begin by presenting a brief overview of the NIDL theory and identify some of the shortcomings that the bulk of the chapter will address. The discussion then proceeds to examine the American semiconductor industry in its principal home base *i.e.* Silicon Valley, California. In so doing, it identifies the necessary internal relations (Sayer, 1982; 1984), in this case the labour processes and technical change, which have been among the primary determinants of the reorganization of the industry on a global scale.

The discussion of the industry in Silicon Valley provides a necessary prelude to the subsequent examination of the industry as it has emerged and changed in Southeast Asia. I argue that the organizational and technical form of the industry in Southeast Asia is now in the process of being constituted as a distinct subregional division of labour and that this emergent feature has significant implications for the subsequent development of the industry in the region and for its social, economic and spatial consequences. The chapter concludes by raising some of the implications of the discussion for NIDL theory and research.

THE INTERNATIONALIZATION OF INDUSTRIAL PRODUCTION

The most developed accounts of the origin and significance of the reorganization of industrial production on a global scale are those which, following Jenkins (1984), I shall group under the rubric of the NIDL (*e.g.* Fröbel *et al.*, 1980; Ernst, 1980; Frank, 1980, 1981; Warren, 1980; Schiffer, 1981). While recognizing that there are significant theoretical differences between these various accounts (not least the extent to which they emphasize the dynamics of exchange rather than production as determining the internationalization process), for the purposes of this discussion, I shall focus my comments on the most extensive contribution to the debate currently available, that of the Starnberg researchers, Fröbel, Heinrichs and Kreye (1980). As I have critically reviewed their work and that of others in related papers (Henderson and Cohen, 1982; Henderson, 1985), only the briefest of accounts is necessary here.

The essence of their argument can be summarized as follows:

1. The migration of industrial capital from core to peripheral locations within the world-system has been necessitated by the gradual worsening in recent years of the conditions for valorization and hence capital accumulation in many of the advanced capitalist societies. So serious has this situation been that even medium scale, 'national' firms have had to internationalize their production in order to survive.

2. There have emerged a number of preconditions which have potentiated the globalization of industrial production. Amongst these the most important are first, the existence at the periphery of seemingly endless supplies of labour power which is both low cost and unorganized, but potentially as productive as relatively high cost and organized labour power at the core; second, the development of massively deskilled labour processes which no longer require significant inputs of skilled labour power in order to manufacture a vast range of commodities; and third, the spatial dispersal of particular labour processes within the same firm has been facilitated by innovations in transport and communications technologies which have helped contain transactional costs and enabled organizational direction and control to remain at company headquarters in the core.

3. The internationalization of production has been further encouraged by the provision of investment incentives by international agencies such as UNIDO (United Nations Industrial Development Organisation) and by Third World governments themselves. In the latter case these have often been associated with the construction of export-processing zones and the institution of repressive labour laws and advantageous taxation provisions.

92

4.   The technologies transferred to Third World countries as part of the process of establishing 'world-market factories' are often those that are outmoded and unproductive in the context of core economies.   Rarely, if ever, are 'state-of-the-art' technologies transferred to the periphery.
5.   An important consequence of many of these factors at the level of the world economy is that problems of valorization at core locations can now be overcome by virtue of the creation of new possibilities for the extraction of absolute surplus value at the periphery by means of the 'super-exploitation' of Third World labour.

Though there are many particular aspects of Fröbel *et al's* analysis that have been confirmed by other studies (see Lim, 1978a, b; Luther, 1978; Sunoo, 1978; Ip, 1983 for various East and Southeast Asian countries), there remain a number of significant problems of both a theoretical and empirical nature. Amongst these, their insistently argued capital-logic approach to development[2] and the associated tendency to devalue the role of states and social conflicts internal to Third World countries (in so far as they affect a 'national' development strategy), are especially troublesome.   However, as I have analysed these problems elsewhere (Henderson, 1985), these particular issues (with the exception of the question of the state which is taken up below) need not detain us in the present context.   The following set of related problems are more pertinent for our current discussion.

First, throughout their work, Fröbel *et al.* seem to ignore the fact that the search for new possibilities for the extraction of absolute surplus value may not necessarily be the motivating force behind the internationalization of activities of all firms or industrial branches.   At least as likely in the case of particular branches or firms is the fact that the concern for new opportunities for increasing *relative* surplus value is the principal motivation behind their drive to internationalize.   In addition, even with branches or firms whose initial internationalization developed from a concern with absolute surplus value, it is by no means inconceivable that over time, under technical, market or state pressure, particular operations in specific peripheral locations may come to be organized around a concern with relative surplus value (as when, for instance, technological upgrading takes place).

Second, this exclusive concern with the question of absolute surplus value is one of the elements which leads Fröbel *et al.* to deny the possibility of genuine peripheral development under capitalism, at least in so far as export-oriented industrialization might hold out such possibilities.   In this sense they appear to echo some of the pessimistic conclusions of early dependency theory (for example, Frank, 1971; Emmanuel, 1972; Amin, 1974, 1976), and fly in the face of empirical reality, not least with regard to the experience of economic growth in the 'Four Little Tigers' of Southeast and East Asia (see Schiffer,

93

1981; Hamilton, 1983).

Third, in spite of the wealth of empirical information they bring to bear on the analysis, Fröbel *et al.*'s account of the contours and significance of the NIDL still appears to be pitched at too abstract a level. They seem to assume that, whatever the origins of the internationalization of production within one branch or firm, the course of the subsequent development of the internationalization strategy remains much the same, irrespective of the particular branch or firm one is concerned with. The corollary of this is that they assume that the economic, technical and social impact of a given branch or firm tends to be much the same, irrespective of the particular peripheral country in which world-market factories are established. The account of the NIDL which Fröbel *et al.* provide, therefore, is both profoundly ahistorical and insensitive to the differences in the internal balance of class forces in particular peripheral or semi-peripheral states, and hence to differences in their national development strategies. As a result, Fröbel *et al.* fail to recognize that production strategies of branches and firms change over time subsequent to the initial internationalization, and that they articulate in different ways in different periods with the economic, political and social circumstances of particular Third World countries. Put another way, while the form and content of the NIDL may be much the same from one branch to another at the moment of initial internationalization, both of these may well change over time, depending on the branch one is concerned with. If this is indeed the case, then it may pose significant implications for the role of particular peripheral or semi-peripheral locations within the NIDL.

Finally, a related problem to those detailed above, concerns the type of information required to assess the relative prospects for development within the NIDL. While data which charts changes in GDP, real wages, welfare expenditure etc. are obviously important, what are also required are 'theorized histories' (Castells, 1977) of particular industrial branches and firms as their operations impact on particular territorial units. It is only in this way that we can discover the actual labour processes, technological inputs, connections with local economies, impacts on labour market structure, class formation and other factors that are the consequence of particular forms of investment in the Third World. Only with such theorized histories at hand can we adequately assess the implications of the NIDL for development in particular peripheral or semi-peripheral locations.

I shall return to these points in the last section of the chapter, but here it is necessary to begin to examine the empirical case with which we are concerned: the origins of an international division of labour within the American semiconductor industry, and its changing pattern of development in Southeast Asia.

THE INTERNATIONALIZATION OF AMERICAN SEMICONDUCTOR PRODUCTION[3]

Together with the textile and garments industry, semiconductor production has been the paradigmatic example of an industrial branch that has been internationalized in terms broadly identified by NIDL theory. In this section I examine the determinants of the internationalization of American semiconductor industry as a necessary preliminary to a focus on the development of its 'offshore' plants in Southeast Asia.

   With the invention of the transistor in 1947 and its manufacture in commercial quantities from the early 1950s, the 'solid-state' semiconductor rapidly began to displace the vacuum tube as the building block of electronic machines (Braun and Macdonald, 1982). The powerhouse of semiconductor technology and production was then, and largely remains to this day, the United States. It is there that most of the significant technological innovations have taken place. During the 1960s semiconductor technology became increasingly sophisticated resulting in the creation of the microprocessor, in 1971. Subsequent developments in the 1970s led to the production of LSI (Large Scale Integrated-circuitry) and then VLSI (Very Large Scale Integration-circuitry), which had a capacity to combine in excess of 100,000 transistors on a single silicon chip. In an industry where technological innovation has been, at least until the mid-1970s, an essential precondition for a firm to gain a toe-hold in the market and subsequently expand its market share, it is hardly surprising that the semiconductor market has been dominated by American producers. Though their position of dominance is increasingly threatened by Japanese competitors, in 1982, three of the world's five largest 'merchant' semiconductor manufacturers were American-owned (*Global Electronics Information Newsletter*, 27 December 1982).

   As the American semiconductor industry grew during the 1950s and 1960s it developed a particular spatial focus. The world's most important territorial complex of semiconductor and related electronics production emerged in Santa Clara County ('Silicon Valley') California, with secondary complexes around Boston, Dallas and Phoenix (Bernstein *et al*. 1977; Saxenian, 1981; Henderson and Scott, 1984). From the beginning of the 1960s, however, this spatial focus began to dissolve as increasing numbers of Silicon Valley firms sought to lower costs by investing in 'offshore' production facilities. Their preferred locations were Latin America (particularly Mexico) and Southeast Asia. Beginning with Hong Kong in 1962, by the mid-1970s American semiconductor firms had set up production facilities in every capitalist East and Southeast Asian country with the exception of Brunei (Siegel, 1979). In addition, from the mid-1970s, partly in an attempt to circumvent restrictive EEC tariffs on imported semiconductors, American firms began to set up plants in Western Europe, with Germany, France, but especially Eire and the UK (particularly Scotland) being favoured with their

investment (Siegel, 1980;   Scottish Development Agency, 1983).
     Before turning to analyse the development of the industry
in Southeast Asia, it is necessary to briefly outline the theoretical and methodological issues that will guide our discussion.

Methodological and Theoretical Preliminaries

Understanding the meaning and logic of the development of an
international division of labour within any industrial branch
necessitates attention to the structure of capitalist commodity
production at large;   the central dynamics of labour processes
in the context of the contradictory capital-labour relation;
the internal and external organization of industrial production;
the socio-spatial consequences of these phenomena;   and the way
this ensemble of relations changes over time.   With regard to
the American semiconductor industry, a full account of these
features would necessarily begin with an examination of the
industry in its core location, Santa Clara County, California.
It would focus for instance on the technical and spatial articulation of the industry's component labour processes;   the
extent to which they were capital rather than labour intensive;
conflicts arising from contradictions in the labour process and
in the social and spatial reproduction of the labour force (and
its various sectors);   the nature of the product (the extent to
which it was a low-volume, high-value, customized product or a
large-volume, low-value standardized output) and its market;
and the extent to which there were government and/or planning
regulations which inhibited the possibilities for continued
accumulation in the core.   As these determinants and others
have been analysed in detail elsewhere (Henderson and Scott,
1984), there is no need to traverse that ground in detail here.
Some methodological and theoretical comments are, however, in
order.
     If we wish to avoid the elaboration of theoretically inco-
herent accounts of the spatial development of an industrial
branch we need to take seriously Sayer's (1982,1984) distinction
between relations that are internally necessary to the development of a phenomenon, and those that are externally contingent[4].
This does not mean, of course, that externally contingent relations are to be treated as of no account in social scientific
explanation.   On the contrary, such relations are of importance
in the analysis of particular empirical outcomes. What it does
mean, however, is that these relations do not constitute the
primary determinants of the phenomenon *in general*, and have
significance only in the context of their articulation with the
primary determinants (the internally necessary relations) in
particular empirical circumstances.   For an analysis of the
spatial development and social impact of semiconductor production (or any industrial branch), this methodological prescription
implies that its function as a part of capitalist commodity
production at large is the essential starting point, and hence
relations associated with valorization are crucial. Consequently

our analysis of the internationalization of the American semi-conductor industry begins by focussing on its labour processes and technical change.

Labour Processes and the
Determinants of Internationalization

Semiconductor production involves four component labour processes. These are R & D (Research and Development), wafer fabrication (the process by which the microscopic electronic circuits are etched on the silicon wafer, which is itself divided into 'masking' and 'diffusion' processes), the assembly of transistors, diodes and integrated circuits, and the final testing of the product. These component labour processes have widely varying needs in terms of capital investment, labour skills, special-ized inputs, and so on. R & D, though capital intensive, also demands the application of highly qualified and creative scien-tists and engineers. Wafer fabrication too (especially the masking process) is capital intensive and calls for highly skilled technical labour, though recently it has begun to make use of increasing numbers of semi-skilled workers. Assembly in particular, though also, to some extent final testing, have been predominantly labour intensive processes, given over almost entirely to unskilled labour.

These labour processes were in general all found in geo-graphical association with one another in the early years of the industry's growth in Santa Clara County, California, but the fact that they were technically disarticulated meant that potentially they could be organizationally and hence spatially separated. Even *within* the wafer fabricating process for instance, there is an incipient, if not in some cases actual, internal disarticulation of the process into masking (which employs highly trained engineers and technicians) and diffusion (which depends to a much higher degree on semi-skilled and un-skilled workers). To be sure, there are definite internal economies of scope and scale that tend to keep all the labour processes in the semiconductor industry unified within the single firm. Nevertheless, when linkage costs on their trans-actional activities with one another became sufficiently low, then the possibility of their spatial dispersal could be made real. Cheap air transport and telecommunications made possible exactly this outcome.

That said, there are other strong, though contingent, deter-minants of the location process in the semiconductor industry. The precise ways in which these determinants play themselves out depend very much on which type of labour process we are talking about. R & D requires ready access to highly trained scientists and engineers for its successful operation; as a corollary, it needs the kind of local urban/environmental con-ditions (such as are found in and around Silicon Valley) which can sustain the effective social reproduction of this form of labour (see Saxenian, 1983a) and, of course, the localized training

of such labour in universities and research institutes is a
further major asset. Many of the same conditions apply to the
location of wafer fabrication facilities. However, while there
has been a moderate internationalization of these facilities
(even at the cost of some loss of quality control) in order to
evade certain kinds of tariff barriers (companies such as
Motorola and National Semiconductor have located wafer fabrication plants in Britain as a means of successfully penetrating
the high EEC tariff barrier on semiconductors and of therefore
tapping the lucrative European market), it has been assembly
and testing that have been increasingly relocated out to the
periphery of the world-system over the last two decades.

All the component labour processes of the industry were
effectively confined to the United States in the early period
of development when markets were limited and specialized, and
the military constituted the principal end-user. In 1960,
military end-users consumed half of American semiconductor production, but by 1966, this had dropped to 30 per cent, and then
in 1972 to 24 per cent (Braun and Macdonald, 1982). This relative
decline in military markets had three major corollaries. First,
it was associated with a relative and absolute increase of
large-scale, standardized demands. Second, it induced stronger
price-competition and the necessity for more stringent cost-
cutting measures (since reliability more than cost is the concern
of military purchasers). Third, it opened the way to the
internationalization of production, for military procurements,
by federal law, are almost entirely restricted to domestic
manufacture (Snow, 1982).

With the insistent rise of more standardized commercial
markets, the conditions for internationalization of parts of
the industry were brought to fruition. First assembly, then
testing functions were dispersed to other parts of the globe,
especially to Latin America but above all to Southeast Asia.
Then, in response to the EEC tariff barrier, some wafer fabrication activities followed on to Europe. Given the large amounts
of labour employed in assembly and testing, the low wages (given
potentially high labour productivity) at the sites selected in
the periphery were undoubtedly a prime locational determinant
(Troutman, 1980; Fröbel *et al.*, 1980; Rada, 1982; Ernst,
1983). We must add to this the remark that political stability
and the security of capital investments have become increasingly
important in those offshore locations where firms in recent
years have sought technologically to upgrade their plants.

It is only through an investigation of the articulation of
these various determinants as they have changed over time and
impacted on the industry's component labour processes, that we
can comprehend the waves of internationalization indicated above
and the associated emergent international division of labour in
the semiconductor industry. We now consider in some detail the
specifics of the offshore development of the industry in Southeast Asia.

THE SOUTHEAST ASIAN DIVISION OF
LABOUR IN SEMICONDUCTOR PRODUCTION

Just as Fairchild Semiconductor had been the originator of the Silicon Valley electronics complex in the mid-1950s, so it initiated offshore semiconductor production in Southeast Asia in the early 1960s. Hong Kong was the first Southeast Asian recipient of Fairchild investment in 1962 when the firm established a plant to assemble 'discretes' (the generic term for transistors and diodes) and subsequently, integrated circuits. From this beginning in Hong Kong the industry diffused out to other locations in Southeast Asia, and this diffusion brought in its train a definite subregional division of labour. Before analysing the structure and significance of this subregional division of labour, however, we need to pay attention to the reasons why Hong Kong should have been the initial preferred location for American semiconductor investment.

In the previous section it was argued that the determinants of the internationalization of industrial production at the highest level of abstraction arose out of the need for capital valorization and accumulation. Empirically these determinants have associated with them spatially contingent circumstances; for example, the local reproduction of particular kinds of labour power or, as in Silicon Valley, the development of restrictive planning legislation, which tend to produce particular locational outcomes for industrial investment. In the case of semiconductor production in Southeast Asia the most important of these circumstances by far has been the presence of enormous pools of cheap and underemployed labour (Rada, 1982). But the mere existence of cheap labour was in itself not a sufficient locational inducement. Hong Kong had a number of additional special advantages, which made it a particularly attractive location. (Similar advantages in Taiwan, South Korea and Singapore meant that they were also to develop flourishing semiconductor industries at an early stage). These advantages included political stability, an open financial system with no limits on the repatriation of profits, and excellent telecommunications and air transport facilities (Henderson and Cohen, 1982). In addition, Hong Kong had a further crucial advantage. Over the 1950s, it had developed a flourishing industrial economy based on textiles, garments, plastics, and other labour-intensive forms of production. By the late 1950s, Hong Kong was already integrated into the NIDL and had become a major location for American-owned radio assembly and production of the cheaper varieties of consumer electronics (Chen, 1971). This meant that Hong Kong possessed by the early 1960s a work force that was habituated to the kinds of labour processes characteristic of semiconductor assembly. It had, in other words, what many observers (including manufacturers) wrongly classify as a 'skilled' labour force (see Henderson and Cohen, 1979, for a general account of the ideological significance of labour

99

habituation and 'skill'). Furthermore, the existence of a flourishing informal sector in Hong Kong helped to keep industrial wages down to a level which at that time was quite comparable to wages in many other peripheral areas. Finally, Hong Kong was able to supply the small but crucial demand for qualified engineers and technicians necessary for the successful operation of semiconductor assembly functions.

By investing in a production facility in Hong Kong, Fairchild established an international division of labour in semiconductor manufacture, which though it has altered in form, effectively set the pattern for the subsequent expansion of offshore production. Fairchild and the other American firms which followed in its wake set up factories to assemble semiconductors using largely young female workers (Lim, 1978b; Grossman, 1979). The wafers were fabricated in the United States, air-freighted to Southeast Asia, assembled into discrete or integrated circuits and air-freighted back to the United States for final testing. At that time the vast majority of the output was destined for American markets, though what was not was in any case marketed by the parent companies (Siegel, 1980). The emergence of this spatial division of labour was effectively encouraged by American tariff regulations which charged import duty only on the value added abroad. As the value added to semiconductors assembled offshore was primarily a result of the application of cheap, unskilled labour power, duty charged on their re-import did not substantially affect the economic viability of offshore production.

Another feature of this emergent division of labour, was the form which the investment took. Fairchild and every American semiconductor manufacturer which followed them to Southeast Asia chose to establish wholly-owned subsidiaries in the region, rather than joint-venture or licensing operations. The reasons for firms' preference for this form of production seem clear enough. Reliable production methods and high yields (in circumstances where both production technologies and product specification were changing rapidly) depended on rigorous technical and managerial control. Even at the present time, offshore production of semiconductors is overwhelmingly conducted in wholly-owned branch plants. There has, however, been a limited subsidiary development of subcontracting relations within the Southeast Asian system, particularly in the Philippines. Plants in places like Hong Kong and Singapore, for example those of Motorola and National Semiconductor, have begun to subcontract out assembly of the less sophisticated types of semiconductor to independent producers, especially at times when the former have been unable to cope with excess demand (Paglaban, 1978).

The retention of this arrangement would seem to suggest that even the most 'advanced' of Southeast Asia's electronics production complexes have still not developed to the extent that they can guarantee American manufacturers the types of controls necessary for the high yield production of such a technologically sophisticated product as semiconductors. With the insistent technological upgrading of integrated circuits in particular (such as via the development of VLSI technologies), it seems likely that American semiconductor houses will continue to organize the bulk of their offshore production in the form of wholly-owned subsidiaries.

Throughout the 1960s and up to the 1970s, the pattern of the international division of labour described above was repeated many times over in Southeast Asia. In each case the basic form of American penetration of the local economic system was the same. The offshore plants specialized in intermediate (assembly) processes, but basic managerial and technical control remained firmly implanted in the United States, as did much of the product finishing processes, at least until relatively recent years. Nevertheless, an internal subregional division of labour within Southeast Asia did start to come about. In the more advanced centres of production, Hong Kong and Singapore, branch plants began to specialize more and more in the assembly of relatively small-batch, high cost semiconductors. After 1971 and the first incursions (by National Semiconductor) of American semiconductor branch plants into Malaysia, the less developed locations (Indonesia, Thailand, the Philippines, in addition to Malaysia) took over much of the large batch, standardized, low grade production activities (Siegel, 1979, 1980). At the same time, Hong Kong and Singapore became important centres of final testing, not only for their own products, but also for those made elsewhere in Southeast Asia. Testing is of course a delicate operation that calls for intense levels of managerial and technical supervision, and only the main centres of production could meet the necessary quality control standards. Motorola has been especially active in developing this aspect of the subregional division of labour, and since the early 1970s its Hong Kong plant has been the main local testing centre for the company's output from its Philippine, Malaysian, and South Korean plants. Subsequently, Fairchild and National Semiconductor developed major testing facilities in Hong Kong and Singapore.

In more recent years, however, National Semiconductor and Fairchild, for instance, have dispersed testing functions to other plants in their Southeast Asian networks, while Fairchild has systematically run down its Hong Kong facility, finally closing it in 1983, and splitting its functions between their South Korean and Philippine facilities. However, in spite of this development of testing facilities in countries such as South Korea, the Philippines and Malaysia, the semiconductors they produce remain relatively low grade in technological terms.

Why, we may ask, has this peculiar subregional division of labour occurred? Why, in other words, has more and more of the investment in assembly plants for large-batch standardized low grade outputs tended to go to an increasing degree to countries such as Indonesia, Malaysia, and the Philippines, while Hong

101

Kong and Singapore have tended to be upgraded as to the quality
and complexity of their production technologies and labour processes.   There are two major reasons for this; first,
throughout the 1970s, labour costs in Hong Kong and Singapore
increased dramatically relative to other parts of the region.
Thus, as Table 5.1 shows, both Hong Kong's and Singapore's manufacturing wages shifted strongly in the direction of American
manufacturing wages between 1969 and 1980.   By contrast, manufacturing wage rates in some countries in the region were still
far below those of the United States in 1980, and also considerably below those of Hong Kong and Singapore.   Thus, in the
continued search for cheap labour (combined with reasonable
levels of political security) much new assembly work has shifted
to these low-wage countries.   Second, Hong Kong and Singapore
(along with South Korea and Taiwan) had for long been able to
supply well-trained technicians, engineers, and scientists.
This is a reflection in part of their more advanced level of
development, as it is also in part of their advanced educational
systems that can generate large numbers of highly qualified
personnel.   Thus, critical testing activities can be carried
on in these centres with quite high levels of reliability. By
the same token, Hong Kong and Singapore are also in the process
of becoming local centres for the provision of customer services
throughout the expanding Southeast and East Asian market. This
subregional division of labour can be seen in value-added data
for semiconductor imports into the United States.   In 1979 the
value added to semiconductors partially processed in Hong Kong
and imported into the United States was 56 per cent of their
total price.   For semiconductors imported from Singapore (and
Taiwan), the corresponding figure was 46 per cent. For Malaysia,
Korea and the Philippines, the value added was, respectively,
45, 39 and 32 per cent of the price (Ernst, 1983:166).

Table 5.1   Ratio of American to Foreign Manufacturing Wages
             for a Sample of Southeast Asian Countries

	1969	1980
Hong Kong	10.3	2.6
S. Korea	10.2	3.0
Taiwan	18.2	3.8
Singapore	11.1	4.7
Philippines	na	7.9
Indonesia	na	8.1
Thailand	na	11.9

Source: Rada (1982:186)

We must add to these remarks the comment that Hong Kong
and Singapore are also becoming important centres of local sales
and marketing in the industry. Today, the regional headquarters
of Motorola is in Hong Kong and that of National Semiconductor
in Singapore. Thus these cities function as localized centres
of management and control within the overall global pattern of
the industry.

The Articulation of the Subregional and
International Divisions of Labour

Whatever the contours of the Southeast Asian division of labour
in semiconductor production, and the developmental tendencies
inherent within it, there is no possibility of developing an
adequate explanation of its significance unless it is recognized
that its features and the way they alter over time, are a product
of the articulation of the subregional with the international
division of labour, and of the dynamic development of that
articulation.

In spite of the fact that certain territorial units within
the subregional division of labour, Hong Kong and Singapore for
instance, have emerged as semiconductor production centres producing a technologically more advanced output, employing greater
technical expertise, and exercising greater managerial and marketing control than elsewhere in Southeast Asia, it must be
remembered that this 'advanced' development is relative and
appears to have significant limitations placed upon it by virtue
of the articulation indicated above. The following discussion
outlines some of the features of this articulation as they currently exist.

First, the international division of labour in American
semiconductor production is 'structured in dominance' to employ
Althusser's phrase. The technological and managerial control
centres remain firmly in the United States. It is there almost
exclusively that R & D is undertaken, as well as much of the
wafer fabrication. While some wafer fabrication has been
diffused to Europe (particularly Scotland), fabrication of the
most advanced forms of wafers, those destined for microprocessors, is carried out exclusively in the United States. With
the possible exception of Motorola there seems little likelihood
of American companies establishing wafer fabrication facilities
in Southeast Asia, even for the production of the technologically simpler types of wafers.

The Southeast Asian division of labour in semiconductor
production, therefore, is likely to remain a division between
territorial units that 'specialize' in performing different
orders of intermediate production processes. Some units will
continue to assemble and test technologically more sophisticated
semiconductors than others. The wafers are likely to continue
to be produced in the United States and Europe (National
Semiconductor, for instance, assembles and tests semiconductors
in Thailand and Malaysia from wafers fabricated at its Scottish

plant: Henderson and Scott, 1984). It seems unlikely, therefore, that anywhere in Southeast Asia will benefit in the foreseeable future from American investment in fully-integrated semiconductor production facilities.

Among the developments that have the potential to alter the nature of the international-subregional articulation in the coming years, one in particular needs to be mentioned. With the introduction of VLSI technologies (which require many complex bonding operations in the assembly process) and the gradual shift within much of the industry from the production of customized, small-batch output to standardized large-batch products, the automation of assembly and testing functions is emerging as a technological imperative and beginning to make economic sense. Although there has already been some automation of assembly and testing in Southeast Asia with a consequent shedding of labour (Motorola and Teledyne for instance have both reduced their Hong Kong workforces by over half as a direct result of automation), the most ominous sign for semiconductor production in the region is the announcements by Motorola and Fairchild of their intention to repatriate assembly and testing (facilitated by automation) back to the United States (*Electronic News*, April 16, 1982; *Global Electronics Information Newsletter*, 38, December 1983).

While these developments are likely to alter the international-subregional articulation, they will probably not result in the wholesale exodus of American semiconductor production from Southeast Asia. What some industrial analysts (for example, Ernst, 1983) see as more likely to happen is that it is the assembly and testing of the most sophisticated integrated circuits, such as microprocessors that will be repatriated to the United States, whereas the intermediate processing of the less sophisticated devices will be retained in the periphery/semi-periphery. However, the industry throughout its global domain is likely to engage in further capital deepening which will probably result in a drastic reduction in employment opportunities at the unskilled and semiskilled levels.

THE SOCIAL AND ECONOMIC IMPACT OF THE
SOUTHEAST ASIAN AND INTERNATIONAL DIVISIONS OF LABOUR

The previous section described the topography of the emergent Southeast Asian division of labour within American-owned semiconductor production, and noted that developments within it appear to be locating Hong Kong and Singapore, but also (perhaps to a lesser extent) Taiwan and South Korea at the fulcrum, with the other production areas of Malaysia, Indonesia, the Philippines and Thailand subordinate to them. The point was also made, however, that the features of the subregional division of labour, and hence their significance and impact, could not be abstracted from the global division of labour within American

104

semiconductor production as a whole. Methodologically they had to be assessed in terms of the dynamic articulation of the two divisions of labour. In this section, I examine some of the social and economic implications of these articulated divisions of labour.

Growth of Local Semiconductor Complexes

For much of its brief history in Southeast Asia, the semi-conductor industry has had remarkably little impact on local economic structures. With the exception of minor purchases, linkages to the local economy have been slight, and employment has rarely been numerically significant relative to total population (Lim, 1978a; Rada, 1982; Ernst, 1983). However, the growth and development of the industry in Hong Kong, Singapore (and possibly Taiwan and South Korea also), together with the spatial reintegration of assembly and testing, does not seem to be encouraging the incipient emergence of semiconductor industry complexes. These complexes include firms that supply many kinds of ancillary materials and services to semiconductor plants. They also include equipment manufacturers, the notable example here being the American firm of Kulicke and Soffa (the leading manufacturer of automatic semiconductor bonding equipment) which now has a branch plant in Hong Kong. In spite of the circumstance that the semiconductor complexes of Hong Kong and other areas are still in their infancy, they have nonetheless helped provide the conditions under which locally-owned semiconductor firms have managed to come into existence. There are three such firms in Hong Kong (reputedly backed by the People's Republic of China) and at least one in Taiwan and two in South Korea (Siegel, 1980; Neff, 1982; Engardio, 1984). The Hong Kong firms (and possibly the others also) use wafer masks produced in Silicon Valley, but have in-house wafer diffusion capabilities. They produce low-grade standardized outputs for local (and in the case of the Hong Kong firms, Chinese) markets. Because of core control over the most advanced forms of scientific and technological knowledge, it seems unlikely that such locally-owned firms will be able to technologically upgrade themselves to any significant degree.

During the last two or three years, however, a number of American firms have set up design facilities in Asia in order to service the product requirements of their Asian customers. Motorola, Siliconix and Teledyne have established design sections in Hong Kong as has National Semiconductor in Singapore. With the possible exceptions of Taiwan and South Korea, American semiconductor firms have not developed design facilities elsewhere in Southeast Asia. It is especially significant to note that Motorola is contemplating construction of a wafer fabrication facility in Hong Kong in order to service its other Southeast Asian plants. From field enquiries it seems that some American-owned semiconductor plants in Hong Kong are now vertically integrating downstream, and are starting to produce electronic sub-assemblies using not only locally-manufactured semiconductors (purchased from foreign, largely American and Japanese-owned companies) but also other components including printed circuit boards, switches, rectifiers, and so on. Thus the Hong Kong semiconductor complex is also beginning to merge into the larger and very definitely local electronics complex, which for some years has been assembling watches, consumer electronic equipment and more recently home computers. From recent research in Singapore (Lim and Pang, 1982), it appears that similar developments are underway there, as well as in Taiwan and South Korea also. No similar development appears to be evident in those Southeast Asian countries whose foreign-owned semiconductor plants produce largely standardized, technologically low grade output (see Lim, 1978a for the Malaysian case).

The Role of the State

Earlier it was suggested that the NIDL theorists have tended to devalue the extent to which a peripheral state theoretically had sufficient autonomy within the world-system to affect, to some extent, the course and consequences of world-market oriented industrialization. Their argument in fact seems to be that the state does little more than provide for the infrastructural requirements of foreign manufacturers and the juridico-political context in which they can successfully 'super-exploit' their labour forces. While it is undoubtedly true that peripheral/semiperipheral states have made infrastructural provision (often not to the extent or with the degree of efficiency that foreign industrialists would like to see - witness the telecommunications problems in Thailand and the Philippines for instance) and have developed repressive, and sometimes brutally enforced labour legislation (Luther, 1978; Deyo, 1981 for Singapore; Sunoo, 1978 for South Korea, and Villegas, 1983 for the Philippines), the situation is rather more complex than Fröbel *et al.* (1980) have indicated. It is now clear that while for structural reasons states must intervene in economic and social development in the interests of foreign and local capital, those very same interventions may have positive consequences for the social and material well-being of workers. Even those semiperipheral states that in the dream-world of laissez-faire theorists are economic 'success stories', precisely because of their supposed commitment to non-intervention, have now been shown to have intervened massively, with positive results for both capital and labour. Indeed, in the case of Singapore (Lim, 1983) and Hong Kong (Schiffer, 1983), both of which have developed important welfare, educational and housing programmes, their spectacular economic growth would have been inconceivable without such intervention.

That said, the question of political order and stability in a peripheral state becomes increasingly important for foreign industrialists where they seek to technologically upgrade their operations. For example, in situations where semiconductor firms invest in labour processes that are dependent on large inputs of human labour, *i.e.* they have low capital-labour ratios, then political stability is not as serious a problem as some theorists, such as Frank (1981), have assumed. When firms seek to increase capital-labour ratios, however, the political stability of a state takes on greater significance.

Repression, however, is not the only route to political stability, nor is it the most successful in the long run. 'Legitimation expenditure' on such things as public housing programmes coupled with representative democratic forms are often more reliable routes to political stability. In some of Southeast Asia's 'hosts' to semiconductor and other foreign-owned industrial branches, however, their massive and growing material inequalities and foreign indebtedness coalesce to ensure that repression seems the only possible route to political stability in the context of a capitalist world-system. The Philippines for the present, appears to be a case in point (see Bello *et al.*, 1982; Villegas, 1983). The possibility of technological upgrading of labour processes by foreign semiconductor firms in such contexts seems remote.

There are other ways in which peripheral and semi-peripheral states have indicated by their actions that their policies are not mere reflexes of the structural requirements of the NIDL. There are two types of policy which are of particular interest here. First of all, some states have adopted development strategies designed over time to transfer control of industrial enterprises from foreign to local interests, thereby laying the ground, it is hoped, for a more genuine 'national' development in the future. Malaysia, for instance, has been a case in point, although there 'local' interests have been racially rather than nationally conceived (Lim, 1978a). Secondly, and of importance to the electronics industry and semiconductors in particular, some semi-peripheral states have taken the initiative in encouraging the technological upgrading of their local industries. Such intervention is particularly important in the light of growing evidence that electronics technologies 'freely' transferred from core to semi-periphery/periphery, are almost never of the 'state-of-the-art' variety (Ernst, 1980, 1983), and are unlikely to be so in the foreseeable future. The Government of Singapore has been particularly active in this regard (Ernst, 1983) as has Taiwan whose single wafer-fabricating facility was set up with state funds. Among the Southeast Asian leaders in electronics production, however, the Hong Kong Government in particular has been uninterested in supporting such developments (*South China Morning Post*, June 17, 1984). It has thus stumbled badly in its structural role as guardian of the conditions of (local) capital accumulation.

Labour Force Composition
Evans and Timberlake (1980) have shown that 'dependent development' generates severely asymmetrical labour force compositions

107

and rising relative inequalities in 'developing' countries.
This situation tends to be particularly pronounced in urban areas
where high proportions of the labour force are unskilled manual
workers with significant numbers of them employed in the service
sector. Smaller, though still significant numbers are employed
in low-skilled white-collar jobs, with much smaller proportions
in middle-class professional employment. Significantly in such
urban labour markets, there tends to be little demand for skilled
manual workers, and little emphasis on their training. With
regard to those countries in which export-oriented industrialization is a major part of their development strategy, very high
proportions of their industrial labour forces are female. A
recent UNIDO study has shown that in South Korea for instance,
75 per cent of all workers in export industries are female. In
Malaysia's Beyan Lepas export-processing zone, 85 per cent of
all production workers and nearly 100 per cent of all assemblers
are women (UNIDO, 1980). In the American-owned semiconductor
industry, similar proportions of women in the manual labour
force are evident not only in Southeast Asian locations, but also
in Europe (Scotland) and the United States (Grossman, 1979;
Snow, 1982; Henderson and Scott, 1984).

This utilization of female labour in the semiconductor
industry has had a number of implications. Firstly, it does
appear to constitute an example of 'super-exploitation' of
Third World workers by foreign enterprises and the women employed
tend to be young. Employment of those between sixteen and
twenty-five years old tends to be the most usual (Lim, 1978b;
Grossman, 1979), although our research in Hong Kong suggests
that child labour (girls as young as eleven or twelve) was
probably utilized fairly extensively by American semiconductor
firms during the 1960s. Additionally in Hong Kong as recently as 1983, an average working week of about 48 hours (including overtime) was still usual for workers in the electronics
industry (Hong Kong Government, 1983). Health risks also continue
to pose a serious problem. Eye and muscle-related ailments
tend to be the most common, and usually result in the relatively
older women, those in their mid-twenties, being made redundant
(Lim, 1978b). Although one might expect such health hazards
to decline in those plants that have introduced automated production equipment, circumstantial evidence suggests that this
may not be the case[5].

The absorption of Third World women into semiconductor
production has also had implications for traditional social
relations. As Lim (1978b, 1982) has shown for Malaysia and
Singapore for instance, traditional patriarchal social forms
have been creatively utilized by many firms to assist the habituation of their female work forces to routine factory labour.
Obversely, however, the entrance of women into wage labour has
tended to disrupt traditional social relations. Its impact
seems to have been double-edged. While it appears to have
weakened traditional patriarchal domination in the household,

108

by providing the women with a degree of material independence, it has inevitably helped generate domestic conflict and on occasion placed female factory workers beyond the social and material support system of their families. This situation has been particularly problematic where the women have been thrown out of factory jobs. There is now some evidence from at least one Southeast Asian city of a link between expulsion from factory labour and involvement in prostitution (Phongpaichit, 1981).

The final comment that is necessary at this point concerns the extent to which women semiconductor workers develop useful and transferable ('saleable') skills from their employment. From her study of transnational electronics production in Malaysia and Singapore, Lim (1978a) has argued that employment in the industry has little beneficial effect on skill acquisition. Even in those sections of Southeast Asian industry where there has been some technological upgrading, such as with the introduction of automated testing equipment by Motorola in Hong Kong, work tasks remain largely unskilled. At Motorola, for instance, women are employed merely to manually feed integrated circuits into channels connected to computerized equipment where laser beams test for faults in the circuitry.

If the semiconductor industry, even in its most advanced Southeast Asian locations, does little to upgrade the skills of those women who constitute the vast majority of its labour force, is it any better at developing the skills of its male workers? Other than the employment of small numbers of men in the most arduous unskilled tasks (such as in the warehousing and shipping sections), United States semiconductor manufacturers employ men predominantly as supervisors, technicians, engineers and managers. The numbers employed as technicians and engineers tends to be directly related to the capital intensity of the labour process. For example, in Motorola's Hong Kong plant, probably the most capital intensive American semiconductor facility in Southeast Asia, only about 300 of the 700 work force are manual production workers. The majority of the rest are technicians and engineers.

The availability of well-trained technicians and engineers in such places as Hong Kong and Singapore, and at a much cheaper price than in the United States, has had a number of effects. First, it has led to the increasing employment of local engineers in the industry, to the extent that in the Hong Kong case local personnel are now in charge of at least three of the major American semiconductor operations in the territory. Second, our research suggests that the availability of such labour is an important factor which bears on companies' decisions about whether to technologically upgrade their operation in a particular Southeast Asian location. Finally, the semiconductor industry's (and more generally, the electronics industry's) interest in employing local engineering graduates has encouraged state and private investment in educational resources designed to reproduce a labour force with these skills. The development of the National University of Singapore's Institute of Systems Analysis (partly funded by IBM) is an example of this (Ernst, 1983).

In summary, it seems that the relative dominance of a particular territorial unit within the international and subregional divisions of labour in semiconductor production has few implications for their manual labour forces. Whether the women are employed by, say, National Semiconductor or Motorola in the United States or Scotland, Hong Kong or Malaysia, they are likely to remain the unskilled recipients of relatively low wages (while recognizing significant differences in wage levels depending on the relative dominance of the territorial unit in the international and subregional divisions of labour). For the employment of skilled (and predominantly male) technicians and engineers, however, the prospects seem to be better. In this case, however, the possibilities for the skilling of the labour force and its continued reproduction, do depend on the relative dominance of the territorial unit within the international and subregional divisions of labour. Where the unit has achieved core or semi-peripheral status within the NIDL and where local electronics complexes have begun to develop, then, as Henderson and Scott (1984) have shown, local educational institutes tend (often with state assistance) to adjust their curricula to the demands of the industry, and thus socialize the reproduction costs of a crucial sector of the semiconductor labour force. Once these processes are under way in particular locations within the subregional division of labour, however, once local electronics complexes have begun to develop around semiconductor production, once local educational institutes begin to effectively produce the necessary technicians and engineers, the situation takes on a developmental logic of its own. The growth of such economic, social and technological complexes in such parts of the subregional division of labour as Hong Kong and Singapore, may present foreign semiconductor firms seeking to technologically upgrade their operations with very compelling reasons to do so in those locations. If this is indeed the case, then we must be pessimistic about the possibilities for the upgrading of production in the territorial units currently on the periphery of the Southeast Asian division of labour.

CONCLUSIONS AND DIRECTIONS

This discussion of the emergence of a subregional division of labour within American semiconductor production in Southeast Asia has highlighted some of the key features of that division of labour and some of the developmental problems and possibilities that are inherent to it. I do not wish to summarize that discussion in this final section, but rather to emphasize four important points that arise from it.

First, the emergence of the new international division of

labour, its contours and contents, its problems and possibilities are all much more complex than NIDL theory as currently formulated would lead us to expect. Fröbel *et al.* (1980) have undoubtedly pointed scholarship in the right direction, but their work is only a first approximation and as such is too crude to provide an adequate account. Our study of the American semiconductor industry has shown that a production and consequently a socio-spatial hierarchy are emerging within Southeast Asia. This subregional division of labour seems to contain within it its own developmental possibilities and constraints. The significance of these, however, cannot be adequately assessed unless it is recognized that their form and direction are framed in terms of the articulation of the subregional with the overall international division of labour in semiconductor production. For particular territorial units within the Southeast Asian division of labour, this means that their capacities for real development are greater than one might expect from NIDL theory.

Part of the reason for this is that their production facilities have been technologically upgraded out of a concern with increasing relative, as opposed to absolute, surplus value (on a global scale) and hence tend to contradict the analysis presented by Fröbel *et al.* (Singapore and Hong Kong are cases in point). This said, however, the retention of control over a key factor of semiconductor production, *viz.* creative knowledge, by the core, suggests that such semi-peripheral units are probably unlikely to be themselves transformed into cores of the global division of labour within the industry.

On the other hand, those Southeast Asian countries which are currently on the periphery of the subregional division of labour, are unlikely to reach core status within the subregional let alone the global system. A major reason for this is the emergence of social and technical production complexes with their necessary reproductive support systems in such places as Hong Kong, Singapore, Taiwan and South Korea. These complexes now appear to be developing self-generative dynamics which importantly include the socialization of labour force (particularly technical labour) reproduction costs, and the reduction of linkage costs amongst others. Under such circumstances, other things being equal, further American investment in capital intensive semiconductor labour processes is likely to locate in these parts of the subregion rather than others.

The second point to note is that the above observations stem from the study of one fragment of one industrial branch, albeit a globally important one. In order to develop a total picture of the development prospects of a particular city, country or region, however, we need a series of 'theorized histories' of the way the internationalization of various industrial branches impact on the same territorial unit. But such theorized histories cannot be constructed merely by manipulating data emanating from global and national sources, or from the particular firms themselves. Such data tend to be too abstract, obscuring the rich detail of the embeddedness of particular labour processes of particular firms in particular cities. First-hand investigations in other words should be very much on the research agenda.

Third, such arguments for a particular type of empirical work also relate to the need for empirical work that arises out of a particular methodological orientation. It seems to me to be impossible to assess adequately development prospects in one territorial unit unless they are grasped in relation to the dynamics of the capitalist world-system as a whole. Thus the export of particular labour processes to particular locations by particular industrial branches needs to be understood merely as one moment in the global reorganization of capitalist commodity production. It therefore needs to be understood, for instance, in relation to the restructuring and deindustrialization currently taking place within core economies (see Bluestone and Harrison, 1982; Massey and Meegan, 1982). An additional aspect of this process is the export of human labour to fuel the accumulation possibilities in core, and to a lesser extent, semi-peripheral economies (Piore, 1980; Sassen-Koob, 1982).

The final point to emphasize is that the arguments above point to a massive research agenda. It is an agenda which cannot be accomplished by a series of individual researchers working in isolation. As well as highlighting the need for alterations in our methodological orientations and conceptual apparatuses, NIDL theory, and world-systems analysis of which it is a part, it also highlights the need to alter our scholarly practice. We need to abandon our 'possessive individualism' and create research teams of global dimensions. Given theoretical coherence, the work of such research teams appears to be our best chance of mapping in sufficient detail and subtlety the impact of the changing international division of labour, and within it the role of multinational corporations in social, economic, political and spatial development in various parts of the globe.

NOTES

1. In this chapter I follow the French usage of the term industrial (or production) branch. It refers to the production of one product, *e.g.* cars, trucks, computers or semiconductors. (See Palloix, 1975, 1977).

2. Witness for instance the following comment:

> 'The new international division of labour is an "institutional" innovation of capital itself, necessitated by changed conditions, and not the result

of changed development strategies by individual
countries or options freely decided upon by so-called
multinational companies.' (Fröbel *et al.* 1980:46).

3. This and the following section draw on my work with Allen
Scott (Henderson and Scott, 1984). I am indebted to him
for his assistance in these matters.

4. Interesting, though theoretically incoherent accounts (in
the sense defined here) of the spatial development of
semiconductor production and high-technology industry more
generally, have recently been provided by Saxenian (1983b)
and Hall (1984) respectively.

5. In one relatively automated American semiconductor plant
we studied, a doctor visited for a few hours each day.
This occurred in spite of the fact that the factory employed only 200 workers.

Acknowledgement
I wish to thank Allen Scott for the initial stimulation that
produced some of the arguments advanced here, James Kung for
his research assistance, and the University of Hong Kong's
Urban Studies and Urban Planning Trust Fund for funding the
research on which the chapter is based.

REFERENCES

Amin, S. (1974) *Accumulation on a World Scale*, Monthly Review
Press, New York.
Amin, S. (1976) *Unequal Development*, Monthly Review Press,
New York.
Bello, W., Kinley, D. and Elinson, E. (1982) *Development
Debacle: The World Bank in the Philippines*, Institute of
Food and Development Policy/Philippine Solidarity Network,
San Francisco.
Bernstein, A., DeGrass, B., Grossman, R., Paine, C. and Siegel L.
(1977) *Silicon Valley: Paradise or Paradox?* Pacific
Studies Center, Mountain View, California.
Bluestone, B. and Harrison, B. (1982) *The Deindustrialization
of America*, Basic Books, New York.
Braun, E. and Macdonald. S. (1982) *Revolution in Miniature*,
Cambridge University Press, Cambridge.
Castells, M. (1977), *The Urban Question*, Edward Arnold, London.
Castells, M. (1984) 'Towards the informational city? : high
technology, economic change and spatial structure : some
exploratory hypotheses', *Working Paper*, No.430, Institute of
Urban & Regional Development, University of California, Berkeley.

Chen, E.K.Y. (1971) The Electronics Industry of Hong Kong: An
    Analysis of its Growth, unpublished MSocSc Dissertation,
    University of Hong Kong.
Cohen, R.B. (1981) 'The new international division of labor,
    multinational corporations and urban hierarchy' in Dear, M.
    and Scott A.J. (eds.), *Urbanisation and Urban Planning in
    Capitalist Society*, Methuen, London: 287-315.
Deyo, F.C. (1981), *Dependent Development and Industrial Order*,
    Praeger, New York.
Emmanuel, A. (1972), *Unequal Exchange*, Monthly Review Press,
    New York.
Engardio, P. (1984) 'Galloping forth in semiconductors (South
    Korea 1984)', *Far Eastern Economic Review*, 125(29): 64-66.
Ernst, D. (ed.) (1980) *The New International Division of
    Labour, Technology and Underdevelopment*, Campus Verlag,
    Frankfurt.
Ernst, D. (1983) *The Global Race in Microelectronics*, Campus
    Verlag, Frankfurt.
Evans, P. and Timberlake, M. (1980) 'Dependence, inequality
    and the growth of the tertiary: a comparative analysis
    of less developed countries', *American Sociological Review*,
    45 (4): 531-552.
Frank, A.G. (1971) *Capitalism and Underdevelopment in Latin
    America*, Penguin, Harmondsworth.
Frank, A.G. (1980) *Crisis: In the World Economy*, Heinemann,
    London.
Frank, A.G. (1981) *Crisis: In the Third World*,   Heinemann,
    London.
Friedman, H. and Wolff, G. (1982) 'World city formation: an
    agenda for research and action', *International Journal of
    Urban and Regional Research*, 6 (3): 309-343.
Fröbel, F., Heinrichs, J. and Kreye, O. (1980)   *The New Inter-
    national Division of Labour*, Cambridge University Press,
    Cambridge.
Grossman, R. (1979) 'Women's place in the integrated circuit',
    South-East Asia Chronicle, 66: 2-17.
Hall, P. (1984) 'The geography of high-technology industry',
    Working Paper, Centre of Urban Studies and Urban Planning,
    University of Hong Kong.
Hamilton, C. (1983) 'Capitalist industrialisation in East Asia's
    Four Little Tigers', *Journal of Contemporary Asia*, 13 (1):
    35-73.
Henderson, J. (1985) 'The new international division of labour
    and urban development in the contemporary world-system',
    in Drakakis-Smith D. (ed.), *Urbanisation in the Developing
    World*, Croom Helm, London.
Henderson, J. and Cohen, R. (1979) 'Capital and the work ethic',
    Monthly Review, 31 (6): 11-26.
Henderson, J. and Cohen, R. (1982) 'The international restruc-
    turing of capital and labour: Britain and Hong Kong',
    Paper presented to the International Sociological

Association's Tenth World Congress, Mexico City.

Henderson, J. and Scott, A.J. (1984) 'The growth and inter-nationalisation of the American semiconductor industry: labour processes and the changing spatial organisation of production', Mimeo, Centre of Urban Studies and Urban Planning, University of Hong Kong.

Hong Kong Government (1983) *Quarterly Report on Wages, Salaries and Employment Benefits*, Vol. V, Government Printing Office, Hong Kong.

Hymer, S. (1979), 'The multinational corporation and the inter-national division of labour' in Hymer, S. *The Multinational Corporation: A Radical Approach*, Cambridge University Press, Cambridge: 140-164.

Ip, H.S. (1983) Hong Kong's Development: A Dependency Case?, unpublished MSocSc Dissertation, University of Hong Kong.

Jenkins, R. (1984) 'Divisions over the international division of labour', *Capital and Class*, 22: 28-57.

Lim, L.Y.C. (1978a) Multinational Firms and Manufacturing for Export in Less-Developed Countries: the Case of the Elec-tronics Industry in Malaysia and Singapore, PhD Dissertation, University of Michigan.

Lim, L.Y.C. (1978b) 'Women workers in multinational corporations in developing countries: the case of the electronics industry in Malaysia and Singapore', *Occasional Paper*, Women's Studies Program, University of Michigan.

Lim, L.Y.C. (1982) 'Capitalism, imperialism and patriarchy: the dilemma of third world women workers in multinational factories' in Nash J. and Fernandez-Kelly M.P. (eds.), *Women, Men and the International Division of Labor*, State University of New York Press, Albany: 70-91.

Lim, L.Y.C. (1983) 'Singapore's success: the myth of the free market economy', *Asian Survey*, 23 (6): 752-764.

Lim, L.Y.C. and Pang, E.F. (1982) 'Vertical linkages and multi-national enterprises in developing countries', *World Development*, 10 (7): 585-595.

Luther, H.U. (1978) 'Strikes and the institutionalisation of labour protest: the case of Singapore', *Journal of Contemporary Asia*, 8 (2): 219-230.

Massey, D. and Meegan, R. (1982) *The Anatomy of Job Loss*, Methuen, London.

Neff, R. (1982) 'Hong Kong takes a cut at technology', *Electronics*, 24 March.

Paglaban, E. (1978) 'Philippines: workers in the export ind-ustry', *Pacific Research*, IX (3 & 4): 2-31.

Palloix, C. (1975) 'The internationalisation of capital and the circuit of social capital' in Radice H. (ed.), *International Firms and Modern Imperialism*, Penguin, Harmondsworth: 63-88.

Palloix, C. (1977), 'The self-expansion of capital on a world scale', *Review of Radical Political Economics*, 9 (2): 1-28.

Phongpaichit, P. (1981) 'Bangkok masseuses: holding up the family sky', *South-East Asia Chronicle*, 78: 15-23.

Piore, M. (1980) *Birds of Passage*, Cambridge University Press, Cambridge.

Portes, A. and Walton, J. (1981) *Labor, Class and the International System*, Academic Press, New York.

Rada, J. (1982) *The Structure and Behavior of the Semiconductor Industry*, UN Centre for Transnational Corporations, Geneva.

Sassen-Koob, S. (1982) 'Labor migration and the new international division of labor' in Nash J. and Fernandez-Kelley M.P. (eds.) *Women, Men and the International Division of Labor*, State University of New York Press, Albany: 175-204.

Saxenian, A. (1981) 'Silicon chips and spatial structure: the industrial basis of urbanization in Santa Clara County, California', *Working Paper*, No.345, Institute of Urban and Regional Development, University of California, Berkeley.

Saxenian, A. (1983a) 'The urban contradictions of Silicon Valley: regional growth and the restructuring of the semiconductor industry', *International Journal of Urban and Regional Research*, 7 (2): 237-262.

Saxenian, A. (1983b) 'The genesis of Silicon Valley', *Built Environment*, 9 (1): 7-17.

Sayer, A. (1982) 'Explanation in economic geography: abstraction versus generalisation', *Progress in Human Geography*, 6 (1): 68-88.

Sayer, A. (1984), *Method in Social Science*, Hutchinson, London.

Schiffer, J. (1981) 'The changing post-war pattern of development: the accumulated wisdom of Samir Amin', *World Development*, 9 (6): 515-537.

Schiffer, J. (1983) 'Anatomy of a "laissez faire" government: the Hong Kong growth model reconsidered', *Working Paper*, Centre of Urban Studies and Urban Planning, University of Hong Kong.

Scottish Development Agency (1983) *Electronics in Scotland: Industry Profile*, Glasgow.

Siegel, L. (1979) 'Microelectronics does little for the third world', *Pacific Research*, X (2): 15-21.

Siegel, L. (1980) 'Delicate bonds: the global semiconductor industry', *Pacific Research*, XI (1): 1-26.

Snow, R.T. (1982) 'The new international division of labor and the US workforce: the case of the electronics industry' in Nash J. and Fernandez-Kelly M.P. (eds.), *Women, Men and the International Division of Labor*, State University of New York Press, Albany: 39-69.

Sunoo, H.K. (1978) 'Economic development and the foreign control in South Korea', *Journal of Contemporary Asia*, 8 (3): 322-339.

Troutman, M. (1980) 'The semiconductor labor market in Silicon Valley: production wages and related issues', Mimeo, Pacific Studies Center, Mountain View, California.

United Nations Industrial Development Organisation (1980) 'Women, in the redeployment of manufacturing industry to developing countries', *Working Papers on Structural Change*, No.18, New York.

Villegas, E.M. (1983) *Studies in Philippine Political Economy*, Silangan Publishers, Manila.

Warren, B. (1980) *Imperialism, Pioneer of Capitalism*, New Left Books, London.

Chapter Six

MULTINATIONAL CORPORATIONS AND THE
TRIPLE ALLIANCE IN LATIN AMERICA

R.N. Gwynne

The process of recent industrial expansion in Latin America has
been engineered through a distinctive institutional structure.
This structure has been referred to as 'the triple alliance' -
an alliance between state firms, national private enterprises
and MNCs (Multinational Corporations). The balance between these
elements varies from country to country and is continually changing.
In the larger countries, it would appear that national private
enterprises have been losing some ground to both public enterprises and multinational corporations in terms of their contribution to the industrial product.   In the smaller countries, a
reverse trend seems to be occurring with national private enterprises gaining ground.   As well as these changes in balance
between the elements of the triple alliance, there has also been
a greater differentiation of their respective roles.
     The differentiation of roles has been most apparent in the
latter stages of ISI (Import Substitution Industrialization),
the strategy that came to dominate industrial development in
most Latin American countries during the 1950s and 1960s.   Ad-
herents of this policy envisaged four stages of industrial production. The first stage saw the production of basic non-durable
consumer goods such as textiles, foodstuffs and pharmaceuticals.
This was followed by the production of consumer durable products,
such as cookers, radios and televisions, and the critical motor
vehicle industry; initially all were heavily dependent on the
importation of parts for assembly. The third stage was critical
in the industrializing process as it involved the promotion of
'intermediate' industries producing the inputs for companies
set up during the first and second stages. Typical industries
at this stage include chemical plants making paint, synthetic
fibres, dyes and acids, or engineering works producing small
motors and gearboxes, or parts industries for durable goods
assembly.   The final stage of the process would promote the
development of the capital goods industry which would manufacture machinery and plant installations.   It was the task of
government to plan and synchronize each successive stage in the
process.

STATE FIRMS

As government played such a significant role in the execution of ISI policies, state firms came to have some clear functions within national industrial strategy. The policy of ISI envisaged within its latter stages both a broadening of the range of local manufacturing (to include consumer durables such as the motor vehicle) and a backward integration of production (to build up the intermediate and capital goods sectors). Within this framework, it has been the role of the state enterprise to invest in such intermediate and capital goods and basic infrastructure as continued industrial expansion has required. The state adopted this role because of inadequately developed domestic capital markets which meant that only the state could provide the necessary capital for such large investments. Furthermore, as much of the investment was of a strategic nature (power, communications, steel), governments wished to exclude the multinationals from participation.

The role of the Brazilian state in that country's rapid industrial growth since 1964 is illuminating. A large proportion of Brazil's federal investment funds are managed by the BNDE (National Development Bank). In the late 1960s, this bank was responsible for over one fifth of national capital formation. Investments were directed into steel (now 60 per cent owned by the government), oil refining (wholly government owned), petrochemicals, power and communications. In 1963, 65 per cent of electricity production was under private ownership; by 1982 the state had virtually complete ownership of this vital sector. Powerful state companies have been created. Petrobras controls oil exploration, production and refining as well as the majority of national petrochemical installations. Siderbras was established in 1974 as a holding company to control and coordinate the Brazilian government's majority interests in eight steel companies (Dickinson, 1978). In providing basic infrastructure and by investing in necessary though not immediately profitable industries, the Brazilian government and its state firms have undoubtedly facilitated industrial growth in many other manufacturing sectors.

Such patterns of state investment and control are not exclusive to Brazil. In 1978, the steel produced by state iron and steel enterprises made up 80 per cent of total production in Venezuela, 69 per cent in Argentina and 60 per cent in Mexico (UNECLA, 1979). The share of state enterprises in oil refining is also important. In Mexico, Colombia, Uruguay and Bolivia, all oil refining is carried out by state firms, while the contribution of such firms to the processing of chemical and petrochemical products is also substantial. In Argentina and Mexico, there are large state enterprises that process basic petrochemical products, while in Andean Pact countries, such as Colombia, Peru and Venezuela, all the enterprises that process such products are state-owned.

119

Increased state participation in basic industries can also
be attributed to the conviction that it is a means of increasing national decision-making power in the sector.   This is
particularly appropriate in those countries whose governments
see multinationals as posing a threat to national sovereignty
and who desire complete control over production, income and
capital flows in critical sectors. Nationalization of foreign
interests has been a popular policy in Venezuela in the 1970s
(Sigmund, 1980) with iron ore and oil production being nationalized in 1975 and 1976 respectively. The state firm PETROVEN
controls oil exploration, production and refining through four
subsidiaries that took over the organization of the four oil
companies that previously controlled the industry. Similarly,
the state firm PEQUIVEN controls the production of basic petrochemical feedstock (ethylene, propylene, ammonia, urea) selling
them to mainly private national firms for further processing.
One interesting case of increasing state involvement in
industry is provided by the Venezuelan aluminium industry. The
industry has become majority-owned by the government due to what
could be described as a government monopoly on increased investment in the sector.   Government influence is exerted through
the regional development body, the CVG (Corporacion Venezolana
de Guyana), mainly because aluminium production is concentrated
in the region of Guyana.   In 1962, the CVG established a 50 per
cent partnership with one of the six aluminium multinationals,
Reynolds, to form a joint company, ALCASA, and produce aluminium
at Ciudad Guyana using Caribbean bauxite and power from the CVG
dam at Guri.   In the early 1970s, there were disagreements
between the two partners over provision of new investment and
the participation of Reynolds in providing new technology. Although the partnership continued, the CVG decided that its new
plant would be fully state-owned and created an aluminium subsidiary, VENALUM, for this purpose.   In 1979 the VENALUM
smelter at Ciudad Guyana became the largest smelter in the world
with a capacity of 280,000 tonnes per annum; the CVG was able
to guarantee high capacity utilization after signing a contract
with a Japanese syndicate to sell 140,000 tonnes of aluminium
a year.   With ALCASA's 120,000 tonne capacity plant, the CVG
now had the opportunity to invest in an alumina plant; approximately one million tonnes of alumina are required to produce
400,000 tonnes of aluminium.   In 1983, a new CVG subsidiary,
INTERALUMINA, completed a US$1 billion alumina plant, again
wholly-owned by the state.   In order to feed a one million
tonne alumina plant, two million tonnes of bauxite are required;
the CVG discovered and began exporting a 500 million tonne de-
posit of high-grade bauxite at Los Pijiguaos and created a new
subsidiary, BAUXIVEN to exploit it.   When the BAUXIVEN operations are fully working at Los Pijiguaos, Venezuela will have
the first fully integrated aluminium industry in the Third World
with all three stages (extraction of bauxite, production of
alumina and then aluminium) present in or near the Ciudad

Guyana industrial complex. The six aluminium multinationals that control much of the world market in aluminium have not as yet developed a fully integrated industry in a non-advanced economy principally because they fear easy nationalization.

State firms have thus developed in two very distinct sectors of Latin American industrial economies. On the one hand, they have been established in the extractive industries and in the further processing and refining of the minerals concerned. State firms in this case have developed for strategic reasons and due to a national wish for greater control over the crucial resources of a country. On the other hand, state firms have developed in the basic heavy industrial sectors of the more advanced Latin American economies - producing oil and steel, petrochemical feed-stocks, aluminium and electricity for a wide range of manufacturing consumers.

NATIONAL PRIVATE ENTERPRISES

In contrast to the state firm and MNC, the national private firm is characterized by great diversity in terms of size, technological level and forms of organization. In most large and medium-sized countries, large national conglomerates have developed with a wide variety of manufacturing interests and often important tertiary functions in such areas as banking, insurance, finance, tourism, commerce and the media. Table 6.1 illustrates the wide range of interests of the six major conglomerates that existed in Chile in 1978; even the conglomerate that specialized most in manufacturing, the Grupo Angelini, had nearly 50 per cent of its subsidiary companies involved in other functions. At the other end of the size range, large numbers of small enterprises fill demand gaps left by, or provide low-cost competition for, the large state, national and multinational companies. Due to labour-intensive methods and low capital inputs, these small enterprises generate a much higher proportion of employment than their production levels would indicate. According to Tyler (1981), in 1979, the 135,000 small firms in Brazil, while accounting for only 21 per cent of the total value of production, employed as much as 44 per cent of the total manufacturing employment. The organization of most of these small firms is simple, based around a single entrepreneur or family, and many are highly susceptible to changes in the macroeconomy or the policy shifts of the large companies. As a result, they have to be very adaptable and flexible in order to survive.

In terms of their relationship with MNCs, it is often pointed out that the latter predominate in the technologically more dynamic sectors, leaving the national private firms to specialize in the more traditional industries. In 1979 the 2,700 largest national private firms in Brazil, for example, accounted for 75 per cent of production in the non-durable consumer

Table 6.1 Company Interests of Chile's Six Leading Conglomerates, 1978

Conglomerate	Financial institutions	Agricultural and timber companies	Mining and construction companies	Manufacturing companies	Commercial and other companies	Total
Grupo Cruzat-Larrain	32	12	11	34	20	109
Grupo Javier Vial	27	6	5	15	13	66
Grupo Matte	25	7	1	7	6	46
Grupo Angelini	4	4	0	11	2	21
Grupo Edwards	23	0	0	6	6	35
Grupo Luksic	3	6	3	6	13	31
Total	114	35	20	79	60	308

Source: F. Dahse, (1979) *El mapa de la extrema riqueza*, Editorial Aconcagua, Santiago

good sector but only 33 and 45 per cent respectively in the intermediate and metal goods machinery sectors. However, such a distinction can be misleading. National private firms are active in some very dynamic sectors in Latin America. For example, in the motor vehicle industry, national private firms have specialized in components and parts production while leaving assembly and engine production to the multinationals. In Brazil, national firms figure prominently in the plastics, paper, machinery and microcomputer sectors. In Venezuela, the metal fabrication industry is dominated by such national firms as SIVENSA. Nevertheless, throughout Latin America, the majority of firms producing in the food, beverages, textiles, footwear, clothing, leather, cement, furniture and ceramic sectors are of national origin (see Table 6.2).

THE MULTINATIONAL CORPORATIONS

The third agent of industrialization in Latin America, the multinational corporation, generally has its origins outside of the continent. MNCs have historically been of West European and American origin but Japanese interests have been increasing recently. The role of the MNC as an agent of Latin American industrialization is a crucial one, not least because no other continent has received a major contribution from foreign companies in their process of industrialization. The United States, Japan and the countries of Europe largely industrialized through national agents, whether state or private. Other Third World countries are presently industrializing with the assistance of MNCs, but Latin American countries have already developed complex and diverse industrial structures from the contributions of foreign investment. The only close comparison could be the industrialization of the city states of Hong Kong and Singapore where multinational enterprise has contributed to the creation of complex industrial systems.

The role of foreign companies in contributing to the industrialization of Latin America and other less developed countries has been the focus of much theoretical work. One conceptualization has followed Lenin's (1916) interpretation of MNCs as an agent of rival imperial powers competing for control over peripheral countries. The growth of the MNC reflects the need 'to control raw-material sources and markets in order to protect their dominant position and to secure their investment even on a relatively longer-run profit perspective' (Roxborough, 1979). Such a framework assumes an intimate link between the interests of the core country and the MNC that has its origins there.

A more positive approach towards the contribution of MNCs to industrial development has been presented by the Nobel-prize winner W.A. Lewis:

Table 6.2 Percentages of Assets of the Largest 300 Manufacturing Firms in Brazil and Mexico held by American, Other Foreign and National Companies, 1972

	American companies		Companies from other foreign countries		National share	
	Brazil	Mexico	Brazil	Mexico	Brazil	Mexico
Food	2	20	30	6	68	74
Textiles	6	0	38	5	56	95
Metal fabrication	4	48	21	8	75	44
Chemicals	34	54	35	14	31	32
Rubber	100	100	0	0	0	0
Non electrical machinery	34	36	40	58	26	5
Electrical machinery	22	35	56	25	22	40
Transportation equipment	37	70	47	9	16	21
Total	16	36	34	16	50	48

Source: G. Gereffi and P. Evans (1981), Transnational Corporations, Dependent Development and State Policy in the Semiperiphery: A Comparison of Brazil and Mexico, *Latin American Research Review*, 16 (3): 31-64.

Domestic income increases because the undertaking pays wages and salaries to local people, buys local supplies, and pays local taxes; and these payments not only increase consumption, thereby stimulating local production, but also make it possible to have larger local savings, and also to spend on schools, medical services, and other permanent improvements. If the choice is between local capital and foreign capital the advantage may be with the former, but if, as is more often the case, the choice lies between foreign capital or leaving resources undeveloped, then there is little doubt that foreign investment plays a most useful role in providing income to pay for higher standards of consumption, of education, and of domestic investment (1955: 258).

The Latin American reality is somewhere between these two contrasting theoretical constructs. In the early twentieth century, there is evidence to justify the more negative aspects of international investment. The multinational companies of this era were generally involved in the extraction of raw materials, particularly petroleum (Mexico and Venezuela) and minerals (Chile and Peru). Questionable activities of these companies, such as the refusal to pay increased oil taxes after the Mexican revolution of 1911, (Sigmund, 1980: 51), were backed up by their respective home governments who stressed the need for access to cheap sources of raw materials.

However, since the Second World War and the nationalization of international mining interests in Mexico, Venezuela, Chile and Peru, the flavour and structure of MNCs have radically changed. First of all, there has been a major increase in manufacturing as opposed to mining investment by MNCs in Latin America. In 1950, FDI (Foreign Direct Investment) in Latin American mining and oil totalled US$2,381 million, equivalent to 53.5 per cent of total foreign investment in Latin America. By 1978, although FDI in mining and petroleum had increased to US$5,325 million, it only accounted for 22.7 per cent of total investment. Furthermore, mining and petroleum FDI in Mexico and Brazil accounted for only 15.6 per cent of the total (Gereffi and Evans, 1981). The majority of extractive industry investment was in the smaller countries of Latin America.

While in mining and petroleum FDI decreased in relative importance, in manufacturing it increased from US$0.8 billion in 1950 to US$10.9 billion in 1978 - when it accounted for 46.2 per cent of total investment. However, such foreign investment was particularly significant in those countries that had reached the latter stages of import substitution industrialization - notably Mexico and Brazil. Thus 68.5 per cent of FDI in Latin American manufacturing was concentrated in Brazil and Mexico in 1978 (Gereffi and Evans, 1981). As Table 6.3 shows, 74.1 per cent and 65.3 per cent of total FDI in Mexico and Brazil

Table 6.3   Changes in the Investment Patterns of Multinational Corporations in Brazil, Mexico and Other Latin American Countries (%)

	1950				1978			
	Brazil	Mexico	Other Latin American countries	Total	Brazil	Mexico	Other Latin American countries	Total
Total investment (millions US$)	654	415	3,379	4,448	7,170	3,712	12,595	23,477
Per cent of Total investment	14.7	9.3	76.0	100.1	30.5	15.8	58.7	100.0
Extractive	1.1	29.9	30.1	25.8	3.7	2.6	10.3	7.1
Petroleum	17.2	3.1	32.8	27.7	5.9	1.1	25.4	15.6
Manufacturing	43.6	32.0	10.7	17.6	65.3	74.1	27.1	46.2
Public Utilities	21.2	25.8	20.2	20.9	0.4	0.6	2.1	1.3
Other (including Finance and Trade)	16.9	9.2	6.2	8.0	24.7	21.6	35.1	29.8
Total	100.0	100.0	100.0	100.0	100.0	100.0	100.0	100.0

Source: G. Gereffi and P. Evans (1983), Transnational Corporations, Dependent Development and State Policy in the Semiperiphery: a comparison of Brazil and Mexico, *Latin American Research Review*, 16 (3): 31–64.

corresponded to the manufacturing sector in 1978. In other Latin American countries, an average of only 27 per cent of FDI was directed into manufacturing.

The majority of Latin American FDI in 1976 originated in the USA - 50 per cent in the large countries, 77 per cent in the medium-sized countries and 69 per cent in the smaller countries (UNECLA, 1979). However, both European and Japanese investments are increasing. Japanese investment is still most heavily concentrated in the processing of raw materials (steel, aluminium) but European investment is shifting to high technology sectors such as motor vehicles and chemicals.

Indeed, there is increasing evidence to show that the rapid growth of multinational investment in manufacturing in Latin America (an increase of 146 per cent between 1967 and 1976) has taken place in the more dynamic and technologically-innovative sectors. In the country with nearly 50 per cent of continental foreign direct investment in manufacturing, Brazil, 77 per cent of such investment was channelled into technologically dynamic sectors in 1979 - notably chemicals, vehicles, machine tools, pharmaceuticals, communications and the electrical and medical industries (see Table 6.4). This meant that in Brazil in 1979, MNCs controlled 56 per cent of total assets in the transport sector, 51 per cent in the electrical sector and over 35 per cent in the machinery sector. These were the three Brazilian sectors that recorded the highest growth rates during the 1970s (Cunningham, 1981: 48).

Table 6.4   Percentage Distribution of Foreign Direct Investment in Brazilian Manufacturing by Sector, 1979

Sector	%	Sector	%
Food	3.4	Chemicals	18.7
Textiles, Clothing	4.1	Vehicle and Auto Parts	15.3
Drinks	0.6	Machine Tools	13.6
Cellulose and Paper	3.1	Electrical and Communication	11.5
Others	11.8	Metal Processing	7.7
		Medical and Pharmaceutical	5.2
		Steel	3.5
		Rubber	1.5

Source: S.M. Cunningham (1983), 'Multinational Enterprises in Brazil: Locational Patterns and Implications for Regional Development', *Professional Geographer*, 33 (1): 48.

MULTINATIONAL CORPORATIONS AND THE STATE

Conflicts of interest between MNCs and the State have been frequent in Latin America.   The State is basically interested in
maximizing benefits for its own territory.   The MNC, engaged in
world-wide manufacturing operations, is interested in maximizing
benefits for its own international organization.   In this way,
it attempts 'to find ways of achieving the economic efficiencies
of world-wide specialization of production and development within the political constraints imposed by national policies'
(Gunderson, 1979).   While the State can control its own enterprises and strongly influence national private firms, it can
find it difficult to exert influence over multinational enterprises.   Again there are major contrasts in the experiences of
large and small countries in Latin America with regard to multinational corporations.   The larger countries can often exert
considerable power in bargaining with MNCs as their markets are
valuable and rival companies will compete against each other
for tenders (Vernon, 1978).   Smaller countries generally have
substantially less bargaining power due to their small market
size and the often low level of multinational interest.
       However, in both large and small countries, governments are
increasingly worried about the concentration of MNCs in those
high-technology sectors that also enjoy the highest growth rates.
This is mainly because governments see growth industries in
their countries being dominated more and more by organizations
over which they have little control.   In the booming industrial
economies of the larger countries, the vital technological component to industrial growth is already strongly associated with
organizations that emanate from the more developed world. This
leads Latin American governments to envisage their countries'
future industrial growth as being highly dependent on forces
and decisions external to their territory.
       This common concern of governments has led some to establish
strict controls over the extent and nature of foreign investment.   One of the more elaborate systems of control, that known
as 'Decision 24' of the Andean Group (Venezuela, Colombia,
Ecuador, Peru, Bolivia, Chile) was implemented in 1974; the most
controversial aspect was a 14 per cent profit and dividend rem-
ittance ceiling on registered capital for MNCs.   The major
effect of Decision 24 was to reduce considerably foreign investment and the scope of new industrial projects in the region.
This was particularly the case in Venezuela which could have
anticipated a significant expansion of foreign manufacturing
investment in the 1974-77 period due to its large oil revenues
and its policy of investing a large proportion of them in industrial development.   However, foreign investment remained low
during the period.   In 1977, Venezuela introduced a much less
restrictive foreign investment law, 'Decree 2442', allowing increased profit remittances, removing the elaborate financial
controls and extending the time limits on transfer of technology

contracts (West, 1978:113). As a result, foreign investment in Venezuelan manufacturing has expanded more rapidly in subsequent years.

Controls, therefore, tend to restrict foreign investment and, because such investment tends to be in the more dynamic manufacturing sectors, industrial growth as well. Lack of controls can also have adverse effects, permitting excessive royalties and profit remittances, the financial juggling of costs across national boundaries and an over-reliance on locally-generated capital. Lack of control can also affect the structure of industry, given that some world industries are now dominated by a small number of large corporations that can be described as forming an 'interacting oligopoly' (Knickerbocker, 1973). In this context, a locational decision taken by one corporation can generate similar responses from other members of a world oligopoly (Gwynne, 1979). This can mean that once one member has decided to locate a plant in a new market, other corporations will follow. In Latin America, such oligopolistic reaction has been particularly marked in the motor vehicle and tyre industries (West, 1977). In large countries, such mass entry can lead to competition between firms utilizing much of their installed capacity. But in small countries the tendency has been for a large number of firms to produce at low capacity and high costs, thus considerably adding to problems of achieving economies of scale. Despite this, few countries have attempted to control the number of multinational firms located in their country - even within the framework of import substitution industrialization (Gwynne, 1978a).

MULTINATIONALS AND EXPORT PROMOTION

The last decade has generally witnessed a shift to more open economies in Latin America and this has had major implications for industrial performance. On the one hand, the larger countries, due to their production of industrial goods being internationally competitive, have been able to expand significantly industrial exports without major increases in manufactured imports. On the other hand, the smaller countries with few internationally competitive industrial sectors, have been unable to expand their industrial exports and have often suffered major increases in manufactured imports. The MNCs have responded to these changes by attempting to increase their participation in the larger countries attracted by the bigger domestic markets and good export records. In the smaller countries, they have been distinctly less interested. Indeed as the opening up of the economies of many small countries has caused the decline (and even disappearance) of many industrial sectors, the MNCs involved in these sectors have often decided to leave or sell out to state or private national firms.

Thus the balance of the triple alliance has been changing

in the last decade, but the nature of the change is closely linked to the size of country. In the larger countries, the MNCs have been distinctly ambitious for a greater involvement in industrial development; as a result, the contribution of the MNCs to the industrial product is often increasing at a greater rate than that of private enterprises. However, in the smaller countries, where MNCs have been less enthusiastic in the last decade and where many have been pulling out, the reverse is often the case. In terms of the contribution to the industrial product, private national enterprises have been gaining ground at the expense of multinationals.

These points can be illustrated by examining two examples - the record of MNC interest in Chile since 1973 and recent developments in the Latin American motor vehicle industry.

MULTINATIONAL INVESTMENT IN CHILE SINCE 1973

Since 1973, conditions in Chile would appear to have been conducive for significant investment from MNCs. The policies of the various economic teams of General Pinochet have been constant in their aim to integrate the Chilean economy more fully into the world capitalist economy, in emphasizing the role of the private capitalist as the main motor of economic growth, and in welcoming foreign capital. The desire to encourage foreign investment was a major reason for Chile's withdrawal from the Andean Group in 1976, due to the latter's strict controls on foreign investment. Chile's own foreign investment law (Decree Law 600 passed in 1976), was a much more liberal document, allowing freedom for profit remittances and technology transfer payments. There were no special company taxes over those paid by national companies.

The Marxist government of Salvador Allende (1970-73) had nationalized most foreign companies and intervened in or taken over the majority of Chile's hundred largest companies. The Pinochet government sold these back to private enterprise often at very low prices, thus creating considerable opportunities for investment during the mid-1970s.

However, at the same time, the economic teams of General Pinochet were continuing to open up the economy to outside competition. According to Congdon (1982: 133) 'the move from autarkic to open policies in Chile was perhaps the most rapid and complete ever implemented'. Exports increased from US$850 million in 1972 to US$4,722 million in 1980. Imports increased from US$1,103 million in 1972 to US$5,777 million in 1980. The ratio of the value of overseas trade to GDP increased from 24.7 per cent in 1972 to 45.6 per cent in 1980. Non-traditional exports (principally timber, fish and fruit) grew from US$71 million in 1973 (5.7 per cent of total exports) to US$1,629 in 1980 (34 per cent of total value of exports). The development of these new activities gave impetus to the economy which registered an average annual growth rate of over 7 per cent between mid-1976 and mid-1981.

Conditions seemed set fair for a major return of the MNCs to Chilean manufacturing. But such a return did not materialize. The paucity of multinational enterprise was most evident in the former import-substituting sectors; these sectors had been protected by high tariffs from foreign competition for many years. Soon after the 1973 *coup d'état*, Pinochet's first Finance Minister, Gotuzzo, began to bring tariffs down to between 25 and 35 per cent - still high but much reduced from earlier levels of over 100 per cent. However, in 1977, the Finance Minister, Sergio de Castro, announced that there would be a 10 per cent uniform tariff by June 1979 (with the basic exception of motor vehicles over 850 cc).

Multinational interest in the import-substituting sectors of Chilean industry has as a result been small - even in the favoured motor vehicle sector where a 10 per cent uniform tariff does not come into force until 1986. In 1974, there were eight vehicle plants in Chile; their multinational links were with Ford, Peugeot/Renault, Fiat, Nissan, British Leyland, Chrysler, General Motors and Citroen. The Pinochet government put out tenders for those companies wishing to stay in Chile. Ford, Nissan, British Leyland and Chrysler were uninterested from the outset. Citroen had been working as a joint venture with the government holding company, and did not wish to increase its capital participation. The Peugeot-Renault plant stayed under the control of local interests. Only Fiat and General Motors bought back or resumed control of their plants. With serious competition from Japanese imports (particularly in small cars of less than 850 cc), Citroen and Fiat terminated production in 1982. This is the best documented decline of multinational interest in Chilean industry over the last few years. Imports of Japanese manufactured Datsun, Daihatsu, Suzuki, Toyota and Subaru cars accounted for 40 per cent of the Chilean market in 1982. The two remaining companies, Peugeot/Renault and General Motors, have only a 25 per cent market share and plan to terminate production by 1986, unless the rules are changed.

Direct foreign investment has been attracted into Chile - but the manufacturing sector has not been a major recipient. Between the passing of 'Decree Law 600' in 1976 and end of 1982 US$1,789 million had been invested in Chile by foreign companies. However, in sharp contrast to the Brazilian case, only 23 per cent of this investment had been in manufacturing. Instead, 40 per cent of this investment had been in mining and 30 per cent in services. Much of the US$412 million invested by foreign companies in Chilean manufacturing industry between 1976 and 1982 had been in export-oriented industry such as fish-meal and metal refining. Other major manufacturing investments have been in petrochemicals (Esso, Dow, Shell), cement (Portland, Blue Circle), tyres (Firestone, Goodyear) and food products

131

(Ambrosoli, Coca Cola). Only five of the largest fifty private firms in Chile in 1978 (assets greater than US$20 million) were foreign owned (Dahse, 1979).

When plants and firms were sold back to private enterprise in the mid-1970s it was national rather than multinational companies that bought up the manufacturing installations. For example, Unilever was not interested in repurchasing their old Chilean subsidiary, Indus Lever, and one of the powerful economic groups in Chile, the Grupo Vial, gained control. A small collection of powerful economic groups emerged in Chile. Through access to cheap international finance and control of banks in Chile, they were able to purchase from the government, uninterested multinationals and smaller firms, significant amounts of Chile's manufacturing base. By the end of 1978 the largest group, Cruzat-Larrain, had assets in thirty-four manufacturing companies, and the Grupo Vial controlled fifteen manufacturing companies. The next four largest groups had interests in a further thirty-eight manufacturing companies. As a footnote, one could add that the two most powerful groups, Cruzat-Larrain and Vial, needed to take out huge loans on the international currency markets in order to finance these empires. When the peso was devalued against the US dollar in mid-1982, their dollar debts rose against their peso assets, and they both met financial ruin in January 1983, at which stage the government intervened. As a consequence, the government has once again to decide how to dispose of a significant number of manufacturing companies.

The Chilean example has served to demonstrate how MNCs have become less significant in the manufacturing sector of a small country that opened up its economy to outside competition. A similar pattern has also been noted in other small countries such as Uruguay and Peru and even in countries of moderate size such as Argentina.

THE MOTOR VEHICLE MULTINATIONALS IN BRAZIL AND ARGENTINA

One study of Argentine industry in the late 1970s concluded that:

> There is little evidence of increased foreign ownership in manufacturing industry, largely because Argentina has been seen as an uncertain and shrinking market. Foreign capital may be attracted to specific projects, but its main form of participation during the Martinez de Hoz years was through the financial system (Schvarzer, 1983).

Such a conclusion is more than borne out by the experience of the motor vehicle industry since 1976. In that year there were still eight major producers in Argentina (Chrysler, Citroen, Fiat, Ford, General Motors, Mercedes Benz, Peugeot and Renault)

producing between them 186,000 vehicles (Gwynne, 1978b). Martinez
de Hoz then began to submit companies to increased competition
from imported vehicles, by lowering tariffs. Citroen and General
Motors closed down their plants and switched to becoming importers. Chrysler sold its Argentinian operations to Volkswagen
who have been studying ways of linking the plant to its large
Brazilian works. Fiat began to make large losses and sold
majority control to Peugeot, who in turn, sold a majority stake
to a local group, Francisco Marci; the new group was labelled
'Sevel' and is now the fourteenth largest firm in Argentina. Ford
(fourth largest firm in Argentina) and Renault (sixth largest)
are now the only multinationals operating car plants in
Argentina, while Mercedes Benz (seventeenth largest) concentrates
on truck manufacture.

The major problem of the Argentinian motor vehicle industry
(as with the Chilean) has been its inability to achieve significant economies of scale within an import-substitution framework.
In 1965, the industry's output was higher than that of Brazil
and in 1973 nearly 300,000 vehicles were produced. Subsequently,
however, vehicle production declined, reaching 190,000 in 1976
and 130,000 in 1982. The virtual dependence of the Argentine
motor-vehicle industry on the home market has caused it to become locked into a downward spiral, where a declining market
signifies lower production and consequent reductions in economies of scale, which in turn act to increase prices and lower
demand still further.

In contrast, the Brazilian domestic market increased to an
average of over 800,000 vehicles a year by the latter half of
the 1970s, a figure that allowed more than one manufacturer to
benefit from significant scale economies. As a result, and in
contrast to Argentina, multinationals have been actively competing to stay in production and to enter the Brazilian market.
In 1976 there were five significant vehicle producers in Brazil
- Chrysler, Ford, General Motors, Mercedes Benz (mainly trucks
and buses) and Volkswagen; Fiat had recently entered the market,
building a large plant in Minas Gerais. Subsequently, Chrysler
sold out to Volkswagen in 1978. The five multinationals have
found it difficult to achieve the requisite economies of scale
in the Brazilian market, particularly when the domestic market
fell to below 600,000 in 1981. In October 1982, after Fiat had
announced that it was pulling out of all its Latin American operations apart from Brazil, both Robert Garrity (President of
Ford do Brasil) and Joseph Sanchez (President of General Motors
do Brasil) stated that the Brazilian market was only large
enough for four big manufacturers, not five (*Latin America
Weekly Report*, October 29, 1982). The obvious target for the
remark was Fiat who since their entry into Brazil in late 1976,
had not managed to carve out a significant market share in
Brazil. In 1982, its domestic sales were only 44,000 and it
survived by exporting 103,000 cars back to Europe. As a
result Fiat made significant losses in Brazil in both 1981

and 1982, but according to the head of Fiat's international operations in 1983, Vittorio Ghidela, 'The key country in the South American car business will continue to be Brazil, and we are determined to stay there, even if the losses continue' (*Latin American Weekly Report*, April 2, 1983).

Vehicle MNCs have therefore differentiated between large and smaller countries as Latin American economies generally have become more open. During the closed import-substitution phase of industrial development, MNCs achieved greatest success in terms of reducing costs and increasing demand in the larger countries of Latin America. Their record in the smaller countries was generally much poorer. As Latin American economies became more open in the 1970s, MNCs have responded by staying and competing fiercely in the larger countries. In the smaller countries, they have either virtually left (Chile) or have left the market to a much smaller number of producers (Argentina). As a result, it is the larger countries that appear to have benefited most from the contribution of MNCs to the triple alliance. In the smaller countries, the MNCs that remain still basically focus on the domestic market and exports of vehicles and components are minimal. In the larger countries, however, the MNCs (as with the Fiat case) are forced to export in order to survive in the market they regard as vital. In the case of Brazil, the need for the MNCs to export meant that the full effect of the 1981 crisis (when domestic sales fell by 40 per cent) was reduced when vehicle exports rose by 37 per cent. While MNC vehicle exports had been just over ten per cent of domestic sales in 1980, in 1981 this ratio rose to nearly 25 per cent. In the smaller countries, meanwhile, a domestic crisis in sales is usually followed by the departure of one of the multinational producers.

The progressive opening of the Latin American economies to the world market has resulted in the triple alliance evolving differently according to size of country. In the larger countries (most notably Brazil and Mexico), MNC interest in production is high and government policy aims to control and often restrict multinational participation - as with the mini-computer industry in Brazil. Governments concentrate on pre-serving the interests of the other two sections of the triple alliance. In smaller countries, on the other hand, multi-national interest has been lower and even governments enthusiastic about the involvement of multinational enterprise have been unable to attract much direct foreign investment in manufacturing. In these countries, the national private enterprise has asserted itself as the major element of the triple alliance - as in both Chile and Argentina.

Latin American industrialization, in contrast to the industrialization of Europe, United States and Japan, has developed within the institutional framework of a triple alliance of state firms, MNC and national private enterprise. Within the process of industrialization, each has developed a well-defined role.

To a certain extent, the three contrasting roles have been compatible, particularly in the more mature industrial countries of Brazil and Mexico. Nevertheless, the fact that MNCs are playing such a critical role in the development of the more dynamic and technologically-innovative sectors may have serious implications for the long-term stability of the industrialization process in Latin America generally.

REFERENCES

Congdon, T.G. (1982) 'Apertura policies in the course of Latin America', *The World Economy*, 5(2): 133-148.
Cunningham, S.M. (1981) 'Multinational Enterprises in Brazil: Locational Patterns and Implications for Regional Development', *Professional Geographer*, 1981, 33(1), p.48.
Dahse, F. (1979), *El mapa de la extrema riqueza*, Editorial Aconcagua, Santiago.
Dickinson, J.P. (1978) *Brazil*, Dawson, Folkestone.
Gereffi, G. and Evans, P. (1981) 'Transnational Corporation, Dependent Development and State Policy in the Semiperiphery: A Comparison of Brazil and Mexico', *Latin American Research Review*, 16(3): 31-64.
Gunderson, G.S. (1979) The Worldwide Corporation - an economic catalyst, unpublished paper, IGU Commission on Industrial Systems, Rotterdam Symposium.
Gwynne, R.N. (1978a) 'Government Planning and the Location of the Motor Vehicle Industry in Chile, *Tijdschrift voor Econ. Soc. Geog.*, 69: 130-140.
Gwynne, R.N. (1978b) 'The Motor Vehicle Industry in Latin America', *Bank of London and South America Review*, 12(9): 462-471.
Gwynne, R.N. (1979) 'Oligopolistic reaction', *Area*, 11(4): 315-319.
Knickerbocker, F.T. (1973) *Oligopolistic Reaction and the Multinational Enterprise*, Harvard University Press, Cambridge, Mass.
Latin America Weekly Report, 29 October, 1982.
Latin America Weekly Report, 2 April, 1983.
Lenin, V.I. (1916) *Imperialism: the Highest Stage of Capitalism*, (in Russian), 13th English edn 1966, Progress Publishers, Moscow.
Lewis, W.A. (1955) *The Theory of Economic Growth*, George Allen and Unwin, London.
Roxborough, I. (1979) *Theories of Underdevelopment*, Macmillan, London.
Schvarzer, J. (1983) *Cambios en el liderazgo industrial argentino en el periodo de Martinez de Hoz*, CISEA, Buenos Aires.

Sigmund, P.E. (1980) *Multinationals in Latin America: The Politics of Nationalization*, University of Wisconsin Press, Madison.

Tyler, W.G. (1981) *The Brazilian Industrial Economy*, Heath, Lexington, (Mass.).

United Nations Economic Commission for Latin America (1979), *International cooperation for industrial development in Latin America (1979)*, Proceedings of the Second Latin American Conference on Industrialisation, Cali, Colombia.

Vernon, R. (1978) *Storm over the multinationals: the real issues*, Macmillan, London.

West, P.J. (1977) The Tyre Multinationals: A Study of Foreign Investment and Technology Transfer in Latin America, unpublished PhD thesis, University of Sussex.

West, P.J. (1978) Venezuela: foreign investment policy, *Bank of London and South America Review*, 12(3): 118.

Chapter Seven

MULTINATIONAL CORPORATIONS, THE STATE AND
INDIGENOUS BEER PRODUCTION IN CENTRAL AFRICA

C.M. Rogerson and B.A. Tucker

INTRODUCTION

The appearance of two important collections of material in 1975
marked a watershed in the academic study of MNCs (Multinational
Corporations) in Africa (*Review of African Political Economy*,
1975; Widstrand, 1975). Together these works sharply exposed
the various and often contradictory roles assumed by MNCs in
Africa - as vanguards of modern technology but also as purveyors
of obsolete equipment, as rapacious exploiters of Africa's pre-
cious resources, both of its peoples and raw materials, but also
as vital allies of petty bourgeois and even of 'progressive'
African governments, as sources of sorely needed injections of
capital but also as major agents of surplus extraction and resource outflow. Most importantly, perhaps, the publication of
these two studies was a springboard for further investigations
as they firmly situated the activities and role of MNCs on the
research agenda of African scholars.
     Over the past decade a stream of writings have investigated
and debated aspects of the operations and developmental impress
of MNCs in Africa. At the centre of this literature are those
theoretical discussions surrounding the concepts of dependency,
imperialism and the spread of capitalist relations of production
into a segment of the global periphery (Seidman, 1977, 1979;
Shaw and Grieve, 1977; Fransman, 1982; Leys, 1982). In particular, the trajectory of development and capital accumulation
in the settings of Kenya and Ivory Coast have engendered considerable controversy on the nexus of the internationalization
of capital, class formation and the African State (for examples
see Langdon, 1974, 1977; Campbell, 1975; Godfrey and Langdon,
1976; Swainson, 1977; Masini *et al.*, 1979; Swainson, 1980;
Kaplinsky, 1982; Leys, 1982; Marcussen and Torp, 1982). Com-
plementing this literature has been a host of sector-specific
studies which investigate the penetration of MNCs both into the
traditional colonial spheres of agriculture and primary resource
extraction and the more recent arena of secondary manufacturing.
Investigations of MNCs and Africa's mineral wealth continue to

137

emphasize the vital role of foreign mining companies in reinfor-
cing the continent's underdevelopment (Bonté, 1975; Carlsson,
1977, 1982; Lanning and Mueller, 1979; Graham, 1982;
O'Faircheallaigh, 1984).   Also critical of the developmental
effect of MNC penetration are those works dealing with the role
of agribusiness in Africa, both in terms of export crops production, such as sugar or coffee, or increasingly in terms of
schemes for large-scale food production (Cronje *et al*., 1976;
Tickner, 1977; Dinham and Hines, 1983; Oculi, 1984).   The
entry of MNCs into the newer realm of African manufacturing has
catalysed research into their employment effects (Kaplinsky,
1979a), locational behaviour (Abumere, 1978, 1982; Rogerson,
1981b, 1982, 1985), debates on the impact of 'appropriate technologies' and taste transfer (Langdon, 1975; Kaplinsky, 1979b;
Van der Wees, 1981) and a questioning of the benefits accruing
to African countries venturing along the paths of industrial
import-substitution (Seidman, 1974; Dietz *et al*., 1977; Crush,
1979) and export-processing (Langdon, 1978; Wellings, 1984).
The geographical concentration of MNC manufacturing investments
within South Africa has given rise to a substantial body of
writings chronicling the volume, nature and organization of these
enterprises (Rogerson, 1981a, 1981b, 1982) and their contribution
towards buttressing the oppressive structures of apartheid
(Seidman and Seidman, 1977; Seidman and Makgetla, 1979, 1980).
Along similar lines of analysis, researchers also identified the
scope and support afforded to the illegal white minority regime
in colonial Zimbabwe by MNCs (Clarke, 1980; Makgetla, 1980).
Although the overwhelming mass of MNCs operating in Africa origi-
nate in developed countries, the recent entry of a trickle of
developing country or 'Third World' multinationals (Linge, 1984)
into Africa has attracted some concern both in Nigeria (Nambudiri
et al., 1981; Nambudiri, 1983) and South Africa (Rogerson,
1985).

There now exists a growing body of literature on Africa as
a *host* to MNCs based in Europe, North America or Asia, but much
less attention has been accorded to MNCs originating and based
in Africa. The most notable studies of Africa as a *source* for
the emergence of MNCs are contained in works which examine the
internationalization of South African capital (Kaplan, 1983;
Innes, 1984; Wellings, 1984; Tucker, 1985a).   It is the task
in this paper to augment this relatively meagre literature on
Africa as a source for MNCs.   More specifically, the intention
is to focus upon the commercialized production of a traditional
form of African beer, manufactured from sorghum grain, which is
commonly made throughout the continent.   The Central African
beer industry affords a valuable case study in the commercialization of an indigenous product and of the emergence of an incipient developing-country multinational (see Wells, 1983; Linge,
1984).   The fledgling Third World multinational was short-lived,
however, because the sorghum beer industry was penetrated suc-
cessively by large scale British and South African based inter-

national capital.

The geographical focus of this investigation is Central Africa (Fig. 7.1), specifically the contemporary independent nations of Zambia and Zimbabwe which were formerly the British colonies of Northern and Southern Rhodesia[1].   Temporally, the years spanned by this investigation are those of the politically turbulent decades of the 1960s and 1970s.   This period marked the ending of White settler-colonial rule in Central Africa with the southward march of political decolonization.   The struggle for independence in the former British colonies of Central Africa was punctuated by the dramas of the break-up of the Federation of Rhodesia and Nyasaland, the granting of political freedom to Black-ruled Zambia and Malawi, the unilateral declaration of independence by the White settlers in Southern Rhodesia and the escalating liberation struggle climaxing in 1981 with the independence of Zimbabwe.   The politically fluid environment of African decolonization struggles and the changing nature of the State in transition from colonialism constitutes the essential backcloth to this investigation in the geography of MNCs.

HISTORICAL BACKGROUND

In light of colonial attitudes towards alcohol in Africa (Pan, 1975) it is remarkable that the continent would be fertile territory for the emergence of a nascent international manufacturing enterprise centred upon beer.   Considerable controversy surrounded the introduction, production and consumption of alcohol in colonial Africa.   Indeed, during the late nineteenth century the traffic in liquor from Europe to Africa was denounced alongside slavery as one of the continent's two great evils (Pan, 1975).   The imperial powers in Africa participated at conferences in Berlin (1884) and Brussels (1889-90) considering measures to control by international agreement the flourishing liquor trade, especially in Dutch gin.   In 1890 the Brussels Act established a prohibition zone across the continent between latitudes 20 north and 22 south in which the signatory governments undertook to prohibit the importation and distillation of spirituous liquors in those parts where their use did not already exist.   Concern for the control on alcohol in colonial Africa was again expressed during the Peace Conference following the First World War. A commission appointed to consider the results of earlier efforts spawned the 1919 St Germain-en-Laye Convention which sought to continue the struggle against alcoholism in Africa.   The preamble to the convention declared that it was 'necessary to prohibit the importation of distilled beverages rendered more especially dangerous to the native population by the nature of the products entering into their composition or by the opportunities which a low price gives for their extended use' (Pan, 1975: 41).   Notwithstanding these international pronouncements, the importation and local production of alcohol

139

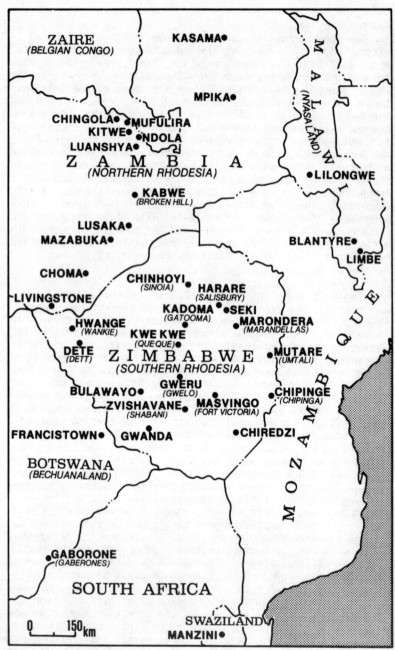

Figure 7.1: Central Africa

140

continued to grow and expanded through colonial Africa during the twentieth century.

The colonizers of Africa were responsible for the diffusion of a range of new spirits and liquors, but there is another lesser known thread which runs through the continent's history of alcohol production. Throughout much of Central and Southern Africa the traditional alcoholic drink was a fermented beer made from malted sorghum or millet (Novellie, 1968). Traditional sorghum beer is quite unlike the lager beers of Western Europe or North America. The period of brewing time for sorghum beer is considerably less than that for lager beers and the final product is pinkish brown in colour, slightly sour in taste and opaque in appearance because of its high content of suspended solids and yeasts (Novellie, 1968). Moreover, the fermentation process of sorghum beer continues right up to the time of consumption. Variously this indigenous form of beer was styled as 'African', 'native' or 'kaffir' beer by the colonial settlers and as *utshwala, doro* or more recently *chibuku* in the local vernacular.

The production of sorghum beer in Central Africa evolved along different organizational channels to that of the European-type lager beers. In rural areas, the manufacture of sorghum beer remained the traditional preserve of the African woman brewer. In the newly mushrooming urban foci of colonial Africa, the role of the woman brewer was supplanted progressively by the initiation of a unique system of local state monopoly in the manufacture of sorghum beer (Rogerson, 1986). The origins of the so-called 'Durban System' of municipal monopoly are rooted in the history of 'native administration' in South Africa (Swanson, 1976). In 1908 the local state in Durban established a monopoly in the production of *utshwala* with the revenues accruing from beer sales being channelled to funding new segregated 'native' townships, barrack-like hostels and other elements of 'native welfare' expenditure (La Hausse, 1984). Quintessentially, the beer monopoly represented a means whereby the urban African labour force subsidized the costs of its own reproduction and correspondingly minimized the costs of 'native administration' to the settler colonial state (Swanson, 1976; Maylam, 1983). Great interest was stirred by the Durban experiment in instituting a municipal brewing monopoly, not only in South Africa and the surrounding British colonies in Central Africa, but also as far afield as Uganda and even Sudan (La Hausse, 1984). The Durban system was gradually extended as a model for native administration in South Africa and, especially in the Transvaal, a system of municipal monopoly in the production, distribution and sale of sorghum beer became widespread (Rogerson, 1986).

Outside of South Africa, the municipal monopoly system was adopted by colonial administrations in the territories of Northern and Southern Rhodesia. Although by no means as extensive as the system of municipal brewing in South Africa, the practice of a local state monopoly in sorghum beer manufacture was established in both of Britain's Rhodesian colonies. Indeed, the less developed participation by the colonial state in sorghum beer manufacture, leaving a niche open for private enterprise and individual brewers, distinguishes the history of the industry in Central Africa from that of South Africa, where the local state monopoly was strongly entrenched.

Prior to the adoption of the municipal brewing system in Central Africa, the sorghum beer industry was dominated by the traditional woman household brewer. On the mines and colonial settler farms the imperative for some control on the availability of alcohol to African workers led to the licensing of individuals, as a class of petty commodity producers, to brew and sell beer in the compounds (Van Onselen, 1976). The foundations for the municipalization of brewing in Southern Rhodesia were laid with the 1911 Kaffir Beer Ordinance (Salisbury, 1911). Bulawayo was the first municipality to establish a brewery in 1913 for beer production along the lines of the Durban system (*Chronicle*, 17 January 1913; Bulawayo, 1913). In the colonial capital, Salisbury, the construction of a municipal brewery was deferred until 1938 (Salisbury, 1938) and for almost a quarter century the municipality commissioned the local malt beer manufacturer to produce sorghum beer for sale in the municipal beer halls (*Rhodesia Herald*, 11 December 1914; Salisbury, 1914). Smaller urban centres chose to license individual Africans to brew sorghum beer for municipal sale (Gwelo, 1926; Umtali, 1926; Fort Victoria, 1953). Only in the late 1950s did such centres as Gwelo and Umtali shift to the replacement of these individual brewers by the erection of formal municipal-run breweries (Gwelo, 1956; Umtali, 1960). In Northern Rhodesia, a similar trajectory of the sorghum beer industry was in evidence. Rural areas were served by the 'informal sector' women household brewers whereas urban municipalities preferred to contract individual African brewers to produce their requirements of 'native' beer (Pridham Jones, 1957). Only in Lusaka and Ndola were there established municipal-run breweries on the South African model. The final component of sorghum beer manufacture in Central Africa was the small-scale illegal township brewers of *chibuku* who operated throughout the colonial urban centres of Northern and Southern Rhodesia (Jules-Rosette, 1981).

THE EMERGENCE OF HEINRICH CHIBUKU BREWERIES

By the mid-1950s the sorghum beer industry in Central Africa comprised a diverse mix of municipal breweries in the largest urban centres, smaller municipalities commissioning individual brewers, mine-compound brewing and the continuation of the traditional practices of *chibuku* brewing legally in the rural areas and illegally in the squatter settlements and peri-urban areas of the cities. Hitherto, private enterprise was excluded from the sorghum beer industry of Central Africa. From 1955 this picture began to be transformed dramatically by the entry and growth of the independent sorghum brewing concern, Heinrich Syndicate Ltd.

The South African based industrialist, Max Heinrich, founded Heinrich Syndicate Ltd. in Northern Rhodesia in 1955. Preceding the formation of this concern sorghum beer brewing equipment was exported from South Africa to the mines and municipalities of the Copperbelt. Although Heinrich's South African interests were important suppliers of brewing equipment, the company was not directly engaged in the manufacture of sorghum beer, being excluded by the system of municipal monopoly (Heinrich, 1984). In Northern Rhodesia, Heinrich entered into the brewing business, securing contracts to produce sorghum beer, marketed under the name *chibuku*, both for the town management board of the Copperbelt centre of Kitwe and of a local mine, operated by the Rhokana Mine Corporation. Rapid expansion of the company's operations ensued with further Copperbelt mine contracts at Nchanga, Mufulira and Luanshya. So successful was the Heinrich Kitwe brewery in supplying the requirements of the mines that it began to threaten and eventually took over the Ndola municipal brewery. The absorption of the Ndola brewery greatly expanded Heinrich's activity in Northern Rhodesia, affording a springboard for the company to begin distribution of *chibuku* throughout the colony (Van Blommestein, 1984). By 1960, only five years after its inception in Northern Rhodesia, Heinrich's *chibuku* was sold in virtually all urban townships of Northern Rhodesia, except the capital Lusaka where the municipality retained its sorghum beer brewing monopoly. Three years later Heinrich's was operating a total of nine sorghum beer breweries to serve the African market in Northern Rhodesia. The growth of the company's operations within Northern Rhodesia was accompanied by a programme of corporate diversification. The first investments by Heinrich outside of sorghum beer production were situated at Kitwe, which was the company's headquarters. Diversification occurred through the purchase of a local hotel and the building of the first dry ice plant in the Federation of Rhodesias and Nyasaland. Further expansion took Heinrich into a range of manufactures, including matches, yeast and nails but most significant was the company's purchase of two of the colony's leading newspapers (the daily *Zambia News* and the weekly *Zambia Times*) which gave Heinrich Syndicate an influential position in the critical watershed years of the early 1960s when Zambia achieved political independence (*Development*, 1963).

In terms of the geography of the sorghum beer industry in Central Africa, the event of greatest significance was the first expansion of Heinrich outside of its Northern Rhodesia core area of operations. The initial move outside Northern Rhodesia was an abortive entry into the Nyasaland colony where in 1960 the company was granted permission to construct a brewery at Limbe. The Nyasaland venture was short-lived, however, for within months of Malawi's independence the licence for Heinrich's

Nyasaland operation was summarily withdrawn and the sorghum beer plant closed (Van Blommestein, 1984). Not for the last time in its evolution, the corporate geography of Heinrich's brewing would be shaped by the politics of Central Africa.

More successful was the spread of Heinrich's sorghum beer operations into the colony of Southern Rhodesia. The establishment of Heinrich within Southern Rhodesia occurred in 1961 amidst considerable opposition from the four municipal authorities (Bulawayo, Gwelo, Salisbury and Umtali) which had by this time initiated municipal breweries under their aegis. Until 1961 the colonial government had not permitted private enterprise to participate in the business of sorghum beer manufacture. After securing the blessing of the colonial state with the grant of a licence, Heinrich secured a contract to supply *chibuku* beer to the municipality of Fort Victoria. The Mayor of Fort Victoria opined that the major advantage of contracting to private enterprise was 'that the risk of sour beer is reduced to a minimum and, in fact, if the beer is not to the palate of the consumer, the suppliers undertake to replenish the stock with palatable beer' (Fort Victoria, 1961). From its first foothold in Southern Rhodesia in the small urban centre of Fort Victoria, Heinrich expanded rapidly; by 1962 breweries had been established to supply the municipalities of Que Que and Sinoia (Fig. 7.2). Behind the popularity of Heinrich's *chibuku* beer was the consistency of the product and its status as an alternative to municipally brewed beer.

By 1963, however, the strains of Heinrich's ambitious dual programmes of diversification and geographical spread were becoming manifest. In particular, corporate finances of this Zambian based concern were severely affected by the expansion into Southern Rhodesia, losses on their newspaper interests in Zambia and the unsuccessful adventure into Malawi. In order to secure additional finance to succour further extension of Heinrich's operations, support was sought from larger enterprises. Successful negotiations were concluded with the British-based Lonrho group and in 1963 Lonrho acquired the entire shareholding of the Kitwe-based organization. The era of the incipient developing-country multinational was thus short-lived as the Central Africa sorghum beer industry came under the influence of Lonrho. The absorption of Heinrich's diverse operations into Lonrho was accompanied by corporate reorganization which precipitated the formation of two sorghum brewing subsidiaries, *viz.*, National Breweries in Zambia and Heinrich Chibuku Breweries Ltd in Southern Rhodesia (Cronje, *et al.*, 1976).

LONRHO AND SORGHUM BEER

Lonrho's entry into the sorghum beer industry during 1963 occurred at a time of increasing flux in the political and economic complexion of Central Africa. Following the dissolution of

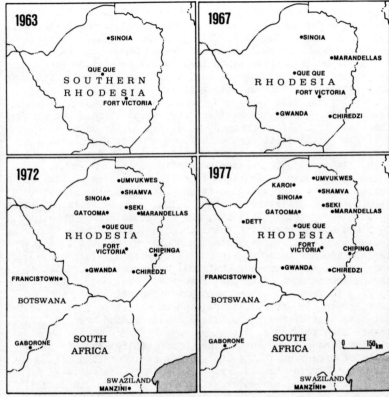

Figure 7.2: The Corporate Growth of Chibuku Sorghum Beer Brewing in Colonial
Zimbabwe, 1963–1977
Source: Heinrich Chibuku, Rhodesian Breweries and Delta
Corporation Annual Reports.

the Federation of Rhodesia and Nyasaland, the two northern colonies moved swiftly to achieve independence, respectively as the new states of Zambia in 1964 and Malawi in 1966. Resistance to the march of African decolonization was propelling the Southern Rhodesian white settler state towards the fateful declaration of UDI in 1965, plunging the region into an escalating situation of political and increasingly military struggle.

During the 1960s the external environment of ongoing decolonization struggles began to affect the organization of the sorghum beer industry. After the heady early days after decolonization a tide of nationalist fervour gripped much of ex-colonial Africa. The hostility between white-ruled Rhodesia and black-ruled Zambia made increasingly difficult the direction of Lonrho's expanding operations from its Kitwe base in Zambia. In response to this changing political climate Lonrho sought to re-structure its activities in the region. Separate companies were incorporated in Salisbury and Kitwe, splitting the hitherto combined operations of the Heinrich Syndicate: Heinrich Chibuku Breweries Ltd was incorporated in Southern Rhodesia to acquire sorghum brewery interests in Fort Victoria, Sinoia and Que Que, and a new Zambian company, National Breweries was created to manage the network of sorghum breweries developed in the territory. In remoulding the corporate organization of sorghum beer brewing in Central Africa, Lonrho effectively made the two national subsidiaries responsible to its London headquarters rather than to Zambia.

The financial weight of the Lonrho empire launched a new phase of expansion in the Central African operations of its sorghum beer brewing subsidiary. Growth was especially marked during the period 1964-1967 with rapid new corporate expansion occurring in Zambia. From its Kitwe headquarters, National Breweries Ltd developed an impressive geographical spread of *chibuku* breweries in small urban centres along the main communications axis between Chililabomwe and Livingstone as well as in the northern provinces. Consolidation and extension of Lonrho's Zambian operations corresponded to a quiescent and problematic phase of the activities of the newly incorporated Heinrich Chibuku Breweries in Southern Rhodesia. Mounting opposition from local authorities surrounding the competitive threat posed by the company to municipal brewers precipitated considerable tension between local authorities and the central state over the rights granted to private enterprise to partici-pate in sorghum beer manufacture in the territory (Bulawayo, 1963; Salisbury, 1964). A climax was reached in early 1964 when the Minister of Local Government ordered a suspension of the issuance of licences to private enterprise sorghum beer brewers. Lonrho's future expansion and further penetration of the lucrative Rhodesian market was thus threatened by this pro-tection of the municipal brewing monopolies and consequently the company actively lobbied against this action (Van Blommes-tein, 1984). Support for the continuing participation of private enterprise in the sorghum beer industry in Southern Rhodesia was particularly strong in the Lowveld where the sugar plantations favoured the organized supply offered by Heinrich Chibuku instead of their existing network of 'informal' African brewers. In light of the considerable influence exercised by the Lonrho group in Central Africa (Cronje, *et al.*, 1976) the reversal of the central state's decision on the issuance of brewing licences was perhaps not unexpected. The decision allowed the further advance of Heinrich Chibuku operations within Southern Rhodesia with new breweries constructed at Marandellas, Gwanda and Chiredzi (Chibuku, 1976).

With technological and management experience in the sorghum brewing industry in Zambia and Southern Rhodesia, Lonrho was well equipped to embark on an expansion of their operations into Malawi, Botswana and Swaziland. In 1964 Lonrho began negotiations with the Malawian government in an attempt to create a further 'national' sorghum brewing subsidiary. Although an earlier attempt to set up brewing facilities in Malawi by the Heinrich Syndicate had failed, Lonrho was awarded licences to brew at Lilongwe and Limbe - two centres which afforded excellent bases for the marketing of *chibuku* beer. The Malawian operation was financed by Lonrho's headquarter offices in London but management and technological agreements tied the enterprise to National Breweries of Zambia. The growth of Lonrho's brewing activities in Southern Africa was spearheaded by Heinrich Chibuku Breweries in Southern Rhodesia who negotiated with government officials for the establishment of brewing operations in the newly-independent states of Botswana and Swaziland (Van Blommestein, 1984). In neither of these former British colonies had there evolved a system of municipal brewing as existed in South Africa and the former Rhodesian colonies. Instead, the brewing of sorghum beer remained largely a traditional pursuit supplemented by groups of petty commodity producers. During 1967 Lonrho entered a joint investment venture with the Tati Trading Company to brew sorghum beer in Botswana. The consortium floated a new company, Botswana Breweries, and within a year of the licensing approval, had established a brewery in Gaborone. Paralleling the expansion into Botswana were developments in Swaziland where Lonrho established Heinrich Swaziland Breweries, and commenced for the first time brewing operations in the country.

If the creation of new national subsidiaries was a response to the changing political environment in Africa, it failed to disguise the extensive operations by Lonrho in White-ruled Rhodesia, the focus of international sanctions. The Rhodesian sorghum beer breweries increasingly became a sensitive issue for Lonrho, more especially as opposition from Black Africa mounted towards international investment in the rebel colony (Cronje *et al.*, 1976). Against the external backdrop of political tension and an internal liquidity crisis at London head office, Lonrho decided to dispose of some of the company's lucrative, but readily saleable, enterprises in Rhodesia. Accordingly, between 1968 and 1972, Lonrho progressively divested itself of interests in sorghum beer brewing within Botswana, Swaziland and, most importantly, Rhodesia. Significantly, it was South African capital, in the form of South African Breweries Ltd, which stepped into this niche vacated by British capital. The entry of South African Breweries, the major producers of malt beers both in South Africa and Rhodesia, marked the company's first venture into sorghum beer since the municipal takeover of brewing in Salisbury, where until 1938, South African Breweries was under contract to manufacture sorghum beer (Salisbury, 1914; South African Breweries, 1972). It was ironic that in Rhodesia South African Breweries was entering into a sphere of brewing operations in which they were entirely excluded in South Africa by the system of state monopoly.

The importance of these events was that they ushered in a new corporate geography of sorghum beer manufacture in Central Africa. Henceforth the industry was divided geographically between Lonrho and South African Breweries with British capital in a northward retreat in Africa, leaving South African capital to establish a sphere of influence of its immediate hinterland. Beyond expanding to a total of twenty breweries in Zambia, the major attention of Lonrho was directed to the new possibilities for sorghum beer manufacture in Black Africa; during the 1970s the first thrusts occurred with the opening (and in some instances the rapid closing) of breweries in Kenya, Ghana and Uganda (Cronje *et al.*, 1976; Van Blommestein, 1984). With the withdrawal of Lonrho the geography of sorghum beer manufacture became dominated increasingly by the operations of the restyled Salisbury-based Heinrich Chibuku Breweries (1968) Ltd which by 1972 was under South African control. The international politics of Southern Africa thus resulted in a recast of the corporate spatial organization of the sorghum beer industry within less than a decade.

SORGHUM BEER - THE SOUTH AFRICAN CONNECTION

South African corporate control of the sorghum beer industry south of the Zambezi was achieved from 1967 onwards through progressive share purchases by Rhodesian Breweries, the local majority owned subsidiary of South African Breweries Ltd (Tucker, 1985b). After securing control of Heinrich (1968) Rhodesia in 1972 (Rhodesian Breweries Ltd, 1967, 1969, 1971; Heinrich Chibuku, 1972) the evolution of the sorghum beer industry in Rhodesia becomes dominated by South African corporate involvement in a pariah international state which was in the final throes of sloughing off White settler colonial rule. Accompanying the success of the liberation struggle and the shift towards a rhetorically 'socialist' regime in Zimbabwe, the transformed political landscape in the region vitally affected the prospects

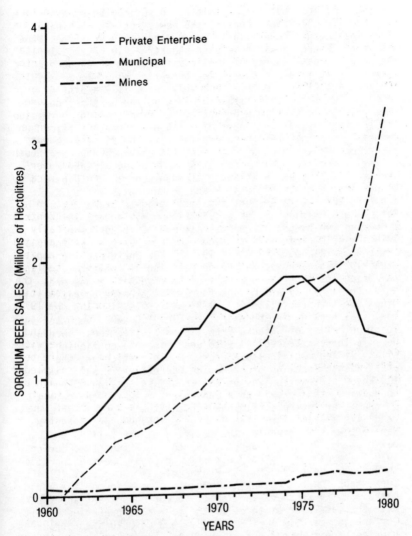

Figure 7.3: The Changing Structure of the Sorghum Beer Market in Colonial
Zimbabwe, 1960–1980.
Source: Rooney, 1977; Delta Corporation Annual Reports.

for South African capital, not least in sorghum beer manfacture.

Under South African control the newly restyled Chibuku Breweries began to consolidate and further extend its position within the Rhodesian sorghum beer industry (Fig. 7.2). In 1972 the proportionate shares of the industry which were contributed by municipal, mine and commercial breweries were 56 per cent, 3 per cent and 41 per cent respectively (Fig. 7.3), a distribution which would be radically transformed over the next decade (Rooney, 1977). Chibuku Breweries embarked upon an aggressive growth strategy, at the heart of which was the acquisition of competing sorghum brewing enterprises. The first task was to secure monopoly status as the country's only private enterprise brewer. The foundations for attaining this goal were laid in the transition years when South African control of Chibuku was being established. In 1969 and again in 1971 the company absorbed through take-over, two small private breweries at Gatooma and Chipinga. The acquisition of six additional sorghum breweries run by private enterprise made Chibuku Breweries by 1978 the sole commercial producers of sorghum beer in the country (*Rhodesia Herald*, 2 April 1977). Now the thrust of corporate expansion was directed to the competition of the extant municipal breweries (increased from four to five with a new brewery at Victoria Falls) and of the four small brewing operations at mines (Delta Corporation Ltd, 1981, 1982, 1983). The demise of municipal brewing in Rhodesia (see Fig. 7.3) owed much to the location policy of Chibuku Breweries who sited their sorghum beer factories strategically to undermine the continuing viability of the municipal producers. In particular, the policy of strategic location of breweries was evident in Salisbury where the Chibuku Breweries was established just outside the municipal boundaries, thus providing a convenient base for the sale of sorghum beer to the contiguous African townships. A massive (and illegal) infiltration occurred of Chibuku products into Harare township weakening the position of the Salisbury municipal brewery (Rufaro Brewery, 1976) to the extent that during 1979 the municipality sold out its municipal brewing operations to Chibuku (Heinrich Chibuku Press Release, 30 July 1979). Further steps towards Chibuku's complete domination of the sorghum beer industry south of the Zambezi occurred in 1981 and 1982 with the take-over of three of the four mine breweries (Delta Corporation Ltd, 1981, 1982). By 1983 Chibuku's corporate expansion programme had established the company as the country's leading sorghum beer producer (Fig. 7.4), with almost three-quarters of the market; the only serious challenge to Chibuku was the Bulawayo municipal brewery which produced approximately a fifth of Zimbabwe's production (Bulawayo, 1984). Accompanying this major growth in sorghum brewing over the decade 1972-1982 was a programme of corporate diversification taking the company into allied spheres of production to beer (Fig. 7.5). Among a suite of activities managed by Chibuku Holdings, the most important centred around the manufacture of food enzymes, starch,

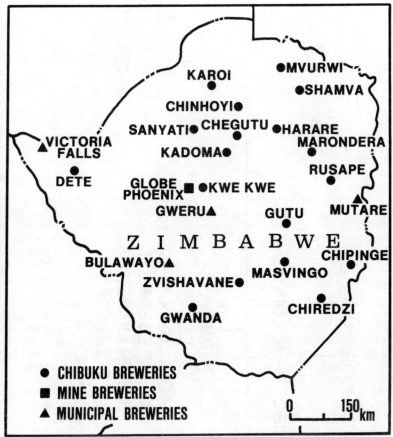

Figure 7.4: The Geography of the Sorghum Beer Industry in Zimbabwe, 1983.
Source: Delta Corporation Annual Report, Mayor's Minutes of
Bulawayo, Gweru and Mutare, 1983.

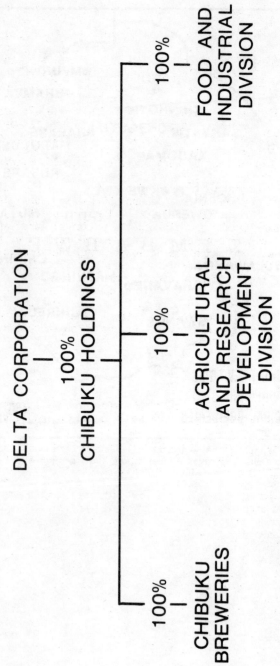

Figure 7.5: The Corporate Organization of Chibuku Holdings.
Source: Delta Corporation Annual Reports

breakfast cereals, beer powder and brewer's grits (Delta Corporation Ltd, 1982).

The international political environment of economic sanctions and hostility towards the illegal Smith regime severely constrained the operations of Chibuku Breweries outside of the rebel colony. Given the blockages on northward expansion in Africa, possible new spheres of growth existed only in those territories such as Botswana, Lesotho and Swaziland, which were quintessentially captive satellites of South Africa (Rogerson, 1981a, 1982). The inherited brewing operations in Botswana and Swaziland experienced mixed fortunes; in Botswana a second small brewery was established at Francistown but in Swaziland the existing sorghum beer brewery was closed down. Eventually, however, in 1978 the corporate spatial organization of beer manufacture was once more restructured with the sale by Chibuku of its Botswana operations to a Johannesburg-based subsidiary of South African Breweries Ltd (Tucker, 1985a). Black majority rule in Zimbabwe further transformed the political landscape confronting Chibuku Breweries. The new environment of post-1981 Zimbabwe was one which was no longer sympathetic to investment from apartheid South Africa. Reacting to these changed circumstances, the Zimbabwean parent company altered its name to Delta Corporation in an endeavour to distance themselves from their South African connections (Delta Corporation Ltd, 1979). South African control was retained indirectly, however, through reshuffling ownership to an offshore non-South African based corporation.

CONCLUSION

The historical investigation of the Central African sorghum beer industry demonstrates the great value of pursuing longitudinal research strategies concerning the growth and evolution of MNCs in the Third World. But the specific case of the commercialization of an indigenous African product is instructive in at least two further respects. First, it points to the existence of groups of small MNCs operating in the Third World whose genesis and continuing *raison d'être* are intertwined with the economic fortunes of products unique to certain cultural tastes or milieux. Expansion for the group of MNCs engaged in sorghum beer production could take place only in culturally similar environs to those of Central Africa thus circumscribing their horizon of future operations to the *regional* African scale. The dismal failure of attempts made during the 1960s to launch sorghum beer into Western European markets (Rogerson, 1986) and the continuing stranglehold of European-type lager beers upon the tastes of Africa's colonial-settlers attest to constraints of cultural barriers upon the potential for 'global reach' of many small MNCs, such as those based in sorghum beer. Second, our case study emphasizes the critical significance which attaches to examination of the colonial and post-colonial State in the Third World in interpreting the historical expansion of certain MNCs. Indeed, the interplay between MNCs and the contemporary State in the Third World appears a critical arena for future investigations.

Acknowledgements

Thanks are due to Phil Stickler for the preparation of all the diagrams which accompany this paper and to the South African Breweries Group for access to archival material in Johannesburg, Harare and Bulawayo.

Footnote

1. In terms of the period under investigation several name changes have occurred as a consequence of independence. The convention followed here is to use the name of the place as it was known at the time. Therefore at various times the same territory may be referred to by different names, *e.g.* Southern Rhodesia/Rhodesia/Zimbabwe.

REFERENCES

Abumere, S. (1978) 'Multinationals, location theory and regional development: case study of Bendel State of Nigeria', *Regional Studies*, 12: 651-664.

Abumere, S. (1982) 'Multinationals and industrialisation in a developing economy: the case of Nigeria, in: Taylor, M. J. and Thrift, H. (eds) *The Geography of Multinationals*, Croom Helm, London: 158-177.

Bonté, P. (1975) 'Multinational companies and national development: MIFERMA and Mauretania', *Review of African Political Economy*, 2: 89-109.

Bulawayo, Municipality of (1913-1984) Minute of His Worship the Mayor for the year ending 30 June.

Campbell, C. (1975) 'Neo-colonialism, economic dependence and political change: a case study of cotton and textile production in the Ivory Coast 1960-70', *Review of African Political Economy*, 2: 36-54.

Carlsson, J. (1977) *Transnational Companies in Liberia: The Role of Transnational Companies in the Economic Development of Liberia*, Scandinavian Institute of African Studies, Uppsala.

Carlsson, J. (1982) 'Gränges and the undermining of Liberia: a critique of a joint venture arrangement', *Review of African Political Economy*, 23: 72-84.

Chibuku (1976) 'What is Heinrich's Chibuku?', Internal Company Report, Mimeograph.

Chronicle, The (Bulawayo), Daily.

Clarke, D.G. (1980) *Foreign Companies and International Investment in Zimbabwe*, Mambo Press, Gwelo.

Cronje, S., Ling, M. and Cronje, G. (1976) *Lonhro: Portrait of a Multinational*, Julia Friedmann, London.

Crush, J.S. (1979) 'The parameters of dependence in Southern Africa: a case study of Swaziland', *Journal of Southern African Affairs*, 4: 55-66.

Delta Corporation Ltd (1979-1984), Annual Reports.

Development, Monthly, Lusaka.

Dietz, A.J., Van Haastrecht, J.M. and Scheffer, H.R. (1977) *Local Effects of Two Large Scale Industrial Projects in the Kafue-Mazabuka Area in Zambia: the Kafue Estate and Nakambula Sugar Estate*. Geografisch en Planologisch Instituut, Katholieke Universiteit, Nijmegen.

Dinham, G. and Hines, C. (1983) *Agribusiness in Africa*, Earth Resources Research, London.

Fort Victoria, Municipality of (1953-1961) Minute of His Worship the Mayor for the year ending 30 June.

Fransman, M. (ed.) (1982) *Industry and Accumulation in Africa*, Heinemann, London.

Godfrey, M. and Langdon, S. (1976) Partners in underdevelopment?: the transnationalisation thesis in a Kenyan context, *Journal of Commonwealth and Comparative Politics*, 14: 42-63.

Graham, R. (1982) *The Aluminium Industry and the Third World: Multinational Corporations and Underdevelopment*, Zed Press, London.

Gwelo, Municipality of (1926-1956) Minute of His Worship the Mayor for the Year ending 30 June.

Heinrich Chibuku Press Release (1979) Heinrich Chibuku Breweries (1968) Ltd., Press Release.

Heinrich Chibuku (1969-1976), Heinrich Chibuku Breweries (1968) Ltd., Annual Reports.

Heinrich, J. (1984) Interview, Chairman, Heinrich Group of Companies, Johannesburg, 28 February 1984.

Innes, D. (1984) *Anglo: Anglo American and the Rise of Modern South Africa*, Ravan, Johannesburg.

Jules-Rosette, B. (1981) *Symbols of Change: Urban Transition in a Zambian Community*, Ablex, Norwood, New Jersey.

Kaplan, D.E. (1983) The internationalization of South African capital: South African direct foreign investment in the contemporary period', *African Affairs*, 82: 465-494.

Kaplinsky, R. (1979a) *Employment Effects of Multinational*

Enterprises: a Case Study of Kenya, International Labour Office, Geneva.

Kaplinsky, R. (1979b) Inappropriate products and techniques: breakfast food in Kenya, *Review of African Political Economy*, 14: 90-96.

Kaplinsky, R. (1982) Capitalist accumulation in the periphery: Kenya, in Fransman, M. (ed.) *Industry and Accumulation in Africa*, Heinemann, London: 193-221.

La Hausse, P. (1984) 'The struggle for the city: alcohol, the emetsheni and popular culture in Durban, 1902-36', unpublished MA thesis, University of Cape Town.

Langdon, S. (1974) 'The political economy of dependence: note toward analysis of multinational corporations in Kenya', *Journal of East African Research and Development*, 4: 123-159.

Langdon, S. (1975) 'Multinational corporations, taste transfer and underdevelopment: a case study from Kenya', *Review of African Political Economy*, 2: 12-35.

Langdon, S. (1977) 'Multinational firms and the State in Kenya', *Bulletin, Institute of Development Studies*, 9 (1): 36-41.

Langdon, S. (1978) 'Export-oriented industrialization through the multinational corporation: evidence from Kenya', in Idris-Soven, A., Idris-Soven, E. and Vaughan, E. (eds.) *The World as a Company Town: Multinational Corporations and Social Change*, Mouton, The Hague: 295-319.

Lanning, G. and Mueller, M. (1979) *Africa Undermined: Mining Companies and the Underdevelopment of Africa*, Penguin, Harmondsworth.

Leys, C. (1982) 'Accumulation, class formation and dependency: Kenya', in Fransman, M. (ed.) *Industry and Accumulation in Africa*, London, Heinemann: 170-192.

Linge, G.J.R. (1984) 'Developing-country multinationals: a review of the literature', *Pacific Viewpoint*, 25: 173-195.

Makgetla, N.S. (1980) 'Transnational corporations in Southern Rhodesia', *Journal of Southern African Affairs*, 5: 57-88.

Marcussen, H.S. and Torp, J.E. (1982) *Internationalisation of Capital: the Prospects for the Third World*, Zed Press, London.

Masini, J., Ikonicoff, M., Jedlicki, C. and Lanzarotti, M. (1979) *Multinationals and Development in Black Africa: A Case Study in the Ivory Coast*, Saxon House, Farnborough, Hants.

Maylam, P. (1983) 'Shackled by the contradictions: the municipal response to African urbanization in Durban *c*. 1920-1950', Paper presented at the workshop on African life in Durban in the Twentieth Century University of Natal, Durban, October.

Nambudiri, C.N.S., Iyanda, O. and Akinnusi, D.M. (1981) 'Third World country firms in Nigeria', in Kumar, K. and McLeod, M.G. (eds.) *Multinationals from Developing Countries*, D.C. Heath: 145-54.

Nambudiri, C.N.S. (1983) *Third World Multinationals: Technology and Employment Choice in Nigeria*, International Labour Office, Geneva.

Novellie, L. (1968) 'Kaffir beer brewing: ancient art and modern industry', *Wallerstein Laboratories Communications*, 31 (104): 17-32.

Oculi, O. (1984) 'Multinationals in Nigerian agriculture in the 1980s', *Review of African Political Economy*, 31: 87-91.

O'Faircheallaigh, C. (1984) *Mining and Development*, Croom Helm, London.

Pan, L. (1975) *Alcohol in Colonial Africa*, Scandinavian Institute of African Studies, Uppsala.

Pridham Jones, H. (1957) 'Latest developments and trends in urban native administration in Northern Rhodesia', in *Record of Proceedings of the Sixth Annual Meeting of the Institute of Administrators of Non European Affairs, Southern Africa*, Margate, Kent, 9-12 September: 43-58.

Review of African Political Economy (1975) Special Issue on Multinational Corporations in Africa.

Rhodesia Herald, Daily, Salisbury.

Rhodesian Breweries Ltd (1967-1971), Annual Reports.

Rogerson, C.M. (1981a) 'Industrialization in the shadows of apartheid: a world-systems analysis', in Hamilton, F.E.I. and Linge, G.J.R. (eds.) *Spatial Analysis, Industry and the Industrial Environment: Vol. 2 - International Industrial Systems*, John Wiley, Chichester: 395-441

Rogerson, C.M. (1981b) 'Spatial perspectives on United Kingdom investment in South Africa', *South African Geographical Journal*, 63: 85-106.

Rogerson, C.M. (1982) 'Multinational corporations in Southern Africa: a spatial perspective', in Taylor, M.J. and Thrift, N. (eds.) *The Geography of Multinationals*, Croom Helm, London: 179-220.

Rogerson, C.M. (1985) 'Decentralization and the location of Third World multinationals in South Africa', Paper presented to the Workshop on South Africa's Regional Strategy, University of the Witwatersrand, Johannesburg, September.

Rogerson, C.M. (1986) 'A strange case of beer: the State and sorghum beer manufacture in South Africa', *Area*, 18 (in press).

Rooney, J.P. (1977) 'Feasibility study on possible acquisition of Rufaro Brewery by Heinrich Chibuku Breweries (1968) Ltd', Internal Company Report, Mimeograph.

Rufaro Brewery, Municipality of Salisbury (1976) Annual Report.

Salisbury, Municipality of (1911-1964) Minute of His Worship the Mayor for the Year Ending 30 June.

Seidman, A. (1974) 'The distorted growth of import-substitution industry: the Zambian case', *Journal of Modern African Studies*, 12: 601-631.

Seidman, A. (1977) 'Post World War II imperialism in Africa: a Marxist perspective', *Journal of Southern African Affairs*, 2: 403-425.

Seidman, A. (1979) 'African socialism and the world system: dependency, transnational corporations, and international debt', in Rosberg, C.G. and Callaghy, T.M. (eds.) *Socialism in Sub-Saharan Africa: A New Assessment*, University of California, Institute of International Studies, Berkeley.

Seidman, A. and Makgetla, N. (1979) 'Transnational corporate involvement in South Africa's military build-up', *Journal of Southern African Affairs*, 4: 153-173.

Seidman, A. and Makgetla, N. (1980) *Outposts of Monopoly Capitalism: Southern Africa in the Changing Global Economy*, Lawrence Hill, Westport, Connecticut.

Seidman, A. and Seidman, N. (1977) *US Multinationals in Southern Africa*, Tanzania Publishing House, Dar es Salaam.

Shaw, T. and Grieve, M. (1977) 'Dependence or development: international and internal inequalities in Africa', *Development and Change*, 8: 377-408.

South African Breweries Ltd (1972), Annual Report.

Swainson, N. (1977) 'The rise of a national bourgeoisie in Kenya', *Review of African Political Economy*, 8: 39-55.

Swainson, N. (1980) *The Development of Corporate Capitalism in Kenya, 1918-77*, Heinemann, London.

Swanson, M.W. (1976) '"The Durban System": roots of urban apartheid in colonial Natal', *African Studies*, 35: 159-176.

Tickner, V. (1977) 'International-local capital: the Ivory Coast sugar industry', *Review of African Political Economy*, 8: 119-121.

Tucker, B.A. (1985a) 'The international expansion of a semi-peripheral based enterprise: South African Breweries Ltd', in Taylor, M.J. and Thrift, N.J. (eds.) *Multinationals and the Restructuring of the World Economy*, Croom Helm, Beckenham.

Tucker, B.A. (1985b) 'Interaction behaviour and location change in the South African brewing industry', *South African Geographical Journal*, 67: 60-83.

Umtali, Municipality of (1926) Minute of His Worship the Mayor for the Year Ending 30 June.

Van Blommestein, J. (1984) Interview, Former Managing Director, Heinrich Chibuku Breweries (1968) Ltd, Johannesburg, 21 February 1984.

Van der Wees, G. (1981) 'Multinational corporations, transfer of technology and the socialist strategy of a developing nation: perspectives from Tanzania', in Hamilton, F.E.I. and Linge, G.J.R. (eds.) *Spatial Analysis, Industry and the Industrial Environment: Vol 2 - International Industrial Systems*, John Wiley, Chichester: 520-547.

Van Onselen, C. (1976) *Chibaro: African Mine Labour in Southern Rhodesia 1900-1933*, Pluto, London.

Wellings, P. (1984) 'Development by invitation? South African corporate investment in Lesotho: progress, problems and prospects, unpublished paper', Development Studies Unit, University of Natal, Durban.

Wells, L.T. Jr. (1983) *Third World Multinationals: The Rise of Foreign Investment from Developing Countries*, MIT Press, Cambridge, Mass.

Widstrand, C. (ed.) (1975) *Multi-National Firms in Africa*, Scandinavian Institute of African Studies, Uppsala.

Chapter Eight

MULTINATIONAL RESOURCE CORPORATIONS, NATIONALIZATION
AND DIMINISHED VIABILITY: CARIBBEAN PLANTATIONS,
MINES AND OILFIELDS IN THE 1970s

R.M. Auty

MULTINATIONAL RESOURCE CORPORATIONS
AND STATE ENTERPRISES IN THE CARIBBEAN

Economic Development and Corporate/Host Relations

Vernon (1971) has identified the obsolescing bargain as an inherent source of friction and instability in corporate/host
relations, especially in developing countries.   Prior to the
investment, negotiations favour the investor since that party
usually has most information about the relative profitability
of the prospective enterprise and can use this advantage to
bargain hard for concessions from the usually capital-scarce
host country.   However, once the investment is successfully
completed and the risk of failure has receded, the investor's
position weakens considerably. The typical project requires five
years or more to recoup the initial investment and several years
of profitable operation thereafter to secure a competitive return.   Meanwhile, the host country can threaten legal sanctions, with nationalization as the ultimate threat, if clauses
it finds objectionable in hindsight, are not rectified to its
satisfaction. Where the rules of the game are tightly prescribed,
as during the colonial period, the resulting instability associated with the obsolescing bargain may be minimal, but in the
aftermath of political independence the scope for testing the
newly defined corporate/host relationships proved considerable.
The resource-based enterprises were especially susceptible to
pressures for renegotiation because of the large scale of capital investment typically involved.
    Firms exploiting natural resources were particularly vul-
nerable to the anti-MNC rhetoric of the late 1960s and early
1970s (Williams, 1975) for three reasons.   First, MNRC (Multinational Resource Corporations) investment in natural resources
has evoked a much stronger emotional response from newly independent, nationalistic countries than foreign ownership of
mere depleting capital assets because historically MNRC ownership meant foreign ownership of large tracts of fertile land, or
of a sizeable and depleting mineral asset. The tendency of mines

and plantations to exhibit enclave characteristics invited their depiction as a state within a state (Porteus, 1973) and therefore as an affront to political independence. Second, the all-pervasive influence of the foreign-dominated lead sector on the rest of the economy, public and private, compounded the sense of external domination. Third, many MNRCs adopted a vertically-integrated product strategy, linking resources to markets in an unbroken chain, in order to minimize the risks of entry and operation in imperfect markets (Auty 1983a). The characteristically large capital investments required protection from costly disruption through the maintenance of a reliable and competitive materials throughput from canefield to sugar refinery, from mine to fabricating plant, or from oilfield to petrol pump. Consequently, the stakes in renegotiating corporate/host contracts in vertically-integrated resource-processing industries have been particularly high, reflecting the MNRC's need to retain, and the host country's need to capture, the entire resource-market production chain (Auty, 1981).

Hirschman (1969) has suggested that, even without the twin spurs to state ownership of the obsolescing bargain and newly acquired independence, the utility of MNCs to developing countries declines as their economies broaden and deepen. The MNC provides an initial package of management, technology, capital and marketing that is critical for the establishment of new production. But, according to Hirschman, this initial positive stimulus wanes as foreign ownership impedes the acquisition of skills by host country nationals and discourages corporate lobbying for gradual institutional change while prompting over-reaction against pressures for fundamental necessary reform such as land redistribution. Hirschman's broad thesis concerning the declining utility of MNRCs through time seems reasonable, though MNRCs have shown considerable sensitivity and flexibility in accommodating demands for 'indiginization' and greater host country ownership than his late 1960s view suggests, so that the expected benefits of MNRC withdrawal may not outweigh the disadvantages.

This chapter will argue that the disadvantages of MNRC withdrawal are likely to be especially severe in the case of the smaller and less diversified developing countries. Hirschman neglected an important dynamic aspect of the corporate/host relationship, namely, the relationship between the host country's level of development and its political sensitivity to foreign direct investment. In particular, as a developing country's economy becomes larger and more diversified, so the relative importance of the individual MNRC declines and the host country's political tolerance for powerful foreign economic agents increases. Political resentment of the greater strength of the MNC relative to that of the state is potentially most intense in the small, undiversified developing country that, ironically, has the greatest need of the MNRC's package of benefits. The resulting heightened corporate/host government tension is likely to be particularly acute in those smaller and less diversified economies where plantations, mines and oilfields are important and where the exploitation of a natural resource by one or a handful of MNRCs dominates national economic activity. The Caribbean is characterized by just such economies and the experience of three of them, Jamaica, Trinidad and Guyana, will be used to explore the resulting problems.

The Caribbean Context

In the Caribbean, the late-1960's surge of anti-corporate sentiment was given intellectual backing by a group of young economists which embraced the newly-formulated dependency theory. Critiques of bauxite mining (Girvan, 1967 and 1971), tourism (Bryden, 1973) and plantation agriculture (Beckford, 1968 and 1972) were widely circulated. Girvan's work was the most influential and argued that oligopolistic competition permitted the aluminium multinationals to suboptimally locate their refineries, smelters and fabricating plants in OECD countries, away from the tropical bauxite mines. Citing Jamaica as an example, Girvan calculated that less than 5 per cent of the final added value from the aluminium chain based on that country's bauxite actually accrued to Jamaica. Worse, half the value of bauxite that was generated in the mining country leaked immediately abroad to service capital and purchase centralized supplies of inputs. Rectification, according to Girvan, required national ownership to ensure the location of all stages of production within the bauxite-producing country and thereby maximize backward linkage through the domestic production of machinery and chemicals (notably caustic soda) and through the establishment of a domestic steel industry based on the transformation of the large red mud alumina refinery residues into iron.

Bryden (1973) also criticized the high rate of revenue leakage associated with foreign ownership and expatriate hotel management in his analysis of Antigua's tourist industry, and in addition, drew attention to the high social costs borne by small farmers as a consequence of tourist-related land speculation and the provision of tourist-oriented infrastructure out of local taxation. In a more polemical vein, Beckford attempted to add the crippling psychological legacy of slavery (the 'plantation mentality') to the shortcomings of economic loss and high social cost identified by Girvan and Bryden. These dependency-based arguments were allied to the Black Power movement which spilled over from the USA into the Caribbean during the late 1960s to produce strong political pressure for the transformation of the constitutional independence achieved earlier in the decade into full political and economic independence.

The threat of nationalization was not new to the Commonwealth Caribbean. For example, from the 1950s Booker McConnell's chief executive in Guyana considered nationalization inevitable.

It was the speed with which state ownership was extended in the 1970s that was surprising. The governments of the Commonwealth Caribbean countries were overtaken by events, so that key policy decisions were implemented in response to intense short-run political pressures rather than as the measured application of carefully considered strategy. For example, street violence and an attempted coup early in 1970 pushed Trinidad's powerful PNM (People's National Movement) government into more populist and nationalist policies than its cautious leaders wanted (Auty, 1984a). A Black Power pressure group within Guyana's ruling PNM government pushed it into unexpected and acrimonious negotiations with Alcan, the country's leading bauxite producer, that culminated in nationalization in 1971 (Auty, 1981). The reformist Manley government in Jamaica was strongly influenced by the preshock negotiations between the OPEC countries and the major multinational oil corporations (Byer, 1972). The Iranian strategy of negotiated entry of state enterprises into resource-based industry was initially favoured, but as negotiations dragged into 1974 and intense balance of payments pressures built up a militant policy was implemented. Jamaica unilaterally imposed a large bauxite levy and spearheaded the formation of an OPEC-style producer organization (Auty, 1980). Nationalization in the Commonwealth Caribbean was a response to short-run political pressures rather than a clearly considered long-term strategy.

CHARACTERISTICS OF STATE ENTERPRISES IN DEVELOPING COUNTRIES

Recent Research Findings on State Enterprise Efficiency

Although the motives for nationalization in the developing countries are well understood, the consequences are only now beginning to come to light. Much information has recently been assembled on the functioning of state enterprises in developing countries as part of a more general investigation of managerial efficiency in developing countries launched in the response to the severe problems triggered by the recession of the early 1980s (Jones, 1982; Radetzki, 1983; Shirley, 1983; World Bank, 1983). The preliminary findings are summarized briefly below.

State enterprises are distinguished from the rest of government activity, such as health and educational services, by their need to earn most of their revenues from the sale of goods and services and by their separate legal identity. They are self-accounting and expected to realize a return on their investment, though rarely under profit-maximizing assumptions (Shirley, 1983:2). So defined, state-owned enterprises in the developing countries account for around 10 per cent of their GDP and are heavily concentrated in utilities, mining and large-scale manufacturing - but not in agriculture (World Bank, 1983). Since state enterprises vary in their organizational structure, attempts at generalization concerning their objectives and

163

levels of efficiency require heavy qualification.

Although behavioural researchers and others have attributed multiple objectives to MNRCs (Thomas, 1980) and, in the short run, priority may be given to differing goals such as product differentiation or expansion of market share, profit maximization is the dominant long-term objective and the return on equity provides a single clear-cut indicator of corporate performance. In contrast, the goals of the state-owned corporation are likely to be more numerous with less significance attached to any one of them. Typical goals might include, in addition to some minimum rate of return, the maximization of foreign exchange earnings, the diffusion of skills, the purchase of local inputs, priority for domestic over foreign investment, the maximization of employment, the furtherance of regional policy and the provision of explicit favours to the ruling party via price controls, localized investment and employment maximization. Sometimes these objectives may conflict and this can handicap industries that are exposed to international competition such as the Caribbean region's resource-based industries. For example, the goal of maintaining employment levels may hamper cost reduction while restrictions on overseas investment may preclude vertical integration and thereby severely handicap state-owned producers (Vernon, 1982).

In the absence of any single measure of performance, such as the return on capital, the health of the state-owned enterprise is difficult to monitor. For example, attempts by Rumania to apply multiple performance targets to state-owned enterprises have proved extremely complicated to administer (Shirley, 1983: 38). With numerous and often imprecise objectives to satisfy sub-optimal performance in any number of areas can be excused on the grounds of demands made by other goals, so that overall efficiency is likely to suffer. There is considerable evidence that state enterprises are less efficient than private firms in the same industry (Shirley, 1983) - though this outcome is not inevitable (Trebat, 1983). Moreover, lower efficiency need not be a disadvantage where production is primarily for domestic consumption in a relatively closed economy and where the reasons for such reduced efficiency are understood and the cost of the trade-off is clearly identified. However, the consequences of reduced viability are potentially disastrous in industries which dispose of the bulk of their output on international markets.

A second important area of potential difficulty for the state enterprise, related to that of multiple goals, lies in the relationship between those charged by the government to call the state firm to account, the board, and the employees, both management and workers. The operation of the firm as a corporation, rather than as a government department, is usually meant to reduce the inefficiency and/or corruption of large central bureaucracies, enhance flexibility through decentralization, and attract personnel different from those in the civil service. However, representatives from several different government departments invariably oversee the enterprise and thereby add to the number and complexity of the objectives set. The management of state enterprises may be given insufficient autonomy or incentive to pursue an effective strategy, while insistence on nationals in the top positions may unnecessarily restrict the quality of management appointed. This is particularly likely to be the case in small countries with an internationally mobile elite, such as most of the countries of the Caribbean. Even where an able management team seeks to function effectively, the intrusion of short-run political pressures arising from the need to placate powerful interest groups or boost flagging revenues may prevent it from doing so. The balance between managerial autonomy and state control is difficult to set, and too much autonomy may be as harmful as too little. The over-extension of Indonesia's state oil corporation in the mid-1970s and the uncoordinated acquisition of capital by Brazil's many state firms during that entire decade had serious negative consequences for their governments' macro-economic policies.

State-ownership has often been expected to elicit a more accommodating worker response, but there is little evidence of this as yet. Nationalization injects a political component into the determination of remuneration, sometimes through the sheer size of the labour force, as in the case of large plantation sectors, or through formidable financial muscle as in the case of capital-intensive mineral sectors. Consequently, the management's negotiating position tends to be weakened by interference from several government departments, usually resulting in overgenerous pay settlements. However, occasionally an inflexible stance may be exacerbated by over-hasty recourse to the physical force at the state's command. Information on state-labour relations is scarce at the general level, but the experience of the Commonwealth Caribbean shows that the introduction of state ownership has rarely elicited better worker-management relations than has private ownership and has, in some instances, been associated with a sharp deterioration as unions explore the flexibility of the new constraints arising from nationalization.

A third area of potential difficulty for the state enterprise lies in its use of capital and labour. Typically, state enterprises have favourable access to capital because they can borrow under government guarantee or gain privileged access to domestic credit. This encourages the selection of unnecessarily capital-intensive projects by state enterprises and crowds out small private firms from capital markets. In other words, the underpricing of capital to state enterprises contributes to the misallocation of resources. When such an investment bias is combined with pressures for maximizing employment and for softened resistance to union wage demands, there are clear negative implications for viability.

The state firm's use of capital and labour differentiate its response to changes in international demand from that of

MNRCs. The state enterprise's greater tendency to regard labour costs as fixed, together with its use of a relatively high debt: equity ratio and political pressure to maximize foreign exchange inflows, encourages sustained production during recession. Where state enterprises are responsible for a sizeable share of global output, as in the case of copper, there are implications for market behaviour. During the recession of the early 1980s, some 25 per cent of copper capacity outside the centrally planned economies was closed, but Zambia maintained full production forcing competitors to bear more of the adjustment burden. Since competitors of the state firm are forced under such circumstances to radically improve their break-even cost of production and yet no corresponding efficiency improvement is required of the state enterprise, its competitive position deteriorates (Radetzki, 1983).

A fourth important characteristic of the state enterprise, the low expectation of liquidation, provides further reason for expecting reduced efficiency. By totally removing, or severely weakening, the likelihood of failure, management and labour lose a significant spur to innovation and improvement. In a large and diversified mixed economy, the presence of several relatively uncompetitive state firms might not pose a serious long-term drag on national economic development. However, for those countries with small and undiversified economies, state ownership of firms in the lead export sector can be disastrous if close attention is not given to ways of countering those characteristics of the state enterprise that discourage sustained efforts at improved public enterprise competitiveness.

The Effects of Nationalization

Although the benefits from the post-independence wave of nationalization have been generally disappointing thus far, there is considerable debate on what long-term conclusions can be drawn. Some observers, like Radetzki (1983), are optimistic about the eventual outcome. Radetzki suggests that the launch of state enterprises results in a decade or two of impaired performance until the difficulties of mastering the new task are overcome. He postulates an initial disruption in operations after the state take-over, followed by a gradual movement towards a new and acceptable equilibrium. The initial poor performance is regarded as a learning experience and the resulting sacrifice a worthwhile one. Others, such as Shafer (1983), conclude that state enterprise imposes very severe costs because governments fail to recognize the important dual role played by foreign corporations in insulating developing country enterprises from debilitating domestic political pressures and in providing efficient access to international finance and markets. For Shafer, nationalization implies a compounding decline in operational efficiency with no guarantee of stabilization, let alone subsequent improvement. The state enterprises of the three Commonwealth Caribbean countries are now explored in order to

determine where they lie along the spectrum of views represented
by Radetzki and Shafer.

THE CARIBBEAN STATE ENTERPRISES

The Need for Caution in Evaluating
Commonwealth Caribbean Experience

Attention has already been drawn to the difficulties of gener-
alizing about state enterprises and, before examining the evidence from the countries of the Commonwealth Caribbean, some
further qualifications are required. First, there is some bias
towards both the older and the very newest industries among the
state enterprises in the region. While the sample of industries
is small, there is evidence that the MNRCs were chary of com-
mitting capital to new resource-based ventures in a region which,
like the Caribbean, was experiencing rapid, large-scale extension of state ownership, but less reluctant to cede ownership
of older, heavily depreciated enterprises. Table 8.1 summarizes
the overall pattern. Most of the three countries' long-
established sugar industry passed into total state ownership,
along with cement manufacture and a sizeable part of Trinidad's
oil refining. Steel, the principal new gas-based industry, is
100 per cent state-owned along with methanol and urea production.
Since ammonia has been produced in Trinidad since the late
1950s, the fertilizer industry can be classified with bauxite
as one of the region's mature industries, and an active MNRC
presence remains in both. Jamaica's largest bauxite mines and
Trinidad's two large new fertilizer plants operate with MNRC
management, but majority state equity, while the Jamaican government also has a minority holding in alumina refining. The

TABLE 8.1   Degree of State Ownership and Enterprise Vintage
             for Resource-based Industry

State Equity %	Enterprise Vintage		
	New	Mature	Old
95 - 100	Steel, Urea, Methanol	Guyana Bauxite, Guyana Alumina	Guyana Sugar, Jamaican Sugar, Trinidad Sugar, Cement, Trinidad Oil
51 - 94	-	Jamaica Bauxite Ammonia	-
10 - 50	Trinidad Gas Fields	-	-
0 - 9	-	Jamaica Alumina	-

anomaly of the Guyanese government's outright ownership of the country's bauxite industry may be partly explained by the fact of the bitterness of the 1969-70 contract renegotiations and partly by the fact that the Guyanese mines are considerably older than those in Jamaica so that Guyanese export mining was being marginalized by the high costs of overburden removal (Auty, 1981). The fact that there is not a rough balance between state and MNRC ownership in the region's declining, mature and new industries is one reason why care must be exercised in drawing conclusions: the state enterprises are particularly prominent in both declining industries and in pioneering ones, where the risks are highest.

A second reason for caution lies in the coincidence of a general deterioration of the international economy with the first decade of Caribbean state ownership. As will be shown, this exacerbated the adjustment problems of the old-established industries and created extremely hostile conditions for the launch of the new ones. Finally, both the sugar and oil refining industries prior to nationalization show that MNRCs could operate with many of the characteristics commonly ascribed to state enterprise, so that even private foreign ownership cannot guarantee insulation from debilitating political interference, though it makes it less likely and persistent. These qualifications require that the evidence presented must be carefully sifted and allowance must be made for the potential distortions caused by the impact of factors other than state ownership on enterprise performance.

An Ageing Industry: Overmanning, Failure to Liquidate and Rapid Decline in Sugar

An examination of post-nationalization developments in the Commonwealth Caribbean sugar industry illustrates the problems of state ownership in an ageing industry. The sugar industry presents particular difficulties in isolating the impact of ownership from other factors for three reasons. First, a long-term decline in efficiency was underway before nationalization (Table 8.2), reflecting a softening in real sugar prices and declining work discipline on the plantations (Landell Mills, 1979). Second, the sugar MNRCs had acquired many operating characteristics usually associated with state enterprises, and functioned by the mid-1960s more like mini welfare states rather than the exploitive enclaves of dependency theory (Auty, 1976). Third, market conditions immediately following the major extension of state ownership in the mid-1970s were especially difficult because the long-term reduction in efficiency was aggravated by amplification of the sugar price cycle, to which reference must be briefly made.

Post-war world sugar prices have followed a seven-year cycle that largely reflects the length of time over which cane can be harvested without the heavy expense of replanting. The price cycle typically has one or two years of high prices followed

Table 8.2   Estimated Sugar Production Costs in 1979
            (US$/tonne)

Producer	Field	(Labour)	Factory	(Labour)	Total	Wage US$/ hour	Yield tonnes/hectare 1960	1979
Barbados	222	(134)	193	(36)	500	1.60	8.19	7.37
Guyana	181	(77)	113	(12)	355	0.70	8.60	5.30
Jamaica	160	(44)	130	(11)	350	0.38	7.39	6.19
Trinidad	191	(80)	178	(56)	445	1.40	6.75	4.22
Cuba	138	(38)	78	(17)	260	0.73	na	5.33
Australia	131	(39)	80	(79)	240	6.20	6.20	10.59

Source: Landell Mills (1979)

Note: The actual cost for Trinidad was around US$ 800 per tonne

by five years of lower ones.   In the wake first of the Cuban revolution and of the 1973-74 oil shock, the price cycle became more erratic (World Bank, 1983:66-67): the peaks of 1963 and 1975 were especially high, while the trough of 1966 was unusually low and there was no significant trough between 1969 and 1975.   Before the early 1960s the cyclical pattern was more regular and the real price of sugar was higher. Although Caribbean producers received a negotiated price for the bulk of their sales, the price they received was linked to long-term trends in the world price, while a significant fraction of output was sold directly on the world market.   Thus, although the Caribbean sugar producers were cushioned from the extremes of short-term swings in international prices they remained sensitive to long-term trends.

Significantly, the partial withdrawal of Tate & Lyle from the Jamaican and Trinidadian sugar industries in 1970 was made after a modest price peak, while the major state take-overs of the mid-1970s (the establishment of Jamaica's National Sugar Corporation, the nationalization of Booker McConnell in Guyana and the extension of the Trinidad government's share of Tate & Lyle's Trinidad subsidiary to 97 per cent) overlapped with a very high peak followed by a singularly difficult trough. Cost increases incurred during the boom years, notably wage bonuses, were difficult to reduce in leaner years, creating acute cash flow problems later in the decade.

Nevertheless, despite the analytical difficulties raised by the long-term decline in efficiency, the blurring of MNCR/ state enterprise characteristics and the medium-term cyclical problems, there can be little doubt that state ownership aggravated the problem of structural adjustment in the industry in all three countries. In particular, the understandable reluctance of governments to undertake timely factory closures resulted in mounting losses and a quantum leap in the scale of the ultimate and inevitable adjustment required. The Guyanese industry will be examined first since it commenced operation under state ownership as a highly efficient industry and its subsequent problems testify to the debilitating influence of political interference even when the government involved had shown itself appreciative of the dangers of such involvement. The Jamaican industry provides a clear instance of the repeated capitulation of the state to politically powerful unions and the invariable paramountcy of short-run political objectives over long-term economic necessities. Finally, the experience of the oil-rich Trinidad government shows how quickly and massively the problems can multiply if there is no threat of plant closure and no effective limit on government funding.

The post-war years ushered in a boom period for the sugar MNRCs in the Commonwealth Caribbean as the British government introduced a price and quota regime that stimulated rapid expansion. The pursuit of economies of scale led to the concentration of factories and firms so that, by the mid-1960s Booker McConnell owned 90 per cent of the Guyanese sugar industry's productive capacity while Tate & Lyle achieved a similar dominance of the Trinidad industry and owned one-third of the Jamaican industry. The United Fruit Company owned 10 per cent of the Jamaican industry through one 50,000 tonne factory. While the MNRCs operated large factories, the local owners operated smaller ones that were closer to the economic margin (Auty, 1976). Consequently, the MNRCs were expected to treat their workers better and by the 1960s they had acquired the characteristics of 'mini welfare states', especially in the case of Tate & Lyle. Overmanning the high fringe benefits were not offset by higher productivity so that the MNRCs' cash flow was insufficient to cover proper maintenance and provide a satisfactory return on capital. By the late 1960s the Commonwealth Caribbean sugar industry had lost its post-war dynamism and was a relatively high-cost producer with declining levels of efficiency (Smith, 1976). This was less true of Guyana where Booker McConnell's strategy of horizontal integration and product diversification removed the pressures for wage capitulation associated with Tate & Lyle's vertically-integrated strategy and fostered tighter management through the successful pursuit of remaining the region's lowest cost producer (Table 8.3).

On the eve of nationalization in 1976 the Guyanese sugar industry was the most efficient producer in the Commonwealth Caribbean and Booker McConnell generated a significant positive cash flow from its Guyanese operations (Auty, 1981). Unlike Trinidad and Jamaica, therefore, the Guyanese state-owned corporation (Guysuco) inherited a well-run, efficient industry in

Table 8.3   Global Sugar Production Costs 1975   (£/tonne)

Caribbean Region		World Range	
Barbados	130	Australia	75
Belize	115	Brazil	85
Guyana	115	EEC	140
Jamaica	150	Louisiana	155
Trinidad	150	Nigeria	155
		Congo	180

Source: Smith (1976)

which the Caribbean region's basic long-term problems of yield decline and prolonged inadequate cash flow were not yet severe. An important condition of the nationalization agreement was that the departing MNRC would not poach the excellent eleven-man managerial team, most of whom were Guyanese nationals.

Guyana: Unsatisfactory Government/Workforce Relations and Lost Viability

The autonomy given to the management team proved insufficient and recurrent political intervention had damaging results. Five years after nationalization, and in the teeth of executive opposition the new corporation's mission was finally published in Guysuco's 1981 Annual Report, and defined as the development of a diversified agri-business that would expand import substitution, disseminate new crops and production techniques, and promote worker participation. Half the 1981 corporate plan was given over to non-sugar activity which severely stretched managerial resources. The non-sugar activity was largely the result of government efforts to appease some political constituency and commercial viability was of secondary concern. By 1983 six of the original eleven-man executive team had left Guysuco and adequate local replacements had not been secured.

Nor did the transfer to state ownership improve labour relations: high wage costs and overmanning began to emerge as severe problems in the late 1970s. Whereas Booker McConnell had reduced factory employment by 10 per cent to 2,000 between 1969 and 1974 and field labour rose a modest 6 per cent to 16,400, the state firm boosted factory employment by almost 20 per cent and field labour by 25 per cent in the late 1970s following a protracted strike in the first full year of Guysuco's operations. Industry wage rates soared to more than 25 per cent above the national average and labour costs tripled between 1976 and 1981 (Guysuco Annual Report, 1982) even as output declined. The government resisted managerial pleas for closure of the smallest factory, and then finally conceded, only to balk at calls for

171

two additional closures needed to boost capacity and sustain efficiency in the surviving factories.

In its first five years of operation, which coincided with a trough in sugar prices, Guysuco returned profits of between US$0.5 and 2 million except for the strike year of 1977, when it registered a loss of US$7 million.   At first glance this appears a creditable performance; however, the corporation was not provided with adequate foreign exchange for the purchase of chemical and machinery inputs so that efficiency levels were adversely affected.   By the present decade costs were significantly above revenues and in 1981 a loss of US$27 million was incurred on revenues of US$105 million.   In the following year revenues dipped to US$97 million and losses increased to US$31 million.   The continued viability of the industry was queried (H. Davis, 1982) and reports on the efficiency of Guyanese agriculture were commissioned from IFAD (International Fund for Agricultural Development) and the IADB (Inter-American Development Bank).   Both studies concluded that sugar represented the Guyanese government's best immediate prospect for raising the country's foreign exchange earnings and strongly   recommended that the government provide adequate resources for it to perform this task.   The IADB report concluded that viability could be restored by a 50 per cent devaluation of the Guyanese dollar, the reduction of overmanning and the restoration of sugar industry wage rates to national levels (Reca and Maffucci, 1982). However, to maximize the likelihood of restoring viability a new relationship was urged between the government and Guysuco that would raise managerial autonomy, permit the retention of an adequate cash flow and provide sufficient foreign exchange to purchase essential imported inputs.

Jamaica: The Consequences of
Sustained Political Intervention

The Jamaican government was initially drawn into sugar factory ownership through efforts to maintain employment rather than through ideological commitment.   The problem of putting short-run employment maximization above long-term viability existed before the MNRCs withdrew, but increased state ownership expanded the scale of the resources the sugar industry unions could pre-empt so that the situation worsened.   Small factories of suboptimal size were subsidized in areas of low alternative employment during the 1960s, and this set a precedent for the large-scale extension of state factory ownership in the 1970s. When the two large MNRCs sold their large estates to the conservative JLP (Jamaica Labour Party) government in 1970 it was intended that they should be sold to private farmers in plots of 40 to 200 hectares on the highly successful Australian model (Harbridge House, 1971).   However, under the leftward-drifting PNP (People's National Party) government, elected in 1972, this policy was replaced by one of establishing co-operatives. Three trial co-operatives were set up in 1974 and two years later the number was expanded to 23 just ahead of the general election, accounting for the bulk of the former MNRC plantation lands. The three large sugar factories were bought by the state and the NSC (National Sugar Corporation) was established to run them as well as two small units taken over in the 1960s (SIA, 1976). Three more private sugar factories closed permanently in the mid-1970s and four more were added to the NSC group, leaving just two privately-owned factories of around 20,000 tonnes capacity each in operation. These two private factories, Worthy Park and Hampden, provide a base against which to gauge the performance of the state sector.

The long-term decline in agricultural efficiency accelerated through the 1970s in Jamaica, mainly as a result of poor management but also because of difficulties in acquiring foreign exchange for imported inputs as the Jamaican economy deteriorated sharply under the PNP government (Kincaid, 1982). The co-operatives performed badly since they were expanded too quickly: yields were well below the modest 34 tonnes of cane per hectare targeted, and less than half those considered technically feasible (McNeely Engineering Ltd and Proctor Redfern, 1976). Input shortages, labour difficulties and apprehension about further extension of the co-operatives reduced investment, yields and output on the remaining privately-owned farms.

The National Sugar Corporation was unable to generate sufficient capital to install the US$18 million of equipment provided for under a rehabilitation agreement with the World Bank so the condition of the state factories deteriorated. Breakdowns and strikes reduced the efficiency of sucrose extraction so that more cane was required per tonne of sugar produced. From a peak of 500,000 tonnes in 1965, and a plateau around 350,000 tonnes in the early 1970s, Jamaica's sugar production dropped to 275,000 during 1977-80 and continued on a decline to 201,000 in 1981 (Hutchinson and Drum, 1982). All factories experienced declining throughput, but the two private factories were among those with the least production fall-off. Labour productivity was especially low in the state factories because of overmanning: though on the average larger than the private factories, the NSC factories averaged 45 tonnes of sugar per factory worker, compared with 100 for the small privately-owned factory at Worthy Park.

While the tightly-run small privately-owned factories continued to make profits despite their suboptimal size, the larger state factories lost money. For the period 1979-81, total NSC costs were 37 per cent above revenues and by 1982 the accumulated losses were in excess of US$100 million. A management survey completed in 1982 (Hutchinson and Drum, 1982) recommended the termination of the debt-ridden co-operative experiment and the devolution of operational autonomy from the NSC to the individual factories. The success of the two privately-owned factories was attributed in large measure to more effective management. Determined to restore the industry's viability, the newly-elected JLP government set a target of 330,000 tonnes as a reasonable objective for a cost-conscious Jamaican sugar industry. However, a report commissioned from Gulf & Western in June 1982 concluded that US$250 million would be needed to restore the NSC to viability and that the number of factories should be reduced and the factory labour force halved. Faced with a chronic lack of investment funds and convinced of the merits of free market discipline, the JLP government proposed divesture in order to restore the industry's competitiveness and improve its long-term employment prospects. A management contract was negotiated with the former dominant MNRC, Tate & Lyle.

Trinidad: State Ownership Without Financial Discipline

Following the government's acquisition of majority ownership in Tate & Lyle's Trinidad subsidiary in 1970, industrial unrest was initially contained by a three-year moratorium on strikes. The air of uncertainty over the future of the industry resulted in a high turnover in management, and a chronic shortage of skilled staff developed. Between 1973 and 1975, the industry's workforce frequently disrupted operations and secured a doubling of wages during the 1975 boom year. Worker attendance became unreliable, averaging fourteen days per month and the decline in agronomic practices accelerated with yields falling to 3.7 tonnes of sugar per hectare by the early 1980s compared with twice that two decades earlier and three times that level in contemporary Australia (Landell Mills, 1979). Production increasingly fell short of the industry's installed 220,000 tonnes capacity from the mid-1970s, dropping to two-thirds of that level by 1979 and to one-third by 1982. Despite falling output and cumulating losses, work disruptions in support of higher wages continued and rates tripled between 1976 and 1979 with a further high settlement made in 1983.

Although cumulative losses did not mount until after 1976, the government's acquisition of majority ownership in 1970 signalled to the militant unions a significant extension of the potential financial resources to be bargained for. The two oil shocks gave the Trinidad economy a windfall equivalent to 40 per cent of its non-mining GDP and, since the government - now the owner of 97 per cent of the sugar industry - was the main recipient of the oil windfall it appeared to have almost limitless financial resources (Auty, 1984a). Falling throughput and rising fixed costs pushed the average cost of Trinidad's sugar to almost US$800 per tonne in 1979 compared with around US$350 in Guyana and post-devaluation Jamaica, and US$260 in Australia. A rationalization plan was proposed that would cut the industry's capacity to 70,000 tonnes, sufficient to supply the domestic market and sustain one large factory (Rampersad, 1981), but no action was taken even though costs in 1982 were reported to be over US$1800 per tonne. The magnitude of the Trinidad sugar industry's costs and losses is in no way typical of state-owned enterprises, since it results from the very large oil windfall resources at the disposal of the government. Nevertheless, it is inconceivable that the orderly closure of the least efficient factories would have been indefinitely postponed if the industry had remained in private hands. Such closures would have provided an incentive to the remaining factories to improve their productivity and competitiveness. An anonymous, but well-formed, memorandum circulated within the Trinidad civil service in 1979 commented, 'Evidently, there is need for a clearly defined and agreed mission and corporate objectives. The efficiency of the [sugar] company would also be enhanced if it is provided with adequate resources, and if there is freedom from undue government interference'.

Instead of an orderly adjustment to declining long-term growth prospects, state ownership in all three sugar industries resulted in the use of public funds to postpone difficult political problems. Scarce financial resources were thus mis-allocated and the ultimate scale and difficulty of the adjustment problem was thereby greatly increased. The evidence from the sugar industry does not support Radetzki's (1983) hypothesis of initial dislocation giving way to a steady improvement in operating conditions. Rather, a smooth transition to state ownership is followed by several years of apparently successful operation which mask an underlying deterioration in the quality of management, equipment and labour practices and leave the state firm vulnerable to rapid collapse in the face of unexpected shocks. The state-owned bauxite industry in Guyana offers further illustration of just such a pattern.

MATURE INDUSTRY:
CAPITAL SHORTAGE AND MARKET LOSS IN BAUXITE/ALUMINA

Guyana: Accelerated Decline After a Smooth State Launch

Faced with the sudden deterioration of its position in Guyana in 1969, Alcan at first resisted major change, but finally offered to concede majority ownership of its Guyanese subsidiary in exchange for government investment in calciner expansion as its share of the proposed joint venture. However, the negotiations broke down in acrimony and the MNRC provided minimal co-operation during the state takeover. Although two-thirds of the senior management left the fledgling state enterprise in 1971, its first operating year, Guybau (Guyana's state mining enterprise) was launched without major dislocation and achieved commendable results during its first five years of operation.

The total volume of bauxite mined rose two-thirds between 1968 and 1974 and revenues almost tripled as the new state corporation continued Alcan's strategy of raising the share of calcined bauxite (in which Guyana had a near world monopoly) as a share of total output. Net foreign exchange earnings improved from 40 to 60 per cent as local input purchases were increased and depreciation and profits were internalized. The accounting rate of return on investment averaged almost 12 per cent between 1971 and 1975 and paved the way for raising a US$24 million loan for calcining expansion in 1975. However, as the late-1970's recession rendered marketing increasingly difficult underlying operational problems surfaced and eroded the state corporation's credibility as a dependable supplier.

Despite showing five good years in the annual accounts, the state corporation had faced a cost squeeze from the outset: during the early-1970s Guybau's profits and depreciation were a significantly smaller fraction of total revenues than when the firm had been a subsidiary of Alcan. Whereas under Alcan management the bauxite workforce achieved rates of pay twice the national rate this differential was steadily reduced by Guysuco and particularly severe strikes occurred in 1977 and 1979 as worker discontent mounted. A rapid turnover in management commenced and only half were replaced, some of these being political appointees (Caldwell, 1982). Shorn of its access to Alcan's vertical production chain, Guybau was unable to maintain its metal-grade bauxite sales in the glutted alumina market of the late-1970s and resorted to large price increases on calcined sales where it retained monopoly advantage. By the late-1970s calcined sales provided two-thirds of the state corporation's revenues - twice the level under Alcan - yet the volume of calcined bauxite shipped had declined by one-third as operating difficulties mounted and new entrants into calcined production, notably China, took advantage of Guyana's impaired reputation as a reliable supplier to capture an enhanced market share (Table 8.4).

Table 8.4   Changing Share of Guyana and Jamaica in World Bauxite Production, 1960-81

	1960		1967		1974		1981	
	mt	%	mt	%	mt	%	mt	%
World	27.6	100.0	45.2	100.0	84.1	100.0	88.5	100.0
Jamaica	5.8	21.1	9.4	20.8	15.3	18.2	11.6	13.1
Guyana	2.5	9.1	3.4	7.5	3.6	4.3	2.4	2.7

Note: mt = million tonnes

Source: Metallgesellschaft (1982)

Guybau published no annual accounts between 1977 and 1983, but the state firm's losses are reported to have reached US$30 million in 1982 and the government sought an MNRC partner to assist in rehabilitating the industry. An investment of US$60 million was reportedly required in order to renovate the run-down plant and expand the industry's export earning capacity, but the government's poor record in both macro and micro economic management prevented the funding from being raised. By 1983 the Guyanese bauxite industry had collapsed. Its evolution was the very opposite of that hypothesized by Radetzki: a minimal disruption of production masking the underlying accelerating corrosion of the industry's capacity to function.

Jamaica: Majority Equity and Industry Contraction

Although Jamaica opted for majority state equity rather than outright nationalization, the PNP's hostility towards the MNRCs halted the rapid expansion of the industry. Even though management remained with the MNRCs, government intervention in search of higher rents undermined the industry competitiveness. Although three new alumina refineries were constructed in Jamaica in the late 1960s, severe teething troubles resulted in their operation below designed scale so that cost performance, profits and tax revenues were disappointing. Negotiations initiated by the reformist PNP government, aimed at securing state entry into the industry and raising revenues, dragged on through the first oil shock. In mid-1974 the Jamaican government unilaterally imposed a levy on the bauxite industry 50 per cent above that considered viable by the MNRCs. The levy was designed to boost tax yields six-fold over the low pre-shock level to an amount equivalent to 8 per cent of GDP.

Later in 1974 the Jamaican government spearheaded the formation of a bauxite producers' group partly in order to protect its new rent-boosting levy. However, the other leading bauxite producers were less supportive than Jamaica had expected and the MNRCs concentrated their mid-1970's cut-backs on the newly-marginalized Jamaican industry and looked elsewhere for subsequent expansion (Auty, 1983b). Through the unilateral imposition of an excessively high tax, the Jamaican government violated the MNRC's two basic requirements for raw materials flow: competitiveness and reliability.

The negotiations between the Jamaican government and the aluminium MNRCs culminated in the state's acquisition of majority ownership in the two large bauxite-exporting mines in 1977 and of minority partnerships of between 6 and 7 per cent in the Alcoa and Alcan refineries. Although the bauxite levy was intended for investment in further state ownership (C.E. Davis, 1982), the Jamaican government was unable to withstand pressure for the diversion of the levy into current expenditures (Reid, 1978). Although the Jamaican government reserved options to market a fraction of production by itself and to expand the Alcoa refinery, the MNRCs retained wide managerial autonomy. The relatively modest moves into state management reflected growing financial constraints arising from the failure of the government's macro-economic policy (Sharpley, 1983).

177

The original PNP objective of state entry into both refining and smelting was ill-advised for two main reasons. First, the proposed oil-fired smelter would have been rendered obsolete by the first oil shock. Second, investment in alumina refining during the early 1970s generated very little value added/unit of capital compared with mining and smelting except where it triggered bauxite mining expansion (Hashimoto, 1983). For each US dollar invested in the early 1970s, bauxite mining with the levy would add US$0.33 (at 1980 value) to GDP (US$0.07 without the levy); alumina refining US$0.03; and smelting around US$0.12 (Hashimoto, 1983:60). Had the Jamaican government more accurately gauged the rent on its bauxite resource the results of its acquisition of majority state ownership would have been more successful: as production declined the real value of the levy declined, whereas the continued expansion of bauxite production, albeit with the smaller levy favoured by the MNRCs, would have furnished a growing source of government income. Unfortunately, the second oil shock further marginalized Jamaican alumina compared with competing suppliers in Australia so that, even with a government prepared to accept substantial reductions in the bauxite levy, expansion prospects remain poor (Table 8.4). In mid-1984, Reynolds Metals withdrew from Jamaican bauxite production, leaving the government in sole control of a mine with an annual output of 3.6 million tonnes for which there was no longer a market. For the MNRCs Jamaican bauxite had become unreliable and high-priced during the 1970s so that its heyday had passed; it has become an ageing industry with low growth prospects.

New Industry: Overcommitment and
Marketing Problems in Hydrocarbons

The oil windfall provided the Trinidad government with substantial resources for expansion of public ownership either through the acquisition of existing firms or the establishment of new ones. The Trinidad government was cautious, despite strong domestic political pressure for militant measures against foreign investment, and experimented with a wide range of business ventures that involved varying degrees of co-operation with MNRCs. As the full extent of the country's gas reserves became clear through the 1970s, a significant fraction of the government's investment was allocated to gas-based industries including fertilizer, methanol and DRI (Direct Reduction of Iron), with LNG (Liquefied Natural Gas) and aluminium as possible additional options (Auty, 1984a). The Trinidad government's attempts to force the pace of industrialization during the 1970s illustrate the risks of overcommitment by the state and the tendency, common to many mineral-rich countries (including the Caribbean bauxite producers) during the 1970s, to overestimate the importance of resource ownership compared with market access (Auty, 1984b).

A central assumption of the project feasibility studies

executed in the wake of the first oil shock was that, with
continuing high inflation, the price of energy and energy-intensive
products would rise faster than the general rate of inflation.
Access to cheap energy and capital encouraged neglect of market
access, despite warnings about protectionist exclusion on the
grounds of input subsidization (Stauffer, 1975; Turner and
Bedare, 1979). When a critical input is available with low
opportunity cost, such as natural gas, the risk of entry appears
to be reduced because discretionary pricing of the key input
promises to guarantee profitability, with a good chance of earning a significant rent component on the gas. For state enterprises, the prospect of borrowing capital in the late 1970s at
low or negative rates of interest which, once the debt was
retired, promised to yield a sizeable income stream on a modest
capital input, proved an added incentive to early, and often
premature, entry. Although Trinidad carefully researched managerial, financial, technical and marketing needs, and also
sought equity partners, MNRC equity participation was seldom
regarded as vital to project execution.

Trinidad built five gas-based plants (Table 8.5), and all
were sanctioned before the 1980's recession radically changed
underlying assumptions about the rate of inflation. The two
ammonia plants came onstream in the late-1970s and a methanol
plant and urea factory started up in 1984. The two ammonia
plants were undertaken as joint ventures with majority state
equity, but the MNRCs retained management and marketing control.
Satisfactory agreements could not be reached with potential
equity partners for steel, urea and methanol, so the Trinidad

Table 8.5   Main Characteristics of the Gas-based Export
            Industries Established or Planned for Trinidad

Company	Product	State Equity %	Const-ruction	Gas Input (mcfd)	Investment (US$ m)	Unit Cost (1982 US$/tonne)
Tringen	Ammonia	51	1974-77	37	107	140
Fertrin	Ammonia	51	1978-81	65	315	167
ns	Urea	100	1982-84	7	147	170
ns	Methanol	100	1982-85	31	161	240
ISCOTT	Steel	100	1978-81	17	470	410
ALCOTT	Aluminium	90	1981-85p	102	420	1989
ns	LNG	51	1984-88p	750	5359	259

Notes: mcfd = millions of cubic feet per day
         ns = corporate name unspecified
         p = postponed

Source: Auty (1981)

government proceeded with wholly-owned subsidiaries. In the case of the steel plant, a subsidiary of the firm which supplied the technology subsequently brought an anti-dumping suit against the state firm. While marketing problems appear negligible for the ammonia plants and uncertain for the urea and methanol plants, the DRI steel unit provides an alarming example of the risks of overcommitment and inadequate market access for large capital-intensive resource-processing projects.

The initial proposal for steel production in Trinidad, made in 1975, was for 1.2 million tonnes of billet in a joint venture with Kawasaki, Mitsui and Hoesch-Edstel. These three MNRCs would take 33 per cent of the equity and all but 100,000 tonnes of the production. However, disagreement over incentives and prices caused the Trinidad government to assume total responsibility for equity ownership and marketing in 1976. Construction began in the following year on a plant with 750,000 tonnes of billet and a single DRI unit of 450,000 tonnes capacity which, with scrap complement, was sufficient to support 600,000 tonnes of billet production. Fears of scrap shortages and hopes for bulk DRI sales prompted the hurried addition of a second DRI unit which seriously unbalanced the production chain and added 25 per cent to planned capital costs. The technical difficulties and economies of scale of DRI shipment were underestimated by ISCOTT, the new state steel corporation, thereby increasing its dependence on sales of billet and rod.

The ISCOTT marketing survey estimated domestic demand at 60,000 tonnes and local regional sales at a further 140,000 tonnes, so that the large south-eastern USA market was targeted for the bulk of production. The marketing survey was undertaken by one of four North American firms advising the government on the implementation of the steel plant, and concluded that production costs would need to be 3 per cent below c.i.f. competitor prices to offset the foreign source disadvantage, or 10 per cent below when ocean freight was included. However, the survey reportedly found market prospects promising, and projected that continuing cost inflation would provide a significant advantage to producers with low energy and capital costs.

ISCOTT's final capital costs were high at US$900 per tonne, reflecting the burden of the second DRI unit and a 30 per cent construction cost overrun. Cost estimates suggest that, at full available capacity, total production costs would be around US$410 per tonne, some 50 per cent above those of the efficient mini-mills in the targeted south-eastern USA market. The ISCOTT plant could reduce its average cost by retiring some of the loan capital, particularly that incurred to cover the cost overrun which carried high interest rates. Inverting the 70-30 capital to equity ratio would reduce unit costs to around US$300 per tonne, still higher than the US$250 per tonne required for competitive sales in the depressed market of 1982.

As late as mid-1981 the government projected a discounted cash flow rate of return for the project of between 13 and 20 per cent, a maximum nine year payback period and a substantial boost to net foreign exchange earnings. However, four producers in the south-eastern United States market successfully filed an anti-dumping suit against ISCOTT that resulted in the imposition of a 14 per cent countervailing duty. Cumulative losses were reported at US$170 million in April 1982, with the possibility of annual losses running at US$100 million thereafter. When combined with losses from the start-up of Trinidad's other gas-based industries, and from the state acquisition of older industries such as sugar, cement and oil refining, the over-commitment by the state sector was very clear. The procurement of an MNRC equity partner for ISCOTT was viewed as the best practical means of overcoming the market access problem and reducing the size of the state's investment risk.

CARIBBEAN LESSONS FOR STATE OWNERSHIP OF RESOURCE-BASED INDUSTRY

The political objective of increasing national control of economic activity was powerfully advanced during the 1970s, most notably in Guyana, where some 80 per cent of economic activity had been brought within the public sector by the 1980s. The assets of ageing and mature industries were usually acquired at book value and therefore at a fraction of their replacement value, while cheap entry into new capital-intensive resource-based industries was provided through export credit financing at low or negative real interest rates.

The pronounced deterioration of the international economy which overlapped with the extension of state ownership did not present insurmountable problems to well-run firms. In the Commonwealth Caribbean its impact was to expose the growing flaws in the operation of the state firms sooner than would otherwise have been the case. Again and again the evidence suggests that a cumulative run-down occurred in most state firms. Because of the critical role many of the state enterprises played in the economy, the costs of the rapid extension of state ownership were high in terms of growth foregone, especially in Guyana and Jamaica.

Employee relations did not improve with state ownership so that efficiency declined as a result of high management turnover, strikes and looser work practices. Departing management was often not adequately replaced, reflecting the lack of qualified nationals and the operation of political patronage. In Guyana, sharp clashes occurred between the bauxite workers and the government security forces in the mining area which was, before the state take-over, a stronghold of government support. Direct foreign investment was a second casualty of the extension of state ownership, especially in Guyana and Jamaica, where overt government hostility to MNRCs caused this hitherto important source of investment to dry up completely in the late 1970s.

The more catholic attitude of the Trinidad government permitted the extension of state ownership and foreign direct investment to proceed in tandem.

The loss of markets presents a third cost of the extension of state ownership. The advantages of control over natural resources were overstated in relation to those of market access, and the importance of vertical integration was overlooked. Since the industries involved are characterized by high fixed costs, inadequate markets boosted unit costs to become another strand woven with others into the emerging pattern of accelerated decline while credibility as a reliable supplier was lost. The net result has been a significant decline in the capacity of the resource-based industries to generate economic growth under state ownership. The consequences of this were particularly severe in Guyana and Jamaica where sharp declines in real per capita income occurred in the late-1970s. The inefficiencies of the burgeoning state sector were offset in Trinidad by the magnitude of the oil windfall.

The assumption of state ownership was usually a smooth process, even under the tense conditions surrounding the Alcan nationalization, and there is little evidence from the countries studied to support Radetzki's learning thesis of an initial disruption followed by a gradual rise to a new and acceptable efficiency of operation (Radetzki, 1983). The pattern following nationalization in the Commonwealth Caribbean is rather one of an apparently smooth start followed by accelerating decline. Typically, profits and dividends were declared at the expense of maintenance when the state assumed managerial responsibility so that when the subsequent erosion of management, labour productivity and markets began pushing up costs, the earlier skimping on plant maintenance was compounded and competitive performance deteriorated even faster.

Decreased viability resulted from blurred objectives, political interference and overly-flexible financial constraints. The sugar industry provides the clearest instance of the multiplicity of goals that the state enterprise may be expected to perform. Socio-political aims, evident even before nationalisation on the large MNRC plantations, achieved dominance over economic ones for the state enterprise. This ordering of priorities should clearly be inverted since long-term social and political objectives cannot be effectively realised if viability is lost. In an export industry exposed to international competition such as most of the Commonwealth Caribbean's resource-based industries loss of viability is quickly penalised. Shafer's contention that the withdrawal of MNRCs opened firms to debilitating domestic political forces while removing important links to international finance and markets is confirmed by the Commonwealth Caribbean's experience. However, it is important to note, as Shafer (1983) does, that these penalties reflect the weak political systems of the states studied and may not operate in politically more experienced developing countries such as Brazil and Chile.

In addition to requirements to perform political favours at the expense of viability considerations, such as Guysuco's onerous non-sugar activities, there are other less blatant political imperatives that may nevertheless be more enervating. Examples include political appointees on the management of Guyana's two largest corporations; political patronage in labour hiring in Jamaica; and over-delegation to the chairman of Trinidad's National Energy Corporation because he was a favourite of the prime minister. The MNRC can alleviate such pressures, though it may not always be immune to them: the Jamaican sugar industry in the late 1960s provides striking examples of large private foreign enterprises sinking under sizeable socio-political burdens. Manning rates in Texaco's large Trinidad oil refinery are currently ten times those of a modern unit and four times the number that the company requires. These obligations were undertaken in the early stages of investment when profits could easily accommodate such political favours: when the technical supremacy which permitted this action was subsequently eroded the ingrained practices proved difficult to remove (Auty, 1976). For MNRCs that did not get themselves into such a position, like the bauxite corporations, Booker McConnell and the Trinidad government's two ammonia partners, Grace and Standard Indiana, the MNRC's greater accountability to efficiency-enhancing agents, the greater autonomy of its management and the very real prospect of liquidation if competitiveness is lost, reduce its vulnerability to political interference and provide a significant check on the corrosive short-run domestic political pressures.

In addition to insulation against domestic political interference, MNRCs provide two advantages for operating in the competitive international economy that Commonwealth Caribbean governments underestimated in the 1970s; these are access to capital and markets. Technology has not been a major problem in the resource-processing industries discussed here. Although state enterprises could emulate the MNRCs and establish their own vertically-integrated production chains linking resource and markets, the scarcity of capital presents a real obstacle. Even if such capital was available, domestic political objectives to investing overseas preclude such a strategy for all but the capital-surplus oil-exporting countries (Vernon, 1982). Under these circumstances, it would be advantageous to establish joint-ventures with MNRCs that meet the political need for majority state ownership, but assign wide-ranging managerial freedom through a management contract with the MNRC. Trinidad's experience with its gas-based industries suggests that such ventures heighten the sensitivity of state enterprise planners to commercial considerations and reduce the risk of unsound and/or overcommitted investment. Joint ventures with MNRCs may be the only way of reconciling political demands for national economic control with the fundamental requirement of maintaining international competitiveness in small economies dominated by resource-based export industries. In terms of Vernon's analogy: both sides now know that the bargain struck over direct foreign investment in natural resource development was not as obsolete as it appeared to many in the early 1970s. However, this is not to deny that the state must not be vigilant against malpractice: there are unethical companies just as there are unethical governments. For example, one of the four companies which filed the anti-dumping suit against ISCOTT sold the technology to the state firm; while one prospective equity partner in fertilizer production appears to have feigned an interest in a joint-venture partnership in order to offload a surplus factory onto the unwary Trinidad government. In the absence of such joint-venture arrangements there are four measures which governments can implement in order to ensure priority is given to the viability of state enterprises. First, in addition to an annual financial audit, reputable independent assessors should report on the viability of the state firm compared with its competitors and of underlying trends in that relationship. Second, any explicitly social or political objectives assigned to state enterprises should be clearly identified and accurately costed so that the enterprise can be reimbursed by the state to the extent that its performance of these tasks interferes with its prime goal of viability. The adoption of management contracts along the lines used by France and Senegal would reinforce such an arrangement (Shirley, 1983). Third, government intervention to bolster a failing enterprise should be a very last resort and of carefully specified and limited magnitude. Fourth and finally, no significant distinction should be made between management and worker employment conditions in state enterprises and those in the private sector so that career transfer between the two sectors in both directions is facilitated. It is particularly important that political and national appointments should not be made at the expense of ability. Moreover, despite understandable pressures for indigenization, management positions should be staffed with expatriates to the extent necessary for efficient operation.

The experience of the Commonwealth Caribbean suggests that it is often precisely those countries that most need the package of services provided by the MNRC which are under greatest pressure to displace them. As their small and monoproduct economies grow and diversify and the lead sector becomes less dominant, the consequent declining prominence of the MNRC may diffuse the political tensions. Meanwhile, the MNRCs have an important role to play as minority joint-venture partners until effective institutional arrangements are devised to ensure that wholly state-owned enterprises can be viable and, where possible, expand. That is the prudent way to ensure resource-based industries contribute fully to social and political welfare in countries with weak political systems and pork-barrel politics.

REFERENCES

Auty, R.M. (1975) 'Scale economies and plant vintage: toward a factory classification', *Economic Geography*, 51: 150-162.

Auty, R.M. (1976) 'Caribbean sugar factory size and survival', *Annals Association of American Geographers*, 66: 76-88.

Auty, R.M. (1980) 'Transforming mineral enclaves: Caribbean bauxite', *Tijdschrift voor Economische en Sociale Geografie*, 71: 169-179.

Auty, R.M. (1981) 'MNC product strategy, spatial structure and nationalisation: a Guyanese comparison', *Geoforum*, 12: 349-357.

Auty, R.M. (1983a) 'Multinational resource corporations, the product life-cycle and product strategy: the oil majors' response to heightened risk', *Geoforum*, 14: 1-13.

Auty, R.M. (1983b) 'Multinational corporations and regional revenue retention in a vertically integrated industry: bauxite/aluminium in the Caribbean', *Regional Studies*, 17: 3-17.

Auty, R.M. (1984a) 'The deployment of oil rents in a small parliamentary democracy: Trinidad and Tobago', Development Research Department, World Bank, Washington DC.

Auty, R.M. (1984b) 'Resource-based diversification: the energy-intensive export industrial complex in LDC mineral economies', in Barr B.M. and Waters N.M. (eds) *Regional Diversification and Structural Change*, UBC Geographical Series, Tantalus Press, Vancouver: 46-61.

Beckford, G.L. (1968) 'The economics of agricultural resource use and development in plantation economies', *Social and Economic Studies*, 18: 321-347.

Beckford, G.L. (1972) *Persistent Poverty*, Oxford University Press, Oxford.

Bryden, J. (1973) *Tourism and Development: A Case Study of The Commonwealth Caribbean*, Cambridge University Press, Cambridge.

Byer, T. (1972) 'Can Jamaican bauxite learn from Iran's new oil agreement?', Mimeo, Vienna.

Caldwell, T.R. (   ) 'Background to Guyana's bauxite industry crisis', *Caribbean Contact* (September): 13.

Davis, C.E. (1982) 'Energy and the Jamaican Bauxite/Alumina Industry, *JBI Journal*, 2 (1): 33-47.

Davis, H. (1982) 'The future of the sugar industry', Mimeo, Georgetown.

Girvan, N. (1967) *The Caribbean Bauxite Industry*, Institute of Social and Economic Research, University of the West Indies, Mona, Kingston, Jamaica.

Girvan, N. (1971) *Foreign Capital and Economic Underdevelopment in Jamaica*, Allen and Unwin, London.

Guysuco (1982) *Annual Report and Accounts*, Guyana Lithographic, Georgetown.

Harbridge House (1971) 'Blueprint for the future: a long-range plan for the Jamaican sugar industry', Mimeo, Boston.

Hashimoto, H. (1983) 'Bauxite processing in developing countries', in World Bank, *Case Studies on Industrial Processing of Primary Products*, Washington DC: 1-102.

Hirschman, A.O. (1969) 'How to divest in Latin America and why', in Hirschman A.O. (ed) *A Bias for Hope*, Yale University Press, New Haven: 225-252.

Hutchinson, L. and Drum, B. (1982) Management Audit of the Sugar Industry Authority and the National Sugar Co, Mimeo, Jamaica National Investment Co. Ltd., Kingston.

Jones, L.P. (1982) *Public Enterprise in the Less Developed Countries*, Cambridge University Press, Cambridge.

Kincaid, P.R. (1982) 'Conditionality and the use of fund resources', *Finance and Development*, June: 26-29.

Landell Mills (1969) 'Commodity studies: sugar', Mimeo, London.

McNeely Engineering Ltd and Proctor Redfern (1976) 'Clarendon Plains Development: Phase III, Summary Report', Mimeo, Toronto.

Metallgesellschaft (1982) *Metal Statistics*, Metallgesellschaft, Frankfurt.

Porteus, J.D. (1973) 'The corporate state: copper production in Chile', *Canadian Geographer*, 17: 113-126.

Radetzki, M. (1983) 'State mineral enterprises in developing countries: their impact on international mineral markets', Mimeo, Stockholm.

Rampersad, F. (1981) 'The contribution of the petroleum industry to the nation's economy', paper presented to the Geologists' Conference, Port of Spain.

Reca, L.G. and Maffucci, E.A. (1982) 'Guyana: Incentives and Comparative Advantage in the Production of Agricultural Commodities', IADB Loan Contract 660/SF-Gy.

Reid, S. (1978) 'Strategy of Resource Bargaining', *Working Paper*, No.20, University of the West Indies, Kingston.

Shafer, M. (1983) 'Capturing the mineral multinationals: advantage or disadvantage?', *International Organization*, 37: 93-119.

Sharpley, J. (1983) 'Economic management and IMF conditionality in Jamaica', in Williamson J., *IMF Conditionality*, Institute for International Economics/MIT Press, Cambridge, Mass: 233-262.

Shirley, M.M. (1983) 'Managing state-owned enterprises, *World Bank Staff Working Paper*, No.577, World Bank, Washington.

Smith, I. (1976) 'The economics of cane and beet sugar: a rejoinder', *Economy and History*, 21 (2): 126-128.

Stauffer, T. (1975) 'Energy-intensive industrialization in the Persian/Arabian Gulf', Mimeo, Center for Middle Eastern Studies, Harvard, Boston.

SIA (1976) 'The rehabilitation of the Jamaican Sugar Industry', Mimeo, Sugar Industry Authority, Kingston, Jamaica.

Thomas, M.D. (1980) 'Explanatory frameworks for growth and change in multiregional firms', *Economic Geography*, 56: 1-17.

Trebat, T.J. (1983) *Brazil's State-owned Enterprises: A Case Study of the State as Entrepreneur*, Cambridge University Press, Cambridge.

Turner, L. and Bedare, J. (1979) *Middle East Industrialization*, Saxon House, London.

Vernon, R.F. (1971) *Sovereignty at Bay*, Basic Books, New York.

Vernon, R.F. (1982) 'Uncertainty in the resource industries: the special role of state-owned enterprises', Mimeo, Cambridge.

Williams, M.L. (1975) 'The extent and significance of the nationalization of foreign-owned assets in the developing countries 1956-72', *Oxford Economic Papers*, 27: 260-273.

World Bank (1983) *World Development Report 1983*, World Bank, Washington DC.

Notes on Contributors

R.M. Auty, Lecturer, Department of Geography, University of Lancaster.

S.M. Cunningham, Lecturer, Department of Geography, St. David's University College, Lampeter.

R.N. Gwynne, Lecturer, Department of Geography, University of Birmingham.

F.E.I. Hamilton, Senior Lecturer, Department of Geography, London School of Economics and Political Science

J.W. Henderson, Lecturer, Centre of Urban Studies and Urban Planning, University of Hong Kong.

G. Manners, Professor, Department of Geography, University College, London.

C.M. Rogerson, Senior Lecturer, Department of Geography and Environmental Studies, University of Witwatersrand, Johannesburg.

B.A. Tucker, Junior Lecturer, Department of Geography and Environmental Studies, University of Witwatersrand, Johannesburg.

S.W. Williams, Research Fellow, Department of Geography, University of Keele

Subject Index

Uranium   26,28

Valorization   92,93
Very Large Scale Integrated-
        circuitry (VLSI)
        95,104

Wage control   59,62
World Bank (IBRD)   29,173
World material supply system
        33,36

COMPANY INDEX

Company Index

Company Index

AUTHOR INDEX

197

Author Index